Further praise for *Creative Community Planning*

'Wendy and her colleagues have done it again. Raised
to undertake meaningful engagement programs. For ι..., ᴜ ᴜ ᴘlᴀnning practitioner
who spends a lot of time on urban regeneration, often within communities that are
disenfranchised in some way, this new book provides a wealth of creative wisdom
that can help unlock opportunities that we never ever see coming when we begin a
project.'

Dr Mike Mouritz, Head, Sustainable Futures Unit,
HASSELL, Perth, Western Australia

'Wendy Sarkissian is well known as an instigator of imaginative engagement processes
that have enlarged the boundaries of participation theory and practice. In this book
Sarkissian and co-author, poet-planner Dianna Hurford, bring together a set of
participation practices that link the person and the planet through art, poetry, drama,
planned surprises and play. By drawing people away from their standard patterns of
interaction, these inspiring and transformative tools and approaches have the potential
to create plans, policies and agreements that can really make a difference. There is
much to learn from this thought-provoking book.'

Ann Forsyth, Professor of City and Regional Planning, Cornell University

'Wendy Sarkissian and Dianna Hurford are the Margaret Mead and Mary Oliver of
the community development world, combining youth and experience, poetry and
playfulness, toughness and tenderness, to the challenges of living well and sustainably
on our planet. Inviting us to the edge of the known world of community planning
and engagement, they then gently push us off into space and give us the wings to fly:
wings of beauty, creativity and relationship. It's a journey from paralysis to action, from
isolation to connection, from homogeneity to polyphony: no less than a new way of
being for community engagement practitioners committed to healthy communities.'

Leonie Sandercock, professor, cross-cultural planner and film maker

'In *Creative Community Planning* Sarkissian and Hurford deliver an important message
with punch and spice: It's time to go beyond business-as-usual civic engagement. It's
not enough to find out the public's priorities and concerns or seek public buy-in on
community plans and policies. The public represents a tremendously underutilized
community asset: a source of wisdom and creativity in finding solutions to the complex
issues (the "wicked messes") that face communities everywhere. The challenge is to
find ways to bring out the public's wisdom through creative community engagement.
This book launches us on the path.'

Dr Patricia A. Wilson, Professor of Planning and Civic Engagement,
University of Texas, Austin

Creative Community Planning

Tools for Community Planning: The Earthscan Series

Creative Community Planning: Transformative Engagement Methods for Working at the Edge focuses primarily on inclusive creative rationales, approaches and examples for planners and community practitioners to consider alongside existing community engagement approaches. This is the third book co-authored by Wendy Sarkissian in Earthscan's *Tools for Community Planning* series. Her previous books in the series are *Kitchen Table Sustainability: Practical Recipes for Community Engagement with Sustainability* and *SpeakOut: The Step-by-Step Guide to SpeakOuts and Community Workshops*.

For more information about the series visit www.earthscan.co.uk. For information about *Kitchen Table Sustainability* and *SpeakOut*, see www.kitchentablesustainability.com and www.speakoutplanning.com. The website for this book is www.creativecommunityplanning.com.

We are eager to begin an international and cross-cultural conversation about creativity in community engagement with you.

Creative Community Planning

Transformative Engagement Methods
for Working at the Edge

Wendy Sarkissian and Dianna Hurford
with Christine Wenman

Foreword by John Forester

from Routledge

First published by Earthscan in the UK and USA in 2010

For a full list of publications please contact:
Earthscan
2 Park Square, Milton Park, Abingdon, Oxon OX14 4RN
711 Third Avenue, New York, NY 10017

Earthscan is an imprint of the Taylor & Francis Group, an informa business

ISBN: 978-1-84407-846-2 hardback
ISBN: 978-1-84407-703-8 paperback

Typeset by Safehouse Creative
Cover design by Rob Watts

A catalogue record for this book is available from the British Library

Library of Congress Cataloging-in-Publication Data

Sarkissian, Wendy.
  Creative community planning : nurturing inclusion with insight and method / Wendy
Sarkissian and Dianna Hurford ; with Christine Wenman and foreword by John Forester.
    p. cm.
  Includes bibliographical references and index.
  ISBN 978-1-84407-846-2 (hardback) – ISBN 978-1-84407-703-8 (pbk.) 1. Community
development. 2. City planning. I. Hurford, Dianna. II. Wenman, Christine. III. Title. IV. Title:
Nurturing inclusion with insight and method.
  HN49.C6S26 2010
  307.1'216–dc22

This book is dedicated with love
to
Graeme Dunstan
artist, activist and visionary
in recognition of decades of commitment
to community cultural development
and for
lanterns, fire sculptures, flags, banners, street oratory
and a creative fire that never goes out

Contents

List of Acronyms and Abbreviations

BC	British Columbia
CANWA	Community Arts Network of Western Australia
CBC	Canadian Broadcasting Corporation
CCD	Community Cultural Development
CSL	Community Service Learning
CSPVP	Carrall Street Participatory Video Project
DTES	Downtown Eastside (Vancouver, Canada)
ERAG	Eagleby Renewal Action Group
ESD	Ecologically Sustainable Development
FPAR	Feminist Participatory Action Research
IAP^2	International Association for Public Participation
IRC	Internet relay chat
ISOCARP	International Society of City and Regional Planners
MP	Management and Planning
NIMBY	Not in My Back Yard
NLP	neuro-linguistic programming
PAR	Participatory Action Research
PHS	Portland Hotel Society
PSF	Pacific Salmon Foundation
SCARP	School of Community and Regional Planning
SES	State of Emergency Services (New South Wales)
TWS	The Writer's Studio
UBC	University of British Columbia
UNECE	United Nations Economic Commission for Europe
URLC	Urban and Regional Land Corporation (Victoria, Australia)
VAG	Vancouver Art Gallery
VAK	visual, auditory and kinaesthetic
VOJ	Voice of Judgment
VPSN	Vancouver Public Space Network
WOAW	Women Organizing Activities for Women

and so we begin

by turning on stereo speaker
in municipal mountainvalley gymnasium

stumble toward and away toward
and away

toward each other

all of us in this
fluid dance proposal

this collection of multiple
invitations

outside we place ear phone
under ground to feel for root eye
chrysalid text

any hopeful remains

as circle of archaeologists we
begin with art's spontaneous tools

discover

stations of selves

ready

to embark

– dh

Foreword

An old friend from Berkeley, Stephen Blum, used to quip, 'Nature isn't organized the way universities are!' Legal scholar Patricia Williams echoed his point in a deceptively simple way when she observed, 'It is a fact of great analytic importance that life is complicated'. But in Sydney, Australia's largest housing estate, Dominic Grenot put this even more poignantly and practically as he described his day-to-day observations as he worked with residents speaking 80 languages, 'There's always more going on'.

Our educations typically help us in one field to the neglect of others. We presume a lot and often probe far less – various literatures on social learning notwithstanding. And so our typical ways of 'planning' and 'community development' back us into the future; we try to learn from yesterday, as we ought to, but we stay close to our disciplinary trainings. We can count on the fingers of one hand the urban planners who dare to put 'environment' and 'ethics' and 'spirituality' and 'love' in one paragraph, much less one sentence. But we can count on Wendy Sarkissian and her colleagues to do it regularly, persistently, thoughtfully, sensitively and practically – not theoretically, not for the sake of publication but for the sake of improving our lives.

We can count on Wendy and her colleagues to break the rules when they hold us captive, when the rules of our narrow perspectives hide our interdependence, our connections, from us in ways that make us more vulnerable, more alienated, more isolated, less understanding, less respectful, less able to recognize one another and our shared possibilities.

Wendy and her colleagues challenge the idea that first comes knowledge, then comes action – for how can we begin to learn, to listen, to inquire, to wonder, to imagine if we're not already rooted in a place, in a history, in a web of social and political relationships and interactions? Wendy and her colleagues help us to recognize our connections, our interdependence, in far more intricate and intimate ways than most traditional (ecological or 'systems') views do, and so they don't shirk from speaking of 'love' and care and respect and survival when they see all that and more at stake in the ways we treat our places, our planet and one another.

In person and in print, Wendy works by gentle indirection. She knows that we will learn more if we're less able to predict where she's going: if we'll listen more, we'll wonder more, we'll imagine more, we'll hide less, we'll be surprised more, we'll discover more. Lucky us to join her on her journeys, to have her journeys into the world of future possibilities become our journeys too, to have her keen senses of complexity and creativity help us sense too what really matters, help us to see more clearly both the limits of yesterday's education and the real opportunities of what we might do together today and tomorrow.

John Forester

Cornell University and Nicis Scholar at the University of Amsterdam

May 2009

John Forester is Professor of City and Regional Planning at Cornell University. As a student of the micropolitics of planning and participatory governance, his most recent book is *Dealing with Differences: Dramas of Mediating Public Disputes* (Oxford, 2009).

Preface

Transforming community engagement in planning by working at the edge: Finding our way in conversation

It's February 2009. I'm sitting with my dear friend of 30 years, Colette Meunier, in her home in Benicia, Northern California. Colette was a student of mine at Berkeley in the 1970s and has had a long and successful career in local government in Canada and the United States. Despite living thousands of miles apart, we have maintained a close friendship, partly because of our passion for planning – and community engagement. I've asked Colette, my host, to help me understand why creativity is needed in community engagement and to provide some examples of how engagement is undertaken in her adopted country, the US.

> **Wendy**: So, Colette, from your experience, why do Canadian and American planners need to change our approaches to community engagement?
>
> **Colette**: The problems planners are now grappling with – global climate change, Peak Oil, sustainability and global economic interdependency – are very different in scale, complexity and urgency from what most of us have worked on up to now. The urgent, potentially catastrophic, long-term and widespread nature of these problems requires radical rethinking about how we will decide what to do about them and how we will make the changes in our communities and our lives to prevent global disaster.
>
> **Wendy**: Oh, Colette. I so agree! Last year when I was researching and writing Kitchen Table Sustainability, I felt that I could not open another book that began by chronicling the loss of species, the sea level rise, desertification and the magnitude of the catastrophe.[1] It's so urgent. And yet I am certain that we cannot lose hope and

become dispirited. If we lose our creativity in the midst of all these crises, we will be doomed.

Why do *you* think we need to focus on changing *community* planning?

Colette: Finding the solutions to the problems we face will draw on all of our ingenuity and the implementation of the solutions won't just change the physical infrastructure of our communities – it will change how we live our everyday lives. Local government is the governmental level that is most accessible to people in general. It is the one most people have the greatest contact with and the one that has the most direct and visible effect on people's daily lives. I believe that it is at this level that we will most meaningfully grapple with solutions and implement them. However, for us to be successful, we will need to change how we engage people in the planning process.

Wendy: Can you give me a sense of a typical community-planning process?

Colette: The public agencies I worked for or observed have a strong commitment to public participation, often extending far beyond the minimum legal requirements. Part of starting a planning process includes setting up a specific public participation program for the specific planning effort, which may include methods such as a steering committee, a series of public forums or community meetings, administering a questionnaire, stakeholder interviews, publishing a newsletter about the planning process or a combination of methods.

The planning process may vary from municipality to municipality or change based on what the planning process is addressing, but generally, the typical community-planning process starts with professional staff or consultants collecting data, analysing trends and identifying issues. This information is presented to the public. The next step is to develop a range of alternatives that addresses the community concerns and issues. The alternatives are publicly evaluated and discussed to select a preferred alternative or alternatives. The plan is prepared based on the preferred alternative and is then subject to formal public review, hearing and adoption by elected and appointed decision makers who make the final decisions about the plan. The plan policies and implementation programs mostly focus on what is in the control of the local community. Only occasionally do they include coordination with other levels of government and agencies or seeking changes in state or federal legislation and programs. They rarely propose any changes to our free-market economy.

Wendy: And what about adoption of a plan? What typically happens in that phase?

Colette: As proposed plans are considered for adoption, local councils are lobbied by lots of people, each trying to get a change in the proposed plan to address their individual interests. Once plans are adopted, they are often amended to address individual issues but only infrequently comprehensively reviewed and updated. Few communities have processes in place to monitor implementation of the adopted plan's policies and programs. Finally, the adoption of the plan concludes the public engagement process and the participatory program ends.

Wendy: What factors constrain community engagement, in your experience?

Colette: I would say public complacency and limited funding. Only a small percentage of a community's population participates in most planning efforts. People don't participate for many reasons. Some people are already very busy with their jobs, family and friends and feel they do not have time to participate. Others are generally pretty satisfied with their communities, feel no sense of urgency to seek changes and think others will adequately represent their concerns and issues. Some are cynical and disillusioned about whether the plan or their participation in the preparation of the plan will make any meaningful difference. Sometimes, people find the planning outcomes to be technical, abstract or otherwise hard to translate into concrete, foreseeable outcomes.

Wendy: What usually happens when the money runs out?

Colette: That's a good question. Public agencies often cannot afford to allocate sufficient staff resources, training or money for public engagement methods that reach a broader cross-section of the community and draw them into the planning process. Those who do participate are likely to be organized or powerful groups, such as bicycle advocates or business interests, those whose property interests will be directly affected and those with strong opinions and interest in the issues to be addressed by community planning. And, no surprise, many American planning processes are combative and argumentative, conclude with disaffected participants who do not support the adopted plan and result in litigation.

Wendy: Hmmm. That's a good point. When the belts tighten, can we still be creative? We may need to add an additional dose of ingenuity to our creativity. So, how robust do you think current approaches are to address the challenges we see coming down the pike?

Colette: Well, I am afraid that in this country our current approaches will not successfully address problems like global climate change. Our understanding of the causes, mechanisms and rate of climate change is rapidly changing and evolving. The development of solutions to address climate change is occurring in a variety of disciplines, in the public, private and non-profit sectors and in countries around the world. Successfully addressing climate change will require drawing on the wisdom and creativity from all these sources for solutions and likely require significant changes in how we live our daily lives, especially in North America. That's only going to happen with profound common understanding, acceptance and ongoing commitment to making the changes.

Wendy: I totally agree. The same applies in Australia, of course. We're huge culprits when it comes to carbon emissions, for example. One of the challenges for *Creative Community Planning* (and certainly for *Kitchen Table Sustainability*) is to help people come to understand that in many cases 'less is more'.

What changes do *you* think are necessary, Colette?

Colette: I believe that the following changes in community planning and public engagement are needed to address the problems we face:

- Creative, more extensive public engagement.
- Public engagement throughout the life of a community plan.
- Coordination and collaboration across disciplines, levels of government and sectors of the economy.

Generally speaking, the reasons given for public engagement processes include:

- Finding out the public's preferences.
- Incorporating the local knowledge of community members.
- Advancing fairness and justice.
- Legitimizing public decisions as inclusive and democratic.
- Complying with legal requirements for public notice and hearing.[2]

Wendy: And what about simply paying more attention – or listening – to the community? And to communities?

Colette: That's my point, really. The basic purpose of public engagement is *engagement*. Most people will agree that these urgent problems must be addressed if we are to be successful in addressing the challenges of global climate change, Peak Oil, sustainability and global economic interdependency. They will also be interested in learning more and contributing their knowledge and perspectives to the evolving understanding of the problems and will be committed to making the necessary changes in our lives and in our society.

Wendy: Can you spell out some specific reasons or rationales?

Colette: Yes. An important reason for public engagement processes is to develop and share a common understanding. A second important reason is to nurture and mutually reinforce heartfelt, widespread commitment to implementation of the plan's recommendations. We are asking people to make significant changes in how they live. This will best occur if people have had meaningful participation in preparing the plan and its recommendations and an ongoing voice in assessing the efficacy of the plan and its implementation.

Our community planning processes will need to identify and incorporate more community leadership, consensus building and negotiation. This is hard to do where all the public engagement is *advisory*. How do parties negotiate and make tradeoffs when these may be ignored or undone by the ultimate decision makers? Public engagement processes may need to culminate in different decision-making processes.

Wendy: Everyone's talking about diversity these days. To what extent is addressing diversity part of your philosophy?

Colette: It's very important. Diversity will be essential to ensuring that we draw on all of our collective knowledge and consider all concerns and values to craft successful solutions that will be widely embraced. To be successful, we will have to have a level of commonality of purpose, openness and the willingness to listen and learn from others that I have seen only rarely and in relatively small settings.

Wendy: Thanks, Colette. It's been great talking to you about this. From the look on your face, though, you've got something more to say. What is it?

Colette: Oh, Wendy, I wonder, are we up to the challenge? I believe we have to be. Our existing community-planning and public-engagement approaches too often leave us in conflict and without bold enough solutions to really address our concerns. We need to energize and transform our usual ways of doing business and unleash our creativity to engage with each other, finding the paths to making a real difference.

Our conversation made me think of my friend Graeme Dunstan, an Australian activist and artist.[3] A couple of months after my conversation with Colette, Graeme and I are sitting on the deck of our Nimbin house, reminiscing about the projects we've worked on together. We're old friends and we've had some amazing adventures in the course of community engagement. We realize that 20 years have passed since our first project together in Melbourne. I can just hear him listening to my conversation with Colette and exclaiming, 'They haven't got it!'

So no better person to speak with than the man himself. Here's a snippet of our conversation.

Wendy: Graeme, why is creativity important in community engagement? Why do you have to 'act out' things, as we did for VicRoads in Melbourne in 1990[4] and you did in the 2004 Safe Communities conference session?[5]

Graeme: It's about hearing all the voices. *All* the voices. So we are looking to find out what pops into being. I use acting because playfulness and spontaneity are the most revealing. Humans are most creative when they are excited, when they are laughing together and when they are stimulated in some way. I'm after the poetry of the moment.

And we need to be artful about it. So, I say to people, if you want to ask these questions [like ones about safe communities], let's make it artful; let's make it beautiful and let's make it memorable. We want the answers to remain with the participants, surely.

Wendy: Why is beauty important, Graeme?

Graeme: It's uplifting. It brings people together and lifts up their vision of what's possible for themselves. I ask, 'How can we make it beautiful together?' And 'How can we make this interesting and challenging?'

Wendy: What's one lesson you take away from the work we've done together?

Graeme: I've always done CCD [Community Cultural Development] work. That's been my mission since the Aquarius Festival here in Nimbin in 1973. I came back to Nimbin after Aquarius and thought it's all about creating the culture for people with different dreams. You know, they had very different dreams, those Nimbin pioneers in 1973. And I have been here – and doing this work – ever since. Now I am asking, 'How do you create a cultural movement for water in the Murray Darling basin? How do we do that and save that poor river – for future generations?'

Wendy: Why is this work so challenging?

Graeme: It's an empty field. It's an abyss. Most people are asleep in front of the TV. But, with this work, when the change comes, it sweeps them up and carries them along.

Wendy: What sorts of skills do you need for this 'artful' work?

Graeme: You need a good effort, patience and plenty of time. I've seen the transformation of social planning in the time I've been working with you. Now it's changed dramatically in Australia. What we did 20 years ago – at the frontier – is now a sign of good practice.

You know, good energy is never wasted. But you need patience. I say, 'Just do it!'

Wendy: What do you say back to people who say that community cultural development is insubstantial, 'airy fairy' stuff?

Graeme: 'Lofty and impractical' is what they are saying. People often say that. But if they looked inside themselves, they'd find that this loftiness has roots that go deep. And when these [CCD] principles are put into practice, they have great influences.

Reflecting on these two conversations, I realize how grateful I am to the people who helped me keep my creativity alight in my workplace. First would have to be my mentor, Clare Cooper Marcus, whose work I discuss briefly in Chapter 5. I've been blessed with courageous colleagues (among them the bravest would have to be Kelvin Walsh, the *tall koala* in the story about the Aurora project team workshop told in Chapter 6). And I've had courageous clients, especially Bryce Moore and Jill Lim of the now-defunct Urban and Regional Land Authority in Melbourne. More recently, my life has been enlivened by the fire and passion of Yollana Shore, who guides me with her wisdom and whose heart-warming and *heartstorming* approaches to creative visualization we discuss in Chapter 5.[6]

In many ways, this book is a reflection on engagement practices to help us get our communal heads around some of the major issues of our day such as isolation from interactions with Nature and each other, exclusion in decision-making processes, increasing poverty and feelings of individual hopelessness and despair. To protect ourselves and our communities from inaction or spiritual or emotional paralysis, we feel it is important to focus on creativity, beauty, relationships and skilled facilitation. However, we find little support; with much of the existing community engagement discourse preoccupied with hard-surfaced themes such as objectivity, efficiency, risk avoidance, reducing bias and formalizing engagement processes.

Creative Community Planning suggests we slip into a different way of being and acting together in the world – one that is at once practical, musical and light. It provides a needed synthesis of a broad and dynamic field, bringing the discourse up to date for all types of community practitioners working in unique and constantly changing environments.

Acknowledging that many of us identify ourselves as being in a hybrid of fields (more wildflower than mono-crop), we have written this book for people who find themselves cross-pollinated within these various communities: planners, policy makers, community engagement practitioners, community cultural development practitioners, local decision makers, urban and landscape designers, social workers, community group participants, qualitative researchers, artists, activists, teachers and students. We've written it for professionals who want to enhance their practices with more creativity.

With beauty, playfulness and reflection, we offer this book as an invitation to create your own meaningful and transformative work through community engagement practice.

Wendy Sarkissian
Nimbin, Australia
May 2009

Colette Meunier, AICP

With 30 years of experience, planning consultant Colette Meunier, based in Northern California, understands the complexities of the California planning and environmental process, including land-use regulation, policy formulation, environmental compliance, community outreach and conflict resolution. Educated in Canada and at the University of California, Berkeley, Colette worked for local public planning agencies for 28 years before becoming a consultant.

Graeme Dunstan

Australian Graeme Dunstan is an old hippie, still blown along by the winds of the counterculture. A Duntroon (Royal Military College of Australia) dropout and an honours engineering graduate, he was radicalized by the resistance to the US War on Vietnam and graduated skilled in protest organizing and movement building.

He was a key organizer of the transformative 1973 Nimbin Aquarius Festival and ever after explored artful celebration as a means for community cultural development. Graeme has served as a community arts officer in local government at Sydney's south-western suburban frontier and as a cultural tourism and festivals advisor for the State of Victoria.

Gone forth into homelessness, he now lives in his van and travels around Australia, bearing flags and lanterns, burning cardboard sculptures and speaking up and speaking out. Best he can, he organizes and helps others organize resistance to the wars and Earth destruction of corporate capitalism, creating cultural movement for peace, justice and a sustaining Earth as he goes.

Part 1

Traversing the Edge:

Introduction

practice is sensuous activity[1]

as practitioners we have become all types

theatre performer, math teacher,
artist, cartographer, chiropractor,
acrobat, celebrity chef, designer,
photographer, policy drafter,

aromatherapist

we impose: smell
                 c?o?l?o?u?r texture

                    scratch & sniff
the neighbourhood

hold words on tongues to taste
as we walk down seasoned street

leaves wreath heads of publics
absorb colour memory
mud root rain

nature barks geometry
an orchestra of polysound

                              – dh

Why Traverse the Edge?
Creative Underpinnings

Come to the edge.
We might fall.
Come to the edge.
It's too high!

COME TO THE EDGE!
And they came
And he pushed
And they flew[1]

Christopher Logue (1926–)

Introduction:
Creative edges in community engagement

Creativity is an active invitation for all of us to be part of creating healthy communities. As our communities around the Earth shift and grow, we begin to experience the world differently. Our habits, our work, our homes and our social circles change colour and shape. These changes offer us, as community engagement practitioners, an invitation to re-evaluate our work – to continue the work of bridging our relationships with ourselves, with others and with our environments. For us, creativity is the necessary work of evolving community engagement practice using methods that honour people's individual and collective knowledge about their lives and their environments.

Invitation:
We invite you to come to the edge to experience concepts that are contributing to the imagination of community engagement practice: Meg Holden's 'tough and tender minded', Wendy Sarkissian's 'ecotone', Leonie Sandercock's 'borderlands', Norma-Jean McLaren's 'realizing diversity' and John Forester's 'deliberative planning'.

John Forester contends that no formula for effective engagement exists.[2] How could it when every locality, with its own histories, environments and politics, is home to a host of unique relationships? Intuitively and methodologically, we need to examine the differences and emotions that keep people in opposition and we need to provide opportunities to build something new and unexpected. We also need to create open spaces where we can have the types of conversations that will bring people (especially those who tend to remain uninvited in traditional processes) close enough to engage together with an issue. The stories in this book traverse the edge because of the desire to move from paralysis to action, from isolation to friendship and from homogeneous to polyphonic.

Like John, we do not believe in magical formulas for creativity. In writing this book, we offer only an open invitation for each of us to seek clues, to learn in action and to share creative engagement methods with each other. In *Creative Community Planning*, we invite engagement practitioners to share their stories. We also reflect on our own practices. Far from coming to tidy, comprehensive conclusions, these stories present many diverse methods for working at the edge of creative community engagement. They reflect both community engagement methods practised over several decades and some in the experimental stages, illuminating creativity's essential role in bridging conflict, changing the flavour of community discussions, opening participants to new possibilities and forming lasting partnerships to transform our communities and our futures.

Wendy's practice of more than 30 years has also produced some striking examples of what happens when we effectively engage with community. In the 'Gilt-edged Resources' (in the last section of this book), we have included some examples of practices that we have found extraordinary in creating creative space for people to flourish in engagement processes.

Identity politics and debate:
From 'either/or' to 'and–and'

As planning and community engagement are not absent from politics and debate, we expect that creative methods will further dialogues about effective practice. The stories shared here will enrich a contemporary planning debate that questions whether we should be establishing a cohesive identity[3] as planners or interpreting diverse ideologies and multiplicities of method as signs of intellectual advancement.[4] Extended definitions and alternative histories of planning have also resulted in dichotic debates (that sound different to different 'ears') within academic and professional circles – casting planning either as an art or a science. These either/or debates tend to emphasize the importance of rational/emotional, technical/social and singular/multiple approaches to current and future issues such as sustainability.[5]

In this book, we question dichotomies. We wonder, instead, what would happen if we *added* creative methods to our existing engagement processes. Many of the examples in this book would perhaps work best if they were set in a wider context or formed part of a wider approach to capture and cultivate 'missing pieces' of information and knowledge. As we primarily work with people in emotionally charged and diverse contexts, we have found that employing creative methods in planning makes intellectual and practical sense. In a creative spirit, we invite this discussion.

Meg Holden: The tough and the tender minded

In her article, 'The tough minded and the tender minded: A pragmatic turn for sustainable development planning and policy', Meg Holden introduces into the debate William James (1907–1977) and the philosophy of pragmatism. James coined the terms 'tough minded' and 'tender minded' to suggest two ways of understanding the world – ways that were not dichotic but that were present in all of us; ways that could build mutual benefit.[6]

To be tough minded, Meg summarizes, is to believe and trust in 'facts' and to learn through continuous testing and experimentation, whereas to be tender minded is to act on beliefs and intuition, be spontaneous, hopeful and 'idealistic'.[7] In sustainability, Meg argues the work of pragmatism is to bridge these ways of being through 'processes that develop new relationships of trust, respect and regular patterns of action, rather than specific one-time products or outcomes'.[8]

Highlighting James's instructions for each way of being, Meg translates a possible meaning of pragmatism for community engagement and sustainability:

> James instructed the tender minded to take up the good habits of the sciences when determining and 'fixing' beliefs within a group. This meant working as a 'community of inquirers' who share a common investment in understanding and improving their life context by communicating ideas and experiences and testing them against one another's diverse perspectives.

> On the other hand, James instructed the tough minded to adopt the good habits of humanists and political actors, namely critically assessing ends- and means-based values.[9]

Meg suggests that rationality, integration and experience are three components that would benefit us in community engagement practice:

> [S]o that rationality is an invitation to communicate more effectively rather than a straitjacket for channels and forms of communication, so that integration is constructively pursued without making unrealistic demands for comprehensive knowledge and so that personal experiences are recognized as valid and necessary tests and contexts for successful sustainability plans.[10]

She warns of the challenges facing planners in 'interpreting' and 'applying' these components using both tough and tender minded approaches. But we must, she suggests, persist in connecting the tough and the tender minded to engage with publics and build a 'continuous communication and interaction among citizens and experts' and a knowledge 'generated and tested in public contexts' where 'stories have standing alongside scientific models and statistics'.[11]

Although we find tender minded approaches sorely lacking in many community engagement processes, this book is not a book only for the tender minded parts of us. Much of the work also meets the tough minded at the edge, in the pursuit of inquiry,[12] experimentation and testing within wider processes that may include more conventional (even scientific) research models and technologies. Our deepest desire is to meet at a place of creation that calls new, informed and meaningful ideas into existence through rationality, integration, community knowledge and experience.

Ecotone: Adopting an edge metaphor as place of creation

Wendy would like to share a personal story about her discovery of the *ecotone* as a place of creation and how it relates to the work of this book. She says:
I introduce the concept of *ecotone* because in this book we are exploring notions of change and growth, at the margin, at the edge. We are *wayfaring on the margins*, as the American educator and naturalist Florence Krall says.[13]

For Krall, margins are rich and dynamic abodes, places of crossing over and transition, as well as spaces of separation and alienation. Life in an ecotone is all about that.

Our book is all about that – and more. It's about the courage to break away from traditional and prescribed ways of working with communities. It's about finding new ways of working and finding new 'communities' of like-minded souls with whom to work. As the stories in this book reveal, life in an ecotone is always interesting.

Seventeen years ago, spending a year living in voluntary simplicity in the bush of northern Australia, I discovered that I was living in an *ecotone*.[14] An ecotone is a transition area of vegetation between two different plant communities, such as a wetland and a forest. Ecotones are places of differentiation, change and growth. They can support forms of life not found in either of the adjacent systems.

In ecotones, growth and change always occur at the edges. Rich and dynamic, they have an ecology of their own, as well as some characteristics of each bordering community. The response of vegetation to variations in climate will be the most extreme at the boundaries.

In the forest where I lived throughout 1992, the soil and the plant communities to the south-east differed dramatically from those north of the creek. The area around the creek where I lived was my personal ecotone. During this time, living alone in a forest, I found myself – psychologically and spiritually – in my *ecotone*: a marginal place between domesticity and wildness, between conformity and a true meaning of radicalism, rootedness in the natural world. I *was* an ecotone, embodying ecotone. Years before, an ecologist had explained that 'growth and change always occur at the edges – in ecotones'. Thus, I was not surprised to read in Gretel Ehrlich's *A Match to the Heart* (1994) of the richness she found in tide pools: 'Tide pools ... are ecotones, in-between places like those clefts in the brain and the rug-pulled-out limbos in our lives where, ironically, much richness occurs'.[15]

Humpty Doo, 1992

In that place, I was my own 'growing edge'. Sometimes I imagined the creek and its banks as a *mandorla*, an almond-shaped segment created when two circles partly overlap. For Jungian psychologist, Robert Johnson, it's a place of significant soul growth, of overlap between Heaven and Earth. I moved back and forth across the creek, a boundary more visible with the rain but which faded as the creekbed dried up. My life was lived in *mandorla*, negotiating with mandorla-space. My own growth was occurring within its tiny perimeters. Johnson explains that 'the mandorla binds together that which was torn apart and made unwhole – unholy. It is the most profound religious experience we can have in life'.

In this book, we make our offerings and invitations from our place in the ecotone of creative community planning. Here at our growing edge. We invite you to join us in this fertile place, where change is more likely to occur and to be more dramatic than in the communities that border this place.

Leonie Sandercock: Edge as borderland

In 1995, Leonie Sandercock responded to a call to locate new voices for contemporary planning theory. She wrote about the importance of looking to the 'frontiers', 'borderlands' and 'margins' to expand planning theory, to make theory reflective of an ever-changing cityscape. She says:

> We are being challenged in the city and in the academy by frontiers of difference. We must listen to these voices, for they are not only telling us what is wrong with our cities, but also what is wrong with our way of looking at the world and providing clues as to what might be better ways of dealing with both. In other words, we are faced with a challenge to both our theory and our practice by what I call the voices from the borderlands.[16]

These frontiers, borderlands and margins act as a metaphor for the voices not typically heard or even listened to in planning practice. Examining the writings of bell hooks, Gloria Anzaldus, Cornel West and Gueillermo Gomez-Pena, Leonie challenged us to think about new ways of understanding storytelling, planning theory, multiplicity, new and old ways of knowing and dialogical and physical territories.[17]

This challenge remains especially relevant today within the contexts of rapidly changing and diversifying environments. Pooling together all of our knowledge, values and resources and disrupting old patterns of thought are necessary to re-examine and plan for future generations. But have we asked ourselves which voices we have sought out to share their stories and lead us? Have we examined the theories and beliefs upon which we base our practice?

In *Creative Community Planning*, we seek out the frontiers, borderlands and margins to listen for who and what we are missing in our practices, whether it is people with Aboriginal ancestry, nonhuman Nature, children and young people or the plants and soils of a polluted waterfront. Other times *we* may be the voices from a kind of borderland ourselves. All of our stories are contextualized within local territories; in this book, most of our stories are from the margins of 'locals' or communities we inhabit in Australia and western Canada.

Norma-Jean McLaren: Realizing diversity in ourselves

Part of our practice as engagement practitioners is to realize who we are in community, not as static beings, but as an ever growing and ever changing being connected to many social, political, economic and environmental aspects of society. In her cross-cultural planning, anti-racism and diversity training courses, Norma-Jean McLaren invites community participants and graduate planning students to reflect on their backgrounds.[18] She asks us to reflect across multiple categories and to consider how our personal life experiences affect how we listen, to whom we listen and why and how we act (and react) in certain situations. We are invited to explore the words, ideas and personalities that trigger us, the things that cause us to 'shut up' or 'shut down' and refuse to listen.

Maintaining an open sense of curiosity and an open sense of wonder are keys to listening to learn about other ways of being in the world. In a cross-cultural context, we cannot be categorized (as we are by census data) only by race, religion, class, age, housing type, gender or ethnicity. We are a complex intersection of languages, experiences, education, traumas, future plans, emotions, deaths and births, settlement histories, friendships, worldviews and addictions.[19] Within these intersections, we construct stories about what is important to us, what brings us hope, where we harbour fear or oppression. Within us there exists a tangle of connections to each other. Within these connections there will always be more to learn about ourselves and each other.

John Forester: Putting theory into transformative practice

In *The Deliberative Practitioner: Encouraging Participatory Planning Processes* (1999) John Forester asks us as community practitioners to rethink how we learn and act in practice. He invites us to listen with an intimate ear and an analytic mind to the stories we tell ourselves and the stories others tell us and to which we find ourselves listening. He also invites us to step outside the formal settings we legitimize as 'work' and open our eyes to the wealth of our conversations. These conversations are what Forester calls 'participatory rituals', 'encounters that enable participants to develop more familiar relationships or to learn about one another before solving the problems they face'.[20] Developing a caring curiosity towards each other helps us to see people rather than problems, stories instead of issues. Not only does this way of practicing feel better, it is also better practice. As Forester notes, 'Pushing for solutions too soon – before affected parties have been able to listen to one another – can end up taking far more time than preliminary participatory rituals might'.[21]

The invitation to listen in community engagement can be likened to an invitation to a metaphoric campfire. By an edge of forest or sea, we are invited to sit and listen to a story made out of many stories, with friendship at the heart – a friendship that is not necessarily a cultivated intimacy, but a deliberate way of arriving within a circle of people. Here we exchange offerings and watch together how the fire – as a collective organ continuously transforming itself – sparks, births new tongues, forms moving rivers and sustains movements of light in the dark with each shape of wood placed within its range. As practitioners, we may always be asking ourselves: 'How do we keep the firesides inclusive and safe?' and 'What if we have to choose *between* "inclusive" and "safe"?'

Transformative learning through the practice of friendship

Reflecting on Aristotle's *Ethics,* Forester says that, to continue learning through our engagement practices, we need to reach out an arm of friendship to each other. Offerings of friendship in the planning context, he contends, may sometimes be through 'appropriate stories' or those stories that bring 'knowledge, empathy, thoughtfulness and insight to bear on our particular situation, needs and possibilities'.[22] Friends also hold up a mirror, as a river to a face, to show us who we are in the context of our work and our values. By listening to the detailed complexities of our situation, they allow us the opportunity to emote, spin circles of story and reflection around ourselves and eventually dream new possibilities and insights. These possibilities help us to understand more deeply a process we experienced or to address an ongoing issue.

The deliberate work of 'human flourishing'

Forester also invites us to consider community development work as 'human flourishing'.[23] Human flourishing involves creating spaces of trust for different kinds of stories to emerge and for people to express themselves in their own vocabularies. It also means listening deliberately to these stories and applying them to collective and participatory actions. Only then can we act in an imaginative dialogue, flourishing our hearts and minds within the capacity and nourishment of our environments.

In 1979, John Friedmann wrote about the complexity of dialogue in *The Good Society*. Through short textual meditations, John's writing itself asks us to think more deeply about expression in participatory practice and to choose to see the importance of difference and conflict in learning through relationships in community. Friedmann says, 'Meaning does not inhere in the world but arises from the way we choose to see crucial relationships'.[24] To enter deeply into community engagement practice is to enter deeply into relationship.

Building on the experimental participatory models of John Dewey (1930) and Paulo Freire (1970), John Forester established a model 20 years after *The Good Society* was published. Forester's work continues to challenge the way we conduct contemporary practice using methods with emphasis on words such as *expectation*, *success* and *outcome*. Instead, Forester's model focuses on the complexity and messiness of human relationships to teach and guide us. Forester builds on two models. The first is the Deweyan model of creating and testing new learning through ongoing experimentation. The second is the Freirean model of learning in a dialogue with emphasis on a growing awareness of power. Forester's model for learning 'explores not only how our arguments change in dialogues and negotiations but how we change as well'.[25] Central to this learning model is:

> In speaking together in more or less dialogical or argumentative settings, not only do we learn from what others say or do about what they claim, but we learn still more from the way they do it. From the reasons they give, we learn about what others want or believe. But from the way they talk and act, from their style, we learn about who they are, 'what they are like', what sort of 'character someone has (or is)'.[26]

Through these rituals of participation, Forester says we learn more about the circumstances that thread through people's lives, the points of intersection and the places where the seam just doesn't seem to hold. We also rearrange these threads, mapping out new lines, forming new designs and intersections that foster or necessitate new working relationships.

Walking to the edge: Taking a few first steps

Walking out to some of the edges we delineate in this book may seem intimidating, depending on who we are in any given context: the consultant, community member, employee, client or government of the day with whom we are working. We may feel that our reputation and sometimes even our self-identity rely on perpetrating one or more of the myths of what defines *good* professional practice in form, method and approach. The 'risk-management' experts in our organizations will be looking after us as well. In constrained economic times, taking professional risks may seem unwise, even foolhardy.

Risks are risky. There is no denying that. Yet risk taking yields rich results. As the 19th-century Scottish poet, Alexander Smith, famously exclaimed, 'Everything is sweetened by risk'. We strongly believe that to engage more fully and effectively with the diversity of people in our communities, we need to take the risks inherent in venturing outside the safe and stable arenas of normative planning and engagement practice. In Chapter 11, Michelle LeBaron describes a colleague taking the necessary 'one step' outside the expected norm in an engagement process for successful conflict resolution. In other examples (such as the children's party in Chapter 6), an entire professional work atmosphere is dramatically transformed. Working at the edge presents risks in community settings that require both careful preparation and willingness for spontaneity. This work requires us to discern and facilitate multiple spaces for new collective imaginings, depending on our openness to growth, discomfort and ongoing assessment of local cultures and settings.

Adopting a spirit of welcome in practice

Adopting a spirit of welcoming and hospitality in community engagement practice allows us to talk about beauty, poetry and dreams alongside arterial roads, public parks and housing. We can also welcome reflection about the language we use and commit ourselves to ongoing creative inquiry in our practice. As we attempt to re-imagine the lines and spaces of practice – studying and using experimental methods to invite others to listen and share in the multiplicity of voices around them – we discover many points of difference. Our dream is to welcome multiplicity and difference in our engagement processes and to illustrate the power of creativity in nurturing inclusion and community transformation.

Practitioners Working at the Edge: Creativity in Practice

2

Welcoming the edge: Wendy on acknowledging the edges to inhabit

Over the years, Wendy has been considered a pioneering planning professional for her experimental work in community engagement. Her invitation to engagement processes in communities is unique in its spirit of welcoming the knowledge of people typically ignored in public processes. In *On Beauty and Being Just*, Elaine Scarry, professor of English at Harvard University, talks about the etymology of 'welcoming' as acknowledging the presence of beauty and equality in each other.[1]

In this conversation, Dianna Hurford, poet, planner and co-author of this book,

Invitation:
Join Wendy in welcoming people to an edge where they can speak freely and act creatively, bring a spirit and ethic of playfulness to their work and widen their sense of how we should be listening in community engagement processes.

asks Wendy how we, as practitioners, welcome beauty into our community engagement practices.

Wendy: I feel that today life in urban areas has been largely programmed and regulated. Imagine that at the end of the day you leave a regimented job, travel through gridlock traffic and arrive at a community meeting. A gentle person greets you and takes your coat, offering muffins, a hot drink and a comfortable chair. Then a facilitator at your small group table asks how you are and helps you settle in. How much easier is it to bring your community wisdom to the table than if you are marching through the lobby of a hotel to sit in a room of rows where people are already making speeches while gesturing at incomprehensible plans on the stage? This is an entirely different picture. A different model.

As facilitators or workshop organizers, we may not always like what people have to say. They may have views that are contrary to our plans. Maybe they will be rude to us. They may say shocking things, disagree with our engineer's reports and have evidence against what we are saying as planners. But at least if we pay attention to these 'hospitality' issues, we are all on a level playing field when we start these conversations, rather than some of us – perhaps the community members – being at a disadvantage, which is what happens most of the time.

I believe that the only thing that everybody has in common is their human physical reality – their embodiment. The ingredient often left out of community engagement is the ability for people to vote with their hands, vote with their feet, use some physical thing that is different from reading or writing: a process where a participant can march across the room and put a star on issues or topics that are particularly relevant to their lives. Issues that may somehow represent their fears and their dreams. Conventional planning practices are often limited to having participants sitting in chairs and taking turns talking; the body rarely moves in those engagement processes.

Planners are often the reluctant initiators of 'embodied' sorts of engagement processes because I feel they are afraid of the tangible or the visceral when it comes to community contact. People move; they smell; they emote. Swearing is another physical thing that offends us. But it's often part of everyday life and therefore understanding its role has to be part of community engagement.

I remember a workshop we conducted for the Victorian Roads Corporation (VicRoads) in Melbourne in 1990. The Corporation had never invited community members into their building. As it was the first day of spring, Graeme Dunstan and I filled the room with flowers: daffodils and freesias. Staffing the front desk was one of the facilitators with her new baby on her breast. We were trying to say to the community members and the Corporation's planners and engineers that this workshop was about 'ordinary' things. Formally, we were discussing Melbourne's arterial roads, but we also wanted to consider mothers, babies, noise and neighbourhood protection. Intimate, local issues.

Dianna: Fear and disconnection are themes that continue to emerge in our conversations. In your experience, what do people in a community generally fear when coming to a public process?

Wendy: People are afraid they will be misrepresented or that they won't be understood. They may be afraid they won't be able to articulate the fullness of their story for some reason, perhaps because they will be rushed along. Or there won't be a place for them to voice their single solitary issue or complaint. They're afraid they won't be respectfully listened to. I'd say – based on experience – that those fears are often well grounded. We find that people don't come to community workshops wearing an overcoat of inappropriate paranoia. They dress themselves that way for a reason. Community engagement processes can be threatening!

Dianna: Is there an example of an engagement process that acknowledges the beauty of each voice in the room?

Wendy: The Minnesota Block Exercise, part of The Corridor Housing (or Development) Initiative, is one of the most powerful community engagement processes I have ever seen. I had an insight about embodiment at the table where I was observing in Minneapolis in 2006. There were three participants: a white woman, a white man in a suit who looked and acted like a businessman and a well-dressed but informally dressed African–American man. The white man was oldest, then the African–American man and then the white woman.

The woman was quite confident but slightly more deferential to the men, particularly to the white man, and perhaps a little hesitant in how she explained her views. The African–American man was an expansive poetic storyteller; all of his dreams for the site were accompanied by big gestures and powerful poetic language. He imagined himself walking down the street and entering the courtyard, drinking coffee in the corner café, explaining how it would feel to him.

I noticed two things: first, that this process really did accommodate different discursive styles. It was carefully designed to include all voices. And second, I observed that the facilitator was slightly, only slightly, more deferential to the more archetypally 'powerful' voice of the white businessman. He had a presence that perhaps gave a *gravitas* to his suggestions about how development of this site could occur.

As it turned out, everybody's words were heard and everybody's ideas were taken into account. These people were using blocks to 'build' an ideal development for a site across the street. The Minnesota Block Exercise nested within a community capacity-building exercise can be very playful. In that playful context, people were perhaps more 'equal' than they might be in a formal brainstorming session.

Discursive styles nevertheless make their way into community engagement processes. In maintaining a spirit of welcoming throughout our processes, we need to be alert to the risks of inadvertently silencing one voice, one person, at the expense of losing the wisdom all can bring to the project.

If we do this work artfully, we can offer a space in the regimented and programmed life of community members with opportunities to be welcomed, received and listened to. In Australia, we can get hundreds of people to a workshop once word gets out that the processes are fun, relevant and interactive, the food is good, we as consultants are trustworthy and that they, as participants, will be listened to, their views will be taken into account and, in the end, the results will benefit them.

Acting like a child in community engagement

For us, acting like a child is a way to inhabit a side of ourselves that is free to imagine other realities, to create opportunities for laughter and fun and to cultivate our social and emotional intelligence for expression and social engagement. Some of us might hold in the backs of our memories a scolding parent ('Stop acting like a child!') or be daunted by the justification of introducing 'childish' play into our professional work environments. To the contrary, acting like a child in community engagement invites us to liberate inhibitions about expressing feelings and imaginings and to enter into play. Play is an important ingredient in successful work in creative and transformative community engagement, especially as we try to seek out new solutions from new angles and to turn the tensions of conflict into fluid moments of change. Inhabiting a playful spirit and ethic in community engagement can move us in new and unimaginable directions – and into ways of being that we would not have imagined. And it's fun, to boot!

The play ethic

Adopting a play ethic opens new doors, invites us to re-invigorate our thinking and opens up new spaces for regenerating ideas. Play nourishes us and keeps creativity alive in our work. Wendy explains:

When we were initially brainstorming our ideas for this book a couple of years ago, I found myself explaining to Dianna and Christine that one of the reasons I was eager to write about creativity was that I was terrified about what might happen if my workplace could not be creative – and playful. I've carried that concern into a variety of playful and creative approaches to community engagement over the years – making my own workplaces fun and playful.

So it was great to discover Pat Kane – a writer, musician, activist and consultant and author of *The Play Ethic: A Manifesto for a Different Way of Living*.[2] Pat co-directs a creative consultancy, New Integrity, and is one half of the Scottish pop-soul band, *Hue and Cry*. When I heard Pat speak at the 2002 Ideas Festival in Brisbane, his words made a huge impression on me.

Pat spoke passionately about the crisis in the workplace. Work isn't making us happy. It is making us unhealthy. He asked, 'Why believe in work if it doesn't believe in you?' He argued further that, 'play is much more than you think it is'. He claimed that, 'to be literate in play, its forms and traditions is to widen our frameworks of perception'. My experience affirms Pat's contention that 'play is a way of framing what is true'. Important for this chapter is Pat's question: 'Why must we, at a certain point, put childish things behind us?'

As I sat there listening to Pat spelling out 'the seven major rhetorics of play', I found myself drawn to 'play as power and contest' (like to play in sport).[3] That's often what we find in community engagement. I've found that using play is often the best way to get beyond defended positions and interests to a more open understanding of an issue or issues. Pat seemed to agree when he advised us to 'take reality lightly'. Acknowledging that many of us had to work within 'stiff state bureaucracies', Pat supported 'a desire to live an adaptive life of possibility and openness'. Reminding me of the liminal (or threshold) qualities of the ecotone metaphor described in Chapter 1 of this book, Pat explains that 'play is a liminal aspect of the human condition'.

In other writing, Pat argues that:

> ... we're stressed-out, debt-ridden, exhausted. We have less time for our families than we feel we should have... We feel less connected to our communities than we ever did ... we also feel like hollow citizens, too weary to respond to any political entreaty with anything other than a shrug.[4]

I play, therefore I am

Pat challenges us to take our work less seriously. He speaks directly to me and to my work as a community planner. It's important to realize that play is not 'anything idle, wasteful or frivolous'. He exclaims, 'The trivialisation of play was the work ethic's most lasting and most regrettable achievement'. I was encouraged to hear his demand: 'This is "play" as the great philosophers understood it: the experience of being an active, creative and fully autonomous person'.

In my more creative community engagement work, largely influenced by community artist and activist, Graeme Dunstan, I have found that expression of the play ethic is about having the confidence to be spontaneous, creative and empathic across all areas of life – in relationships, in community, in our cultural life, as well as in paid employment. It's about placing ourselves, our passions and our enthusiasms at the centre of our world. And it's about offering the flexibility and fun that play promises to those with whom we work in community engagement processes.

Part 2

Inhabiting the Edge: Dreaming,
Imagining and Embodiment

!remember! our shapes the
colours of finger paint

sea horse

flexible juxtaposition
between alternative and assumed category

constituted of multiple identities[1]
dependently camouflaged

mesmerized by liberated statistician
revealing with her most clever
presentation hand we are numbers

no longer dividable
by one

    (a grape ripens in our mouths)

    taste multiplies
    across zone & grid

                – dh

The Practice of Inhabiting the Edge: Interview with Wendy Sarkissian

3

The practice of inhabiting the edge in community engagement asks artistry to step forward and push us into new territory. Artistry is about many different things. It is about ingeniousness and it's about prowess, practicality, confidence and craftsmanship.[1] Artistry is a superior skill that you can learn by practice and observation. In community engagement, it could be said that operating at the level of artistry means making your projects 'sing'.

Invitation:
Join in on a discussion between Wendy and Dianna on the artistry of community engagement and discover practices like 'Our Bonnyrigg Dream' workshop, where facilitators and participants are comfortable working in silence, breaking the silence and adopting a spirit of play.

When we work together with people in communities, we find that artfulness is also largely about dealing with emotions and conflict. As John Forester is often pointing out, it is critically important to deal with these issues effectively rather than try to run away from them. Misunderstanding and mismanagement of emotions in community engagement cause most conflict. They can also cause processes to become drawn-out and inefficient, resulting in expenses that might have been avoided. Mismanagement can be the biggest waste of time, money and energy for both community members and those who work with them.

The 'artfulness' or practice of inhabiting the edge involves deep listening, nesting creative approaches within a wider engagement process and ensuring that dreams are translated into appropriate action. In a long-distance phone conversation, Wendy at home in Nimbin, Australia, and Dianna on a 93-year-old Dutch barge in France, Wendy shared with Dianna what she has learned through the practice of inhabiting the edges of creative process and where she thinks we need to push the edge further.

> **Dianna**: What makes creative engagement processes practical?

> **Wendy**: The processes I've tried over the years have one thing in common. None has any validity unless it is nested in a carefully designed wider process that allows the community to have a strong ongoing monitoring role – greater than simply 'offering advice'.

> It matters how the material generated in the engagement process is collected, tabulated, analysed and reported on and how it's fed back to the community. Otherwise, discordant voices and nonconforming views may be thrown aside in the interests of saving money, time and moving on with the plan.

> A valid process means that everyone has the opportunity to be part of a representative process. But none of this really means anything if the process itself isn't open and transparent.

> I feel strongly that community engagement processes need to be opened up.

Meaning through movement: Processes using embodiment

Dianna: You refer to opening up processes through embodiment. What do you mean by 'embodied' processes?

Wendy: I am particularly impressed by the effectiveness of processes where people are closely and intimately listened to and where they are made comfortable in a setting that is congruent with their needs – culturally and physically – where they can move around in space to represent their views. This work is both kinetic and kinaesthetic.

So in the 'Our Bonnyrigg Dream' workshop in Sydney in 2005, participants (130 of them – all local residents) lined up to show how long they had lived in the neighbourhood. We placed signs on the walls of this huge gymnasium. And with their bodies, the residents showed when they arrived – from the early 1970s and onward or whether they were new to the area. Then we asked them where their *heart* was. We had placed a large coloured representation of Bonnyrigg (a huge circle) in the centre of the room and signs on the walls for all the Earth's continents. Then we asked where they lived, where they came from, where they had lived before they arrived and, lastly, where their hearts were now.

What I saw touched me deeply: 130 people crowding in the centre of the room, making a dramatic statement that their heart was right there in Bonnyrigg – in the centre of this disadvantaged community slated for community renewal. They showed physically that they wanted to live and stay there. Here were these people – many of them refugees – physically striding across the room and stamping their mark on the territory that represented where their heart was and where they wanted to stay. That's embodied work.

Here's another example. I remember a dramatic community safety forum in a Melbourne community that was not particularly crime-ridden or dangerous. This was some years ago. We were using the Affinity Diagram to move Post-it™ notes around into columns on the wall that represented affinities among local issues and problems. This sorting was done in silence, giving a real power to the physicality of it because there was no talking. We could see what headings were developing although they weren't labelled at this stage. A column on housing and homelessness clearly emerged and there was clearly a column about crime and street crime. There were also other community safety issues centring around housing and child safety, and so on.

Two larger clusters (or affinities) of Post-it™ notes ultimately emerged. One was about housing; the other was about crime: assault, burglary, robbery and street crime. We experienced a powerful dynamic between the youth worker and the head of the local police. One Post-it™ note said 'youth homelessness' and the youth worker kept picking it up and sticking it in the housing column (which was becoming all about housing). The police officer, however, was lifting it up with dramatic gestures and moving it to 'crime'. These two were having a silent tug of war with this piece of paper. Everyone experienced an interesting policy question being played out in this small community centre:

What is homelessness? Are these young people essentially bad? They can't get things together. They're addicted to substances and not adequately socialized and therefore are a danger to the rest of the community. Or are they just people in need of housing?

These questions could have made up an hour's conversation in a workshop. But in my recollection, it was that embodied experience where people had to place the issue where they believed it belonged (in silence, together, with everybody participating) that facilitated the profound experience of the issue. In silence, people really 'heard' the complexity of it.

The Embodied Affinity Diagram

For many years, we have been using the Affinity Diagram in workshops and search conferences with great results.[2] It's a highly effective way of having participants sort their own ideas without the intervening bias of the researcher or facilitator. And now we have taken it to a new level, making it 'embodied'. In the conference where we piloted it, after two days of contributions, activities and reflection, we used this model to help participants identify reflections and lessons.

We found that a wide variety of participants (there were several hundred at the conference) were able to sort their 'lessons' in a short period of time, very efficiently and with a great deal of laughter and good humour.

Lessons tied to balloons

It's really a simple process but it relies on a significant number of props and works well with helpers to manage them. Balloons are awkward, take up a lot of space and are hard to hide from view. But they are the secret to the success of the Embodied Affinity Diagram. In the Sydney Safe Communities Conference in 2004, we encouraged hundreds of participants to sort their 'lessons' amiably and without difficulty, as the photographs below show. We describe this innovative approach in detail in Gilt-edged Resource 2.

Sharing lessons

Wendy coordinating the Embodied Affinity Diagram exercise

The power of silence and breaking the silence

What's amazing (as a facilitator) is to see people discovering that they can sort complex material in absolute silence by using their non-verbal functions, by moving things around, reading, thinking and paying attention to other people. There is a huge place for silence in community workshops.

Dianna: And what happens after the silent clustering of topics in the Affinity Diagram process? Is there a breaking of the silence?

Wendy: Yes, there is a powerful breaking of silence once people surrender to the reality that they have collectively finished sorting. Many factors influence how long it takes: the size of the group, complexity of the issues, tiredness, boredom, taking too long or things just getting naturally sorted. Then comes a powerful auditory process of assigning their labels to each column. That is where you can get huge arguments.

Somebody says, 'That column is about low-income housing or public housing'. And someone else says, 'Well, I think it should be called inclusionary housing or housing for all – anything that goes against the stigma of public housing'.

So you can have a five-minute argument about one heading. You can also find a strong discussion about which topics should be grouped together. Where does youth homelessness reside? In the Melbourne workshop, it ended up in its own column all by itself. That's what the group decided – youth homelessness was such a unique and difficult issue that it needed to be highlighted. It was about homelessness and social support. The police officer retired, admitting that he'd lost ground in arguing that youth homelessness was primarily a crime issue.

So there is a very strong verbal or auditory component after the silence. I've undertaken this exercise with groups of 150 to 200 people and it's often hard to keep everybody focused. But in small groups, there is a breaking of the silence. It is a dramatic moment when I say: 'Now, what have we got here?'

Silence and breaking the silence are two very important components of the process.

From self-reflection to collaborative play

Dianna: In my conversation with Michelle LeBaron, author and currently a professor in the Faculty of Law at the University of British Columbia, Vancouver, she talked about the stages of child development and how, in the first stage of play, a child learns play through solitary play or playing by themselves. In the second stage, children play by themselves in parallel with another person or being. Then the next stage is to play together. It's interesting to think of this theory of play and development when you describe the Affinity Diagram because it seems to me that you are facilitating or orchestrating a process that allows people to arrive at new concepts and solutions together through 'play' development.

Wendy: Wonderful! I always tell people that they are about to experience something 'magical', which is what happens with the Affinity Diagram (and with the Embodied Affinity Diagram – our latest development of the idea).[3] You have identified a very important principle. One thing we need to do better in community engagement is to create space for solitary reflection before joining in the parallel or collaborative stages.

Often when people come to a community workshop, they have a lot of noise in their heads – maybe emotion, distrust or despair. A moment of reflection built into a process – which can be meditative, soulful or both (it doesn't matter) – allows people to bring their attention in a focused way to the purpose of their being there. If our processes always focus on group brainstorming and group decision making (the 'groan zone' of convergent decision making) without opportunities to reflect, my observation is that people often don't offer their best selves to the table.[4]

Often a simple tool like a short, one-page questionnaire asking people to share their opinions can help them, on arrival, leave their 'outside' concerns at the workshop door and focus on the topic at hand. This can be done with interpreters so it doesn't inhibit people who speak different languages. It's often helpful to ask three simple questions:

1   What's the thing you like most about living here?
2   What's your biggest concern about the process for looking at this issue/development?
3   What would you like this community to be like in 30 years?

What this does is help people relieve their other concerns about an exhausting day at work or what happened in traffic on the way to the meeting.

They are able to 'arrive' – to be there.

The appropriateness of dreaming to achieve practical outcomes

I want to return to our earlier conversation about play when you were speaking with Michelle LeBaron. There is a strong movement in community engagement theory and practice – reinforced by some of those in what you could call the 'representative' and 'deliberative' planning camps – that this work should not be fun. It is no laughing matter: that dangerous intersection, the proposed bridge, that community health policy.

Further, there is a view among some practitioners that these processes should not be allowed to wander off into the realms of metaphysics, spirituality and visioning. No way! Intersections are about engineering and construction and we will solve that problem in an engineering way instead of dreaming a better solution for that intersection. Or so some practitioners think. But often processes that involve a component of dreaming are more appropriate – and more effective.

The experiences reflected in this book show that you can undertake embodied, creative, heart-present processes; listen with all your senses; and create community engagement activities that are fun. And that doesn't mean that you won't have findings. It doesn't mean that the outcomes can't be categorized, analysed, interpreted and ultimately applied. There is no evidence that deep, passionate, heart-centered, powerful, emotionally relevant processes do not yield actionable outcomes. We simply need to progress from the 'dreaming' stage to the coming to public judgement and 'giving advice' stages in ways that are not too abrupt for the people involved. And then people will give advice freely.

Dianna: So they dream about the wetlands...

Wendy: Right. Let's say the wetlands are to be drained. Participants can undertake to dream for or on behalf of the wetlands: this rich matrix of interdependencies – the poetic possibilities of nesting birds that have not visited this bioregion for a hundred years. This is what happened in the Eagleby community in Queensland. A decade ago, the members of the Eagleby Renewal Action Group (ERAG) dreamed of a wetland as a local recreation resource and now they have it. I've visited it and it's marvellous.[5]

Oh! Dianna! Speaking of birds! Listen! I'll turn my microphone toward the window. Can you hear the kookaburras? It's almost sunset and they have just started laughing in the big tree behind my house…

Dianna: Beautiful! Three Great Herons have been fishing in the river here beside our boat all afternoon … they're my absolute favourite.

Wendy: Ah, wonderful! So back to the wetlands. In this sort of community engagement process, we could invite participants to dream about how this fertile but unloved wetland could be transformed into a tourist possibility, as well as a home for migrating birds and a rich source of biodiversity in plant and animal life. There is no reason that rich dreaming can't also be about biodiversity values. And there is no reason why they cannot then develop a tourism action plan.

The application of that dream is perfectly possible if you are listening.

It's totally wrong to argue that creative processes cannot yield practical planning and design guidance. I *know* they can. There are many reasons to be more lateral, creative, embodied and fluid and to allow more space in our processes.

Community Visioning as Engagement: Why a Conversation is Merited

> We look back and analyze the events
> of our lives, but there is another way
> of seeing, a backward-and-forward-at-once
> vision that is not rationally understandable.

Rumi[1]

Introduction: Why do we need community visioning as a community engagement method?

We will never perceive the world in the same way again, knowing that the future will be very different from the present. Further, future thinking is now an established part of planning processes and this applies to planning education as well as planning practice. Global factors and forces such as climate change, Peak Oil, the financial meltdown, pandemics, storms, floods and drought are contributing to community anxiety about the future.[2] Particularly in hard times, we can use creative and innovative approaches to help local communities imagine and come to grips with their futures. *Community visioning* as a community engagement method has been used in a number of ways to infuse hope and support palpable action. But as with the word 'sustainability', the widespread use of 'visioning' has resulted in unclear meanings that are sometimes confusing and may not lead to 'solutions' to planning or other community problems. We need a clear and collective means to dream our way forward. Beginning with an apology to the Mayor of Antwerp, this chapter explores some definitional problems associated with the term 'visioning' and then presents a brief history of where visioning came from and where it is headed.

Invitation:
Come and see what all the visioning confusion is about with Wendy's apology to the Mayor of Antwerp, a discussion on definitions and background to the practice of community visioning in planning and a few gems from *Theory U* to guide us in future practice.

Wendy's apology to the Mayor of Antwerp

For some years, I've been concerned about the use of the word 'visioning' and the implication that rational, left-brain activities such as brainstorming and identifying goals and objectives are often miscast as 'visioning'. I was particularly sensitive to this issue after spending a day at a conference in Europe where everyone seemed to be speaking about visioning but I felt we had no common definition. Our problem was not translation. We were simply talking about different things.

For me, visioning involves something *visionary,* something out-of-the-present and ordinary reality. Clearly, not everyone shares this view.

The situation boiled over in September 2007, when I inadvertently offended a distinguished European politician over the meaning of the term 'community visioning'. This is my formal apology to the Mayor of Antwerp, Patrick Janssens, and my explanation of *what* happened – with respect to visioning

– and my guess at *why* it happened. To refresh my memory, I've reviewed the 2007 conference transcript before writing about this incident.

In a panel discussion at the annual ISOCARP (International Society of City and Regional Planners) conference, held that year in Belgium, I was listening to Janssens explain his approach to citizenship and citizen engagement.

To a large audience of planners from around the world, Janssens – a well-educated and experienced politician and a powerful player in complex Belgian politics – explained that strategic planning projects are the City's key development motivators and triggers. He argued that it was important to focus on a vision because quality of life in an urban environment is often difficult to realize. Involvement of the private sector and different levels of government is essential. Further, it's essential to create a community of interest between all the different players – thus, Antwerp's logo: 'The City that belongs to Everyone'. Janssens had taken a principled stand against gated communities.

So far, so good. I'm sitting on the stage as part of the panel, awaiting my turn, fascinated by this charismatic politician, regretting that I'd missed his morning presentation. I'm curious about this man, who holds degrees in political science, economics and statistics and had managed a market research company before becoming Mayor. The following year, he was shortlisted for the World Mayor Award.

Janssens explained that communication, consultation and participation were an integral part of the process. Of his total City budget, he explained, fully 3 per cent was allocated for community engagement.

Then a question arises from the floor and a participant asks Janssens what he hopes to gain from participation, given that he has been elected with a clear vision and policy mandate.

Janssens responds with several strong explanations of the value of participation.

I think ... that most people are unhappy with the actual situation that they are in but they don't want change. They are against change. They are afraid of it.

So what I expect from participation is, first of all, the best possible understanding of why they are unhappy. And secondly ... as politicians and planners ... when we listen well, when we understand well why people are unhappy in a certain situation, we should be able, through our professionalism, to come up with a solution which is partially able to create a better world for them.

And you need conviction.

But then to be able to realize the vision you will need support... If we don't start to build participation early enough in the process, you will lose an enormous amount of time in the execution... I really believe very much in participation... I think that is what leadership is about... You keep on being legitimated if you have proven, first of all, that you have a vision.

And you sell hope in the beginning – hope that with a team of people you are able to make the world better through a number of policies.

Then you have to prove that you aren't only selling hope but that you can change something in reality.

The Mayor's focus on a vision led another participant to ask how a long-term vision and the time required for genuine participation processes could possibly be compatible with the short periods of elected terms. The Mayor reiterated that a long-term vision was needed to be effective. He did not believe in being held 'hostage' to elections.

Then it was my turn to speak:

At the risk of saying something provocative, I'm going to suggest that there is an elephant in the room here...What I've heard so far, not from anybody in particular is ... that we are using the term 'vision' when we actually mean 'plan'.

I think it's the new buzzword for the plan. What I'm hearing is something that is 'social marketing'... It sounds (this is how I feel) ...

top-down ... it sounds 'promulgated'; it sounds like it has rational and alienating technical language attached to it.

And it doesn't seem to be anything about a dream that was dreamed by the community or parts of the community.

Martin Luther King did not say, 'I have a strategic vision'. He said, 'I have a dream'.

And then people laid down their bodies in deeply emotive processes that weren't rational, that were non-linear, that were about their lives – to embody and put flesh on the bones of the dream of this leader.

I think what we have here are two conceptually different ways of looking at the world. One is the 'Path of Explanation', where the whole focus is to reach clarity, to help the community to get to clarity and then endorse the vision (which I think is the 'plan'). And then let's move forward speedily and efficiently...

And then there is the 'Path of Expression', where the aim is to go deep, to reach a depth of understanding of what is going on. Communities are asking for depth. And with depth (which is about storytelling, imagination and creativity), you don't go quickly to conclusions.

A cold silence filled the room as I regained my seat.

Janssens responded:

Maybe it is not a vision. It is a belief. I would be prepared to buy that. But it is not a plan. I am not prepared to compromise on beliefs or on vision.

Later, when the session had drawn to a close, I explained to him that I'd missed his morning session and wasn't particularly directing my comments about 'visioning' at *him*. But the damage was done. Scuffing my way down the corridor to my hotel room that night, I heard myself mutter 'culture shock'. Now I realize the problem was more complicated than that: 'vision shock', more likely.

It was one of those misunderstandings that plague planning – and community engagement: an honest mistake not meant to be offensive. Nevertheless, I sincerely apologize to Patrick Janssens. I believe that I – and all the 2007 ISOCARP participants, to some degree – became entangled in confusion about what a community vision is, what a visioning process might involve and what it might be expected to deliver.

Definitions and definitional problems

I believe that this story illustrates that definitions can often be a problem in community engagement discourse. Others agree with me. As Peter Senge and colleagues explain, '[a]s the idea of vision has become popularized in recent years, its essential meaning has often been lost'.[3] In the past decade, researchers have been critically inquiring into the notion of community visioning, teasing out definitions from a range of concepts and identifying its origins. Canadian academic Robert Shipley has made an extensive study of community visioning, asserting that the abstract conception of *visioning* has as many as 20 meanings and that there is virtually no consistency among them. Although there is among planners a 'tacit assumption' about the meaning, the terms *vision* and *goal* are often used interchangeably. It's also often confused with the term *mission*.[4] Shipley concludes that the meaning of various vision words is poorly understood[5] and in a later work claims that vision and community visioning are 'part strategic planning, part participation and part public motivation'. More than that, it's 'old wine in new bottles'.[6]

Where did community visioning come from?

The research into the origins of the concept of visioning explains that it's nothing new. Shipley identifies both the scriptural and classical connections, as well as origins in utopianism and utopian thinking. The use of *backcasting* and setting a social situation in the future are traced back to Edward Bellamy's *Looking Backwards* (1888). At that time, writers wanting to make social commentary speculated about social conditions directly in a story set in the future.[7]

The humanistic psychologists can take some responsibility for the flourishing of visioning in the latter half of the 20th century, with management and sport taking up the challenge and popularizing the notion. Particularly influential was Tom Peters' management text, *In Search of Excellence*.[8] Systems of visioning that had a direct effect on planning began to appear in the early 1990s, with cognitive mapping, Peter Senge's powerful book, *The Fifth Discipline*, and the less well known but thought-provoking notion of Enspirited Envisioning (Warren Ziegler).[9] More 'proprietary' models followed, with consultant Steven Ames's Oregon Model, Visual Preference Analysis (Tony Nelessen), community strategic visioning and community visioning. Only some of these approaches were designed for use in the urban planning context, however.

In planning, community visioning has been a popular planning tool for over a decade. A few models dominate, none of them 'visionary'.[10]

Shipley identifies both inherent weaknesses in some of the theory and an uncritical belief in certain points of 'conventional wisdom' on the part of numerous planners. Many planners, he claims, were not cognitively aware of the antecedents that they picked up intuitively or second-hand. In fact, many of us have probably forgotten exactly where the ideas originated and believe that we are using a new technique.[11]

With roots in management theory, community visioning has evolved from three local-level activities: futures projects, strategic planning and community architecture and planning.[12] The key features are:

- Extensive participation
- An emphasis on community values
- Wide use of graphics and visual materials
- Exploration of alternative futures
- An emphasis on a shared vision.

Most community visioning processes are undertaken as part of planning processes initiated by government. Frequently proponents seek simple pro-cesses that are easy to explain to elected members and can be implementable within their short terms of office (three to four years at most).

In *Enspirited Envisioning* (1996), Ziegler says that 'true' vision is an expression of our spirit and not knowledge, wishes or goals. A vision, he contends, can be empty or crass if the spirit is absent. Thus, he implores us, when undertaking participatory work with communities and organizations, to 'listen to the voice of the spirit'. This is because we need to be fully engaged if a vision is to be enacted. To do that, we need to listen to our own voices in the first place. Ziegler says:

> *Envisioning the future is not making a wish-list. It is not forecasting the future, or cognitive mapping, or social engineering, or Delphi, or trend extrapolation... It is also not goal-setting...*[13]

For Ziegler, envisioning is '... a discipline of the spirit that invites serious inner work to tease out, to discern, to generate *compelling images* of the future that leads to transformation through a commitment to new action illumined by that vision'.[14] The components are dialogue, deep imaging (eliciting images of the future), deep listening (listening to yourself or to other people with silence, attention and empathy and without judgement) and deep questioning (listening for whatever questions inside yourself insist on being asked and asking them). The way to undertake this work (both as a practitioner and a participant) is to seek 'paths to interiority' and enter an internal state of listening, emptying, waiting and quieting.[15] We are encouraged to find what lies within us about our future in our hopes, dreams, concern, beliefs, fears and assumptions.

Unlike most practices in planning and development, this practice is all about yielding rather than forcing. Yet there is 'no idle chitchat' in Ziegler's model. The process begins with focused imaging, described as 'a special way of telling stories about the future you want and intend to bring about'. This is followed by a 'leap into the future' and deep listening – a component that requires us to engage with the future without judgement or preconditions and to share our images *in the present tense*.[16]

A potential source of new thinking: *Theory U*

Another visioning approach that brings the spirit into the equation is the path-breaking work of Otto Scharmer and colleagues with *Theory U*. Scharmer argues that we need to extend our ways of operating to include empathic and generative listening. This means a shift from reactive responses and quick fixes on a symptoms level to *generative* responses that address systemic root issues.[17]

Scharmer identifies four types of listening: *downloading, factual* listening, *empathic* listening and *generative* listening. Basically, he argues, we need to stop *downloading* and start *listening*, going 'to the inner place of stillness where knowing comes to the surface'. The *U* is one process with five movements or steps that allow us to reach a place of inner knowing that emerges from within, followed by bringing forth the new. This entails 'discovering the future by doing'.

Scharmer's five steps are as follows:

1 *Co-initiating*: Build commitment. Stop and listen to others and what life calls you to do.
2 *Co-sensing*: Observe, observe, observe. Go to the places of most potential and listen with your mind and heart wide open.
3 *Presencing*: Connect to the source of inspirational and common will. Go to the place of silence and allow the inner knowledge to emerge.
4 *Co-creating*: Prototype the new in living examples to explore the future by doing.
5 *Co-evolving*: Embody the new in ecosystems that facilitate seeing and acting from the whole.[18]

As we drop the non-essential aspects of the self ('letting go'), we also open ourselves to new aspects of our highest possible future self ('letting come'). Australian community development specialists Josh Floyd and Peter Hayward believe that *Theory U* is 'a powerful vision of practice that is ideally suited to attracting and engaging participation with the interior qualities needed for effective social foresight cultivation'.[19]

Scharmer's model connects heart and will: 'While an open heart allows us to see a situation from the whole, an open will enables us to begin to act from the emerging whole'. His intention is the integration of head, heart and hand:[20] '… connecting to one's best future possibility and creating breakthrough ideas requires learning to access the intelligence of the heart and the hand – not just the intelligence of the head'.[21] At the core of presence and *Theory U* is a profound opening of the heart carried into action. The future, now accessible, can shape our present actions, rather than have them shaped by the patterns of the past.

This is not to say that this is simple work or that the voice of the future can be acted upon without reflection and discussion. In fact, as Senge and his co-authors explain,

> *Nothing undermines the creative process more than the naïve belief that once the vision is clear, it's just a matter of 'implementation'. In fact, moving from concept to manifestation is the heart of creating – which literally means 'bringing into existence'. And like a river's path from its source to the sea, it is anything but a straight line. Instead, creating is a sort of dance between inspiration and experimentation...[22]*

Now that we have traced the origins of the concept and practice of visioning, we can ask: What should it be and how might it operate in community engagement? That's the topic we address in the next chapter.

Heartstorming: Putting the Vision Back into Visioning

5

Introduction: Wendy's approach to *heartstorming*[1] and community visioning

In April 2009, I attended the Ideas Festival in Brisbane and heard three speakers who were describing global sustainability challenges by paraphrasing Albert Einstein's statement about the need for *new thinking* to address future problems. Einstein's statement goes something like this:

> We can't solve problems by using the same kind of thinking we used when we created them.

By painful experience we have learned that rational thinking does not suffice to solve the problems of our social life.

Many critics are now echoing Einstein's views, claiming that we must deepen our community conversations about the future. We can no longer rely on 'mental models based on past experience'. We need, claims American planning academic, Patricia Wilson, 'new wisdom about the emerging future'. This is because the new direction of 'deep democracy' involves 'the inner experience of interconnectedness'. The sort of civic dialogue Wilson envisages

> **Invitation:**
>
> Walk into Wendy's multifaceted evolution and clarification of her community visioning practice, an approach she calls *heartstorming*.

moves from civic 'knowing' (learning and sensing together in community) to civic 'willing' (the visioning and what is known as *presencing* of the whole that is wanting to emerge).[2] Finally,

> *... the core practice of dialogue can be deepened until we are listening beyond the words to our own and others' needs, feelings, assumptions and frames; and even deeper until we are listening together to the silence, to the heartbeat of the whole, to what is wanting to emerge and be born... At this point we are listening to the deepest faculty of inner knowing.*

Appreciations and foundations

Exploring the dimensions of community visioning has led me to many wise teachers, some much younger than I.[3] I bow in gratitude to Clare Cooper Marcus, who initiated me into the miracles of guided imagery in 1973. At that time, Clare was a Professor in the Department of Landscape Architecture at the University of California at Berkeley. In an innovative process called an 'environmental autobiography', she invited students to explore their favourite childhood environments. Part of the process was a guided meditation asking students to recall a favourite childhood place.[4] Clare's work is chronicled in a number of professional papers and adaptations of her approach are reported in many publications and in her book, *House as Mirror of Self: Exploring the Deeper Meaning of Home* (second edition, 2006), which contains one of my drawings from such an exercise, which I reproduce on the following page.[5]

British-born Clare taught in California for many years and was adept in a wide variety of healing and therapeutic modalities, having undertaken training in order to use the gestalt therapy technique of role playing as a research tool, which informed her work on the book, *House as a Mirror of Self*. Widely

Wendy's Drawing from a Childhood Fantasy, 1980

experienced in working with planners and designers, she carefully prepared her students to explore their favourite childhood environments: 'I find a period of quiet, relaxed breathing starts to get people out of their normal, academic, logical way of thinking, and opens them up into a more loose, fantasy state'.

In Clare's model, having entered into the visualization, the journeying person sees a figure in the distance walking towards them. They feel slightly curious to discover that the figure is a person – themselves as a child. (I remember looking down to see the small child's hand in mine and feeling a strong and palpable connection.) Then *you-the-adult* fades away and *you-the-child* starts to explore the childhood place, experiencing all its qualities from their unique child's perspective. Carefully worded cues encourage the sense of touch, smell, feeling and recollection of special events. In her script, Clare leaves plenty of silent periods for contemplation and remembering.

Coming back

How do we bring participants back so that they can record what they have experienced? Do they arrive by hot-air balloon? Are they magically transported back to the room? Clare reminds us that, '... this can be a very profound experience ... that takes people into a state of consciousness not normally experienced in the classroom. Therefore, a firm and structured ending is called for to bring them into the next stage, that of recording what they experienced'. Her suggestions are to:

> ...ask them to lie down in their fantasy, in what they consider to be the center or heart of their environment, to close their eyes (still in fantasy – they have them closed already in reality) and then listen to my voice slowly counting from ten down to zero; as they listen, they will gradually leave their child-self and their child-environment and return to the here and now – and open their eyes.

Clare asks participants to draw in silence and to write about their experience both objectively and subjectively. Sharing of insights with other participants adds another dimension.

Wendy's approach to community visioning

My approach to community visioning builds on Clare's work and the work of many practitioners and theorists and reflects years of experimentation.

The method I use is a variation of *guided imagery* or *creative visualization*.[6] A script is used to take a group on an imaginary passage into the future. People close their eyes, clear their minds and at the instruction of a facilitator or leader, either recall and experience the past or imagine the future. It can be useful to give participants the 'feel' for a situation or to understand how things might appear from another person's point of view or at another point in time. It can cut through intellectual blocks by calling on people's imagination and enables people to tap into their own memories and instincts.[7] I use visualization to allow community groups to collectively develop a common strategic vision for an area. Community values and aspirations can be openly tabled as participants articulate the issues and concerns, likes and dislikes, so that special characteristics can be identified for future improvement or protection.[8] My approach aligns with the 'guided visualization' described by the New Economics Foundation in *Participation Works!*[9]

I have found that *everyone* is capable of visioning. In a workshop for builders working in small house-building companies in Melbourne in 1990, participants visualized their ideal suburban environment incorporating sites with a mix of zoning and medium-density housing and then collectively drew their visions, using their non-dominant hands. The result was a splendidly creative representation that surprised some onlookers. An angry builder retorted, 'What makes you think that builders can't dream?!' Also in 1990, in a workshop to create concepts for the future of the Town Centre in the semi-rural community of Eltham in suburban Melbourne, participants visualized themselves walking around the revitalized Town Centre 20 years hence. They were accompanied by a young girl who pointed out its features. After participants drew their collective visions in crayons on large sheets of paper, they were encouraged by means of a *backcasting* exercise to examine the steps necessary to achieve their ideal visions.

Setting the scene for deep work: Hospitality in planning

People often ask me how we encourage community participants to engage in creative processes like community visioning. I usually respond that we take care of the details and allow participants to take care of their own dreams, fears, ideas, contributions, and so on.

Hospitality and welcoming are essential. I cannot overemphasize this aspect. We try to set up the room or working space as though we were welcoming friends for lunch. Setting up is a critical first step. I try to be creative in thinking about how people will feel welcomed into the space where the visioning is to take place. What sort of space would you walk into and feel comfortable? Will this work for 'the guests' you have invited to attend the visioning session?[10]

As we aim to create a sacred place for working deeply on issues of great concern to participants, we need to ensure that our own bodyminds are sacred and receptive places, open to receive their heartfelt contributions. A short period of attunement for workshop staff can make a huge difference for everyone.

Early consultation with participants and their advocates (*coproduction*)

By far the most successful visioning workshops are those that are co-designed with community members and their advocates. They can help us with ideas that have worked before and can support deep work by demystifying the process with other community members. In one workshop in Sydney, Christine Fraser, the Community Advocate, co-designed the visioning exercise with Yollana Shore of my consulting firm. Christine was particularly adept at this work as a long-time student of Jean Houston.[11] When you are 'working at the edge' with community members, this collaborative approach enables them to see you for who you really are and can help demystify your approaches. But more importantly, you can tailor approaches for the people with whom you will be working. Asking for and receiving permission is very important with certain cultural groups for which visioning or role plays may not be appropriate.[12]

Teamwork

In working with so-called 'alternative' approaches such as community visioning, it's important to build participants' confidence and a positive expectation. It will be easier if all members of your team support your approach and can help if another is ill or called away. When I was visited by laryngitis the day of an important dreaming workshop in Sydney in 2005, I was blessed with a co-facilitator, Sophia van Ruth, who not only was adept at these processes, but also had co-written the visioning script. I'm positive Sophia did a better job than I could have. (The visioning script is Gilt-edged Resource 1 included at the back of this book.)

Sophia van Ruth reading the visioning script, 2005

Interdisciplinarity: Many paths to the centre

My approach is highly eclectic and interdisciplinary. I am always searching for new ideas and approaches that can deepen the visioning experience for workshop participants. I rarely find ideas in the work of community engagement practitioners working in planning (William Ziegler is an exception). I do find guidance in the wisdom traditions, from therapist friends and colleagues, from reading in a variety of disciplines, including the 13th-century Persian poet, Rumi, cited at the beginning of Chapter 4.

Building confidence (*preframing*)

Many proponents of creative visualization and guided imagery in community engagement emphasize the importance of *preframing* before undertaking such a process. There are many reasons for preframing. First, it's wise to prepare participants for the intensity of the process they are about to experience. Second, research and experimentation in management and sports psychology have demonstrated the effectiveness of approaches that bridge between linear and lateral ways of being and seeing the world. We can explain that, with our current understanding, we may not be able to perceive every possible alternative or solution to a problem or a situation. If necessary, we can explain that guided imagery is not a strange 'way out' experience but is used often, especially in sports psychology and increasingly in business and organizational development, to help people improve performance and achieve clarity about their goals and plans. There is now widespread and public acceptance of guided imagery. It is used to teach relaxation, alleviate anxiety and depression, relieve physical and psychological symptoms and resolve conflict.[13]

Visualization is a right-brain activity that forces people to break out of analytical thinking patterns, which may be exactly what critical thinkers need to solve their problem.[14] There are ways to reach an understanding of a situation through visualization that are not possible exclusively via rational thought processes. Some things simply cannot occur to us unless we open all our senses to the possibility.

Third, to increase participant comfort and 'ownership', it's valuable to explain what's happening (all the steps of a visioning process) so that people are not frightened or simply 'put off'. It's also important at this early stage to address and confront the *Voice of Judgment (VOJ)*, the voice of the inner critic, which can stifle creativity in groups.[15]

The fourth, and very important, reason for *preframing* is to help people know that what they see is *what they really want*. This is a complex matter and clarification may require several iterations of a vision.

Australian David Engwicht, master storyteller and visioning practitioner, taught me about the importance of knowing what we really want. A story about Brisbane activists is particularly helpful. In 1987, David led a community action to stop a road-widening project (Route 20) in his home suburb in Brisbane. Early in the campaign, David argued that his community should not try to push the problem into someone else's backyard, but should search for city-wide and long-term solutions. He also prompted residents to take personal responsibility for their car use – a factor influencing demands for road widening. Residents discovered, three years after they visualized their success and identified the necessary steps to achieve their aims (using 'backcasting'), that they had achieved all their objectives according to their original script.[16]

Respecting multiple intelligences and learning styles

In a recent book, *Kitchen Table Sustainability* (2009a), we described Howard Gardner's 'theory of multiple intelligences', which initially proposed seven types of intelligences: linguistic intelligence (*word smart*); logical–mathematical intelligence (*number/reasoning smart*); spatial intelligence (*picture smart*); bodily–kinaesthetic intelligence (*body smart*); musical intelligence (*music-smart*); interpersonal intelligence (*people smart*); and intrapersonal intelligence (*self smart*).[17] Later, Gardner added naturalist intelligence, spiritual intelligence, existential intelligence and moral intelligence.[18] The message from this work for community visioning is that we need to be alert to our participants' different learning styles and multiple intelligences. A one-size-fits-all approach will not work. Daniel Goleman's concept of *social intelligence*, which has two major components (social awareness and social facility), expands the notion of multiple intelligences.[19] To ensure that participants are not inadvertently sidelined in visioning exercises, we *must* be alert to their multiple intelligences.

Our intention in developing a vision script is to allow people to experience, feel and see vividly and remember clearly. For this work, we are indebted to neuro-linguistic programming (NLP) for many helpful insights.[20] NLP is an in-depth technique we can use to understand our own and others' systems, which can be broadly categorized as *visual, auditory* or *kinaesthetic*. NLP offers a series of methods that model human experience and communication. When used systematically, the approach is oriented towards sensory channels that provide the individual with the maximum amount of information. We use NLP principles in designing our visioning scripts because it helps us understand how people represent their world so we can appreciate their views. It offers tools to help us communicate effectively with a variety of participants. It also profoundly influences understanding of how we communicate and why it is easier with certain people.

Visual, Auditory and Kinaesthetic (*VAK*)

Using NLP principles in our visioning practice, we work in the following way. We draft a visioning script, bearing in mind the purposes of the process. If the aim is to help people imagine their community following community renewal and/ or redevelopment, participants may be guided to walk around the renewed community 15 or 20 years in the future. Once we have completed our draft, we apply NLP principles to it, taking into account the need to stimulate all senses in the listener, especially the visual, auditory and kinaesthetic sensibilities.

Often people understand and express visioning in multiple ways; however, we are aware that those people who are primarily *visual* will have good access to their inner pictures and may be able to visualize everything. For them, emotions unroll like an inner movie. These people are generally focused on seeing and take an interest in being seen. They love performance and respond to evocative images. There are many ways (as you will see in the examples below and in Gilt-edged Resource 1) to stimulate the imagination of the predominantly *visual* person.

For the predominantly *auditory* person, we take into account that they are already adapted to listening and have a strong preference and feeling for speech. These 'rational' people prefer to understand everything exactly. Making sure that there are no discontinuities in the visioning script and that adequate time is provided for debriefing in 'rational' mode can help these people participate fully.

For the *kinaesthetic* person, the visioning script must simulate a *physical* experience, which can be supported by words or stimulating music. In designing the script, it's helpful to provide cues for opportunities to sense, feel and touch elements in the landscape or the environment of the vision.

We have found that, by using simple NLP principles in designing our scripts, we can help to reduce participants' fears, promote self-confidence, increase mental awareness and create compelling visions of the future. This is 'an emerging future that depends on us' and is seeking to emerge through us.[21] To help people get in touch with the environment of the vision, we can use direct questions such as, 'Can you see the vehicle?' Or we can pre-program the visioning exercise to be directive: 'Feel the wind. Then what else do you feel?' Or we can say, 'Breathe as you would normally breathe'.

How to begin?

As the visioning journey is an important part of the process, its beginning must be well thought-out. Following a *preframing* designed to put people at ease and convince them that this is not a recruitment session for the Church of the Cosmic Banana, I ask people to loosen their belts and uncross their legs. I invite those who are used to doing meditation or yoga to sit in any position that helps them feel centred. There are two ways to proceed. The approach of *Enspirited Envisioning* is to 'leap into the future time' and to find yourself in the future environment. This works well for most people. For those who need a bit more time and perhaps a bit of orientation to this way of working, I guide them along a country road, through an old gate into a secret garden, where they meet a young child who takes them on a journey in a hot-air balloon. Either way works. It's often a matter of timing. The important thing is to guide *with confidence*, demystifying the journeying process and giving the impression that this is the most natural thing to be doing!

Paying attention to wording

It must be clear from the foregoing that the *wording* of the script is critical to success. There is much more to community visioning than sitting around, brainstorming, imagining an ideal future and writing down the key points. Many planning practitioners do nothing more than that and miss the huge benefits of paying attention to wording to prompt participants to look for certain features in the future landscapes they are 'visiting'. This is not 'leading the witness' – quite the contrary. By paying attention to careful wording and the NLP principles described above, we can ensure that we prompt only in a *generic* sense. For example a future 'ecological' vision may have transport or transit components. Rather than guide participants into a bus station or a train, we can ask them to visualize the transport interchange and they can work out for themselves what the mode of transport might be. The same applies to schooling, entertainment, community enterprises, shopping, local food production, and so forth. The key is to cue for a response but keep it generic while stimulating participants' unique learning styles.

Yollana Shore, a therapist adept at this work, employs many therapeutic techniques in her guided imagery scripts. In crafting these scripts, she pays careful attention to language. For example, in setting a scene, she might say, 'I wonder what would happen if you were to find yourself waking up in the year 2012?' The phrase 'I wonder what would happen if' will often allow the participant to picture the proposed scenario without feeling overly controlled or directed. When asking participants to do something actively within the scene (to hear, see, feel, walk forward, and so on), Yollana might say something like, 'Just allow yourself to look closely at the kinds of people who are here with you in the park'. In contrast to direct commands such as 'Now, walk up the stairs' or 'I want you to listen to the sounds on the street...', the phrase, 'Just allow yourself', used liberally in a script, permits participants to feel guided without feeling controlled.

Yollana is often careful to include visual, auditory and kinaesthetic sensing/ feeling prompts to ensure that participants with different learning and thinking styles can engage with the experience. She may also prompt dialogue to encourage people to engage more deeply with the imagined setting – for example: 'If this tree could speak … or if it had a message for you about its place in the park … what would it say?' Using lots of strategic, open-ended questions helps participants to be creative and have their own imaginary experience validated, while at the same time exploring the elements suggested in the script.

Timing and pacing

The temptation is to make a visioning script too long. Twenty minutes is probably too long; 15 is preferable. Inexperienced practitioners tend to rush visualizations, perhaps because they are uncomfortable or are being hurried along by others. It's important to provide enough time without losing your participants in the future! It's often difficult to keep calm when those who are uncomfortable with this way of working seek either to help or to sabotage our efforts. In a corporate visioning process for an organization experiencing a great deal of stress in a highly competitive environment, Yollana and I developed a script that allowed staff to experience working collaboratively and with confidence. In a room of 40 people sitting with their eyes closed, I looked up from my script to see the manager giving me the 'wind-up' signal. I glanced at Yollana, who shrugged her shoulders. I ignored the manager. The next time I looked up, the manager was standing outside speaking on her mobile telephone!

Silence is critically important. Make sure there are many pauses in your script (see the example in Gilt-edged Resource 1) so that participants can feel themselves in and experience the future environment.

Intergenerational and interspecies approaches

As my initiation into guided imagery came via the inspired favourite childhood environment approach of Clare Cooper Marcus, I often choose to guide the visitor to meet a child on a path. The child can then identify different elements and qualities of the environment *from their point of view*, introducing an intergenerational component and a freshness that comes from a child's way of seeing the world.

Another approach is to ask the journeying person to have a dialogue with people and/or beings and elements in the landscape they are encountering. You can ask them to listen to the voice of the forest and respond to what the forest (or any element) says. Again, this component of the journey must be later recorded.

Backcasting (Rumi's *backward-and-forward-at-once vision*)

Robert Shipley wisely notes with respect to *backcasting* that:

> *If forecasting … was an attempt to project current trends into the future and thereby predict what would happen, the backcasting was the exercise of speculating about a future state of affairs and working backwards from that point to reconstruct the steps that must be taken to get there. This concept was one of the pieces that went into the modern approach to visioning.*[22]

Backcasting is a valuable, established visioning tool. It works in the following way. When you have guided your participants to a future time and place and they have experienced its qualities, it's time to return to the present and record the journey. While still in the future time, you can ask your participants to reflect (or to listen to the voices of people and/or beings and elements of that future time): 'How did you get here?' It's often helpful to ask *what needed to change* to bring about this new future (or these new futures). Spending adequate time on this stage of the process is important because it can yield valuable insights. It's critical that this *backcasting* instruction not be lost in the drawing and recording stage.

Handling 'The Return'

How to bring people back? There are many ways, echoing the advice about how to enter the visioning process. You can simply ask people to return to the place they are in, ground themselves and gently open their eyes. Or you can count backwards from ten, as Clare Cooper Marcus recommends in her childhood environment exercise. Or you can use more elaborate methods, again considering time constraints. Participants can return in a space shuttle or a hot-air balloon. One way is to ask people to walk through their future environment, using *backcasting* at each point. In this approach, participants would arrive at the last/first place and 'have a final look around at this place'. They can be cued to listen for 'any final messages that the place wishes to communicate'. You might ask, 'If the animals had something to say, what might they say?' or 'If Nature had something to tell you, what might it be?'

It's critical to end on a positive note. Your participants may have received a message or a gift from the future time. That is a talisman to cherish in the present time. So you may want to cue them as follows: 'Know that your vision is possible' or, 'Remember the beauty and power of this place'. A simple instruction concludes the journey: 'When all parts of you are fully integrated and ready, open your eyes and record (or share) your vision…'

Recording and discussion

You'll probably find a soft-eyed and mellow group when you look up from your visioning script. They will now be ready to record their visions. It's important to tread carefully at this point. I recommend that they draw their vision in silence, using the crayons provided.[23] It's also important to give permission and hold it lightly. As Senge and his colleagues advise, 'the visions don't have to be perfect. They just need to be enough to get started'.[24]

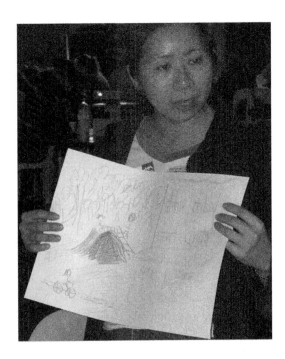

After about 10 or 15 minutes of silent drawing,[25] participants will be ready to share their drawings. This is where the table facilitator comes in. They should carefully record all the qualities discussed as table participants share their visions.

The next steps: Treating material respectfully and respecting individual privacy

What happens next is largely determined by the needs of the project. What is important is that the participants' privacy is respected (they can sign forms to allow us to use the material if we need to) and that all their material is analysed in the most respectful and thorough manner. Drawings may be copied and themes and qualities drawn out for further analysis. We try to return the drawings as soon as possible to participants, so it's helpful to have a colour printer or photocopier on hand. Where permission is given, all contributions must be acknowledged in reports. Participants may feel a strong attachment to the product of a deep process and may be unwilling to have their drawings reproduced.

Final words

It's difficult to capture the quality of a community visioning experience when all participants seem to become attuned to a common desire to seek a happy future. That's very different from a common vision – and it's very powerful. Listening to people share their visions can bring me to tears. Sometimes the qualities in the future scenario are nothing more than community safety and security or, as one woman in Sydney explained to me in 1997, 'not being ganged on'. Another showed me a simple drawing of herself and her female neighbour shaking hands across a fence.

Sitting here in the bush in Nimbin, remembering 'Our Bonnyrigg Dream' – that powerful workshop in Sydney, a thousand kilometres away, four years ago – I sense again that feeling of being drawn to the future. And I sense the power of the future waiting to be born in us.

Not being ganged on

Hello, how are you?

Here's my recollection poem.

Our Bonnyrigg Dream
For Sophia

I lost my voice
The day of the visioning workshop
So I could simply
Listen

Listen.

To bells
Not voices
Inquiring
What might our future be?

Interpreters explaining:
Listen to the years ahead
in eight melodious languages
carried to this place
from all Earth's corners

Their words
Our dreams
consecrating the humble
community hall

Sophia reading the vision script
Sentence by sentence
Pausing, breathing
Interpreters following

Tibetan bells!

A hundred residents
listening
in Arabic
in Vietnamese
in Lao
in Spanish
Khmer, Assyrian, Cantonese, Mandarin
and English

Shawls of prayers
Wrapping round the elder ones
The stolen, forsaken and frightened ones

Dreams rising above
Waiting to be born in us

This gentle listening
all there is to guide us

Acting like a Child: Welcoming Spontaneity and Creativity in the Aurora Team Development Workshop

6

Children and young people have a unique sense of playful leadership when it comes to community engagement. In Chapter 2, Wendy outlined the rationale for acting like a child to invoke the spirit of spontaneity and play. In this chapter, she talks more about welcoming the spirit of play through evoking the spirit of our inner child in the example of the Aurora Team Development Workshop. As this three-day workshop was a process with land development professionals that pre-dated any engagement

Invitation:
Revisit the justifications for play in professional work explained in Chapter 2 by witnessing Wendy's practice of welcoming new spaces for ideas, relationships and sustainable site development objectives. Using this example of working with land professionals in a team development workshop, Wendy encourages us to explore the benefits for community engagement of accessing our inner child.

with the wider community, Wendy evoked imaginative and playful processes to invite the spirit of children and young people into this initial stage. This playful spirit would help the planners and others to create a new culture for achieving innovative and transformative solutions for this residential development in Melbourne.

We first met Pat Kane in Chapter 2. Revisiting his idea of the play ethic, Pat Kane further contends:

> By clearing space for activities that are pleasurable, voluntary and imaginative – that is, for play – you'll have better memory, sharper reasoning and more optimism about the future... The play ethic is ... an attempt to imagine what human beings could do under these coming conditions. Not slumped in front of the television, not lost in a narcotic stupor, not listless or apathetic or passive – but an imaginative, engaged and active citizenry ... meaningful work and serious play become the same thing.[1]

So what to make of this for creative community engagement? For one thing, we need more humour in our work. We also need to get over the requirement to 'act like an adult' all the time. This leads directly to acting like a child.

A team development workshop: our rationale for acting like a child

Wendy shares more of her experiences with the Aurora Project:

Back in 2001, I had an opportunity to bring the play ethic into practice in a team development workshop for members of the land professions in Melbourne. For this work, I engaged a creativity consultant, Kashonia Carnegie, who helped us understand the importance of 'acting like a child'.[2] Kashonia explained that the management approaches pervading both business and bureaucracy constrain the mind to the rational, to reason, hard facts and linear logic. But, she contended, *the rational* is only a small aspect of all the possibilities of the human – useful when dealing with the known and its conventions. It's less effective when we are striving to create something new. Overly engineered communities in the past have let us down. They've planned out disorder and play, leaving behind sterile environments ill-suited to the human scale.

The qualities of a creative person are often dampened by the experiences of adulthood. Expansiveness, openness, fun, wildness, looseness and light – all these qualities receive short shrift in professional life, which becomes associated with limiting beliefs about what is possible. Children laugh on average 400 times a day. Some adults spend days and weeks without laughing. For the child, the future is pure horizon. We wanted to capture that sense of optimism in the planning of a new residential development.

Among the adult themes that need to be overcome so that 'thinking like a child' can be released are the following: *there is a right answer; that's not logical; follow the rules; be practical; play is frivolous; that's not my area of expertise; avoid ambiguity; don't be foolish; to err is wrong; I'm not creative.*[3] In designing the initial experiences for the team development workshop, we paid attention to expressions and activities that could release the characteristics of the creative child within the professional adult.

Over the years, my Australian social planning consulting firm, Sarkissian Associates Planners, has practised many techniques and rituals for lightening up and moving ourselves beyond the limitations of the rational to the infinite possibilities of mind. They range from visioning and active imagination methods that quieten the chatter of the mind, from psychodrama and role plays to playfulness, poetry, collaborative cake making, designing ideal environments with food or simply drawing with crayons.

Bringing forth the inner child is one such approach. Everyone has the remnants of ways of seeing and being, some pre-verbal, that preceded the schooling that trained our minds and equated 'acting childishly' with unreliability and irresponsibility. All of us have experienced that the act of consciously acting in a childish way can bring forth freshness, laughter and insight. The project described below employed this approach.

Introduction to the project

The Aurora site, nearly 650 hectares in size, was one of the largest accessible suburban sites still available for residential development in metropolitan

Melbourne at the turn of this century. To be master-planned by a team of expert consultants, it would eventually house approximately 25,000 residents in an estate with neighbourhoods, shops, schools, community facilities, public transport and generous parklands. It represented a major challenge to the Victorian Urban and Regional Land Corporation (URLC) and its consultants to achieve sustainability objectives which to date had largely eluded developers.

At the time of the workshop (April 2001), the project was highly significant for the Corporation. Everyone saw it as an opportunity to combine a commercial advantage with a strong focus on sustainability, a major emphasis of the Victorian State Government of the time.[4] The Corporation had some previous experience with teamwork approaches and team development workshops, notably for the Roxburgh Park consultant team. That process, facilitated by Wendy Sarkissian, has been documented elsewhere.[5]

The 2001 residential workshop was held over three days in a conference centre in a relatively isolated location north-east of Melbourne. We chose the location so that participants could focus on workshop objectives without the distractions of a working day in the office. A total of 21 people attended the workshop, including:

- Four members of the Urban and Regional Land Corporation management and staff
- The 13 members of the Aurora Project Team (all consultants)
- One guest, a specialist in sustainability (Professor Peter Newman) and
- The three-member workshop facilitation team.

The objectives for the workshop reflected both participants' needs and the objectives of the Corporation to build a strong project team. There was a high degree of congruence between both sets of requirements. For example, when asked for one thing that you would change about previous consultant team experiences, participants suggested increasing levels of inclusiveness and ongoing involvement, as well as increasing opportunities to work together as a team with a 'genuine team approach'. Others asked for 'automatic respect' and 'eager interest in sharing knowledge in a collaborative team committed to delivering a better product that provides economic, social and environmental wins and not 'pie in the sky'.

When we spoke to participants by telephone before the workshop, most said they wanted to engage in team building, process planning, teamwork and open discussions. They were keen to develop a shared vision for future processes and to gain a sense of the Corporation's commitment both to the project and to future team processes. Having worked together on large teams before, many wanted clarification of their exact roles, to build their communication skills and approaches to achieve cohesiveness. They were understandably curious about the Corporation's expectations and vision. Team members were also curious about Ecologically Sustainable Development (ESD)[6] – they wanted to explore real implementation opportunities, rather than theorizing, and sought the latest thinking in other areas of expertise. With eyes on the ball, they also sought after and said they wanted to know about targets and client expectations.

They asked to be able to forge good working relationships within the team, to have their own disciplines recognized as valid and to recognize the difficulties faced by each discipline. They anticipated the experience of being intellectually stretched and contributing towards a healthy collaborative team culture.

As a group, they asked a lot of a short residential workshop. They sought cohesiveness, chances to build team spirit and sense of direction, a successful, open and honest process, real cooperation and support, and a good appreciation of what team members had to offer.[7]

We were somewhat daunted by their passionate commitment and desire for team building. As facilitators, we realized we would need to introduce some alternative forms of engagement to achieve these outcomes.

The children's party: Acting like a child in a team development workshop

The purpose of bringing forth the inner child in this workshop was to nurture creativity and alternative modes of intelligence. The aim of the first session, the children's party, was to locate and release participants' *emotional intelligence*, using methods of applied creative thinking. The fundamentals of emotional intelligence are self-awareness, skilful handling of emotions, empathy and social skills.[8] Too often in our work settings, we form rituals or habits of professionalism that limit our full expression of spontaneous emotions, such as delight, excitement and sometimes disappointment. To act like a child is to accept the chaotic, to let go or lose our mask of pretentiousness and evoke the charm to say and express things in ways less inhibited by whether they are 'right' or 'true'.

By surrounding participants with colour, balloons, music and food reminiscent of an Australian childhood and childhood memories, we aimed to simulate the childhood environment and therefore the creative responses of childhood. We also applied models of creative thinking in the session design, including opportunities for 'incubation' so that our colleagues could sleep on the experience they had in this early session and incorporate their insights into the following days' sessions.

Typical Australian Children's Party Food

One of the ways to foster creativity is to ensure that we engage the full creative potential of the human brain in any exercise. Most researchers believe that there is a much broader range of creativity or creative essence than that attributed to the right half of the brain. Acceptance of the inner creative resource (everyone's creative side) that can be both surrendered to and depended upon, is now firmly established by the new physics, split-brain research and triune brain findings and well established in business and management.

The generic model used for the Aurora workshop acknowledged the variety of learning styles and preferences for ways of being among team members (and related it to recent research on the preferred learning style of planners and members of the land professions).[9] It carefully paced out activities so that participants could tolerate steps that might not be entirely congruent with their learning styles because other steps were more related to their styles. It also provided opportunities for people to monitor their feelings, reflections and moments of self-discovery.

In bringing the creative child into play, we acknowledge that a team needs a variety of approaches to intelligence (beyond being 'smart' or 'clever') to address the complex problems of creating a master-planned community that aims to provide a total environment. Environmental educators agree. Robert Greenway believes that 'to become ecologically intelligent is absolutely essential'. For educational philosopher, David Orr, 'education can be a dangerous thing', as problems inhere in 'the modern fetish with smartness'. The intellect that universities and colleges seek to train fits the demands of instrumental rationality built into the industrial economy.[10] Further, 'we do not know very much about intelligence and … from the perspective of the earth, much of what we presume to know may be wrong, which is to say that it is not intelligent enough'. What we call intelligence and what we test for and reward is more akin to *cleverness*. Intelligence has to do with 'the long run' and is mostly integrative, whereas cleverness is mostly preoccupied with the short run and tends to fragment things.[11]

Modern views of intelligence as 'smartness' began, says Chet Bowers, in the individually centred view of intelligence: the mind processes information and the raw data of direct experience, using different bodily and mental attributes to express intelligence.[12] Bowers' alternative concept of *embodied intelligence* is intended to foreground the symbolic and cultural environment. His *ecological view of intelligence* is based on the long-term sustainability of the Earth's ecosystem as the primary criterion.

Many researchers are now seriously questioning current approaches to developing creativity because of their individualistic underpinnings. We need instead an understanding of creativity based on a more ecologically responsible approach, with an image of the creative person 'grounded in a sense of connectedness and interdependency within the larger biotic community'.[13] Our Aurora workshop aligned with and attempted to work with many of these concepts.

Many avenues can lead to ecological consciousness: traditional ecological cultural practices, mythic attunement with Nature, scientific ecological knowledge (literacy) and spiritual 'world' consciousness. Knowing my professional colleagues, I felt that in this context 'nurturing mythic and spiritual consciousness' might be ever so slightly beyond the realm of trainer or teamwork workshop facilitator. Thus, we prepared a 'normative' workshop agenda for the three days and carefully introduced 'bridging' activities. We reinforced and supported the creative energy released by awakening the creative child in the first workshop session (the surprise, celebration party) in subsequent workshop sessions. We did this to promote the 'epistemological leap'. Then we could nurture more ecological or embodied forms of intelligence and creativity.

Although the workshop was packed with lectures and other more conventional forms of team-building practice, fundamental to these components of the workshop was nurturing creativity. This was achieved through 'giving permission' to Team members to think beyond accepted and inherent paradigms and to think creatively and laterally about their work. We emphasized that 'no idea is a bad idea'. We designed the opening welcome session to encourage everyone to step outside their comfort zones and welcome their inner creative child. The opening session was designed as a surprise children's party complete with typical Australian children's party food, balloons, streamers, whistles, a gift exchange, poetry readings, dancing and music.

The big surprise: Party time!

The element of surprise was another way of heightening excitement and engaging childlike enthusiasm. When the Team members arrived from Melbourne by bus late in the afternoon they were taken to their rooms. They were then gathered in the corridor outside the dining room with the door kept closed until everyone was waiting outside. Then lively music blasted out and 10 to 15 seconds later, the doors opened wide to welcoming by the two workshop facilitators (Kelvin Walsh and Wendy) wearing Wilderness Society koala suits! The tall and squat koalas pulled everyone into the room, where they were bombarded with party hats and children's party food, whistles, party bags, dancing, confetti and streamers until the music ended.

The initial reaction was shock and awe. The dancing left some new arrivals bewildered and others amused. Others looked very uncomfortable. The two koalas were a complete surprise, as was the festive atmosphere and the loud music. Not everyone looked like they wanted to have a party. However, they had signed up for three days, it was clearly 'party time' and the visual cues of

childhood (including the cakes and treats) helped them join in. Discomfort can be a very positive emotion to have in community engagement. Spontaneity can be very valuable: it immediately works to dislodge and disrupt old ways of doing things and to invite new responses.

After the dancing ended, everyone gathered round to see what would happen next. And next were the gift-giving ceremonies. We'd found through our research into high-performance teams that recognition and reward are critical components of effective teamwork. Throughout the workshop-planning process, everyone we spoke to (Corporation staff, the consultants and management associated with the project) commented on the gruelling nature of the consultant-selection process. It had taken months and had been highly competitive and very taxing for all concerned. All agreed that we had to put that unhappiness behind us. As a first step, we needed to recognize and validate the consultants and express the Project Manager's (and the Corporation's) delight in their selection. Kelvin and I knew from experience that the life of a consultant often lacks professionally affirming experiences.

We used the element of surprise in the gift-giving ceremonies. Kelvin and I purchased expensive books for all consultants (following extensive research into their reading tastes) and wrapped them beautifully, accompanying them by signed cards from the Project Manager, Jill Lim. And each participant brought a gift for another (valued at less than $20.00) to recognize their new working relationships as colleagues on this project. (As many of the consultants had worked together before, this was a way of incorporating everyone into the process.) Because children's parties are often associated with gift giving, this component was also part of the strategy to encourage participants to get in touch with their playful, childhood selves and open up to their creative impulses. We also asked each participant to prepare a poem to accompany the gift. The poetry would enhance creativity through gift giving by allowing each member to experiment with wordplay. In preparation for the celebration, we purchased a 'giving tree', under which gifts would be stacked.

After a somewhat formal welcome and distribution of gifts, gradually the sceptical ones seemed to relax and enjoy themselves. Jill presented her gift to each consultant, personally thanked them and warmly welcomed them to the Project Team. The individually selected gifts were received with much pleasure. Then the gift giving between consultants began. Kelvin retrieved the gifts from under the 'giving tree' and each recipient listened while the gift giver read the poem they had written for them. In a lovely touch, some chose to kneel to listen to their poems and receive their gifts. There was much delight in the gifts.

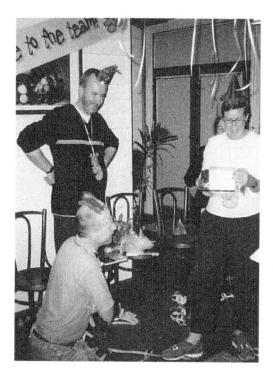

Here are two of the poems: Jim's to Bernadette and Graeme's to Jim:

A cunning social planner Bernadette
Was outnumbered by blokes on the set
So she used wine to dispel fears
in recalcitrant engineers
whilst explaining to them what they'd get.

From Jim

Back in the twentieth century,
Or was it in the first
When armies moved from home or multi-
strada

Years before Madonna, well before the
roundabout,
A toy of singular shape was made
for you.

When thirty thousand trucks into a
cul-de-sac won't go,
And the local transit system is a ...
supermarket.
Don't crack it, chuck a wobbly,
or lose your line and length...

Take strength from a therapeutic toy.

Reach deep into your pocket, squeeze
This little lump.

Pure in form and function, sure to please.
Wrap your hand around it, give
the string a little yank,

It really, really, really is the go.

Jim Higgs, you'll have the answer,
We're really glad you're with us,
For god's sake stay from go
through to woe.

And if it makes a difference,
And we're sure it really can,
Please accept this little yo yo
yo Yo-Yo ....

Graeme Q.

Listening to the silent voices: Children and young people

It felt as though a great sadness had lifted from the consultants' shoulders, as they were celebrated and validated, as well as amused and delighted, by the large and small gifts they gave and received. Everyone loved the gift-giving process and this seemed to enable them to move easily and lightheartedly into the *Listening to the silent voices* session, creating the representations of children and young people as members of the Project Team. As the Aurora project had not yet been publicly launched, no community engagement had begun and so children (and adults) had yet to be formally consulted. This was more of a pre-engagement exercise, a consciousness-raising experience aimed at highlighting issues that would ultimately lead to more meaningful engagement with real children and young people.

Team members created images of a child and a young person for inclusion as members of the Project Team. Our plan was that those representations would accompany the Project Team throughout the development process, would be present at all working sessions and be deferred to for advice. The rationale was that children and young people represented groups of people who would live in Aurora but who would not normally have a say – for example, they would not be allowed to vote. We asked our colleagues to describe a child (aged about 5) and a young person (aged about 15) whom they could imagine living at Aurora. They could use drawings or words for recording. We asked them to describe their personalities, their likes and dislikes, their ethnicity and their abilities.

Team members then self-selected into two groups, one for each young person. Initially, they brainstormed attributes for each of these members and then combined their individual characteristics to create the 'personality' for the two representations.

Attributes of the pre-school child

- 5 years old
- Needs to be valued

- Safe street to play in
- Interesting things to do close to home
- Quiet places
- Trees to sit under, climb, marvel at
- Centre of the Universe
- No boundaries
- TV
- Love from parents
- Exploring and making sense at the World
- Developing new understandings of the World

This child, given the name *Lee*, was neither male nor female but represented both sexes.

Attributes of the young person

- 15 years old
- Peers very important
- Active – sporty / hang out, chill out
- Spaces away from home
- Extend but safe
- Exploration spaces

This young male person was named *Zak*.

Creating the new team members

Then came a new surprise. We pulled from a huge bag two large rag dolls and a selection of carefully chosen clothing and asked each team to agree about the dolls' personalities and dress them accordingly. The aim was to make the children and young people (for whom they would be planning) as 'real' and 'palpable' as possible so that Team members would see them as embodied beings, residents of the future place with dreams and hopes of their own. After a slightly puzzled start, our colleagues took to their tasks with great enthusiasm. They dressed the dolls and annotated their bodies with pens (Zak had pimples; Lee had freckles and a mouth decorated with chocolate). Soon

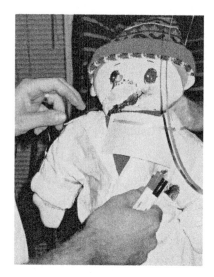 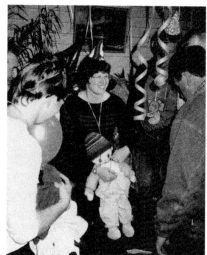

we had two dressed dolls annotated with names, name tags and decorated and labelled bags (backpacks).

These representations were then introduced to the whole Team and accompanied members to dinner and all workshop sessions. They were often referred to and deferred to in discussions throughout the three days, strengthening the team's opportunities to reflect on the needs of these two important groups.

Evaluation: What did participants make of this part of the workshop?

In the debriefing session on the last day, we discussed who found dancing hard and who didn't want to do it. We spoke about introverts and extroverts and expanding comfort zones. I explained that one of the workshop's purposes was to look at things from a new perspective. This was one step: re-igniting the creative spark we all have at birth. With that creative spark ignited, Team members could be fired up to create the best possible planning and design ideas for the Aurora site.

Three months after the workshop, we undertook a formal evaluation, via detailed questionnaires. The results were both encouraging and challenging for the organizers. Team members saw the workshop context as 'very unusual'. Some expressed concern that they might lapse into the more traditional *modus operandi* of the 'expert individual'. They acknowledged that the relaxed but 'intense' environment, away from the 'real world', allowed workshop participants to concentrate and prove 'what a creative group this team really is'.

Some wrote that it was a great feeling to be considered as part of the Team and to be included at such an early stage of the project. Most felt that the workshop was well conceived, well run and achieved a lot. Many suggested another 'review' in 12 to 18 months.

One consultant commented that meeting the rest of the Team in a new environment, gaining an understanding of the Team's direction for the Aurora development and then working on this for two solid days were invaluable aspects of the workshop. Others congratulated the URLC for the resources and commitment they put into the project (this *was* an expensive exercise!) and thanked the facilitators for their passion and effort in making the experience worthwhile, valuable and fun.

Here is what some of the consultants said:

> *I was actually not entirely sure what to expect from the workshop so my own objectives, which were to meet and get to know the rest of the Team, were well met in an interesting and challenging format.*

> *I suppose the fact that they are silent voices means that we need to be acutely aware of their existence. Perhaps we need to invent some method or culture to ensure that they are listened to.*

> *It needs to become second nature to us all (it may already be to some) to always test our decisions in view of the silent voices.*

One participant noted that the emphasis on expressing and/or diluting 'technocracy' was 'a valuable reminder, and brilliantly conveyed'. Finally, one participant commented:

You took me from a very sceptical and slightly jaded person (at first) and very cleverly hooked me in. The koala suits threw me at first; I thought, 'Oh, god, what do we have here?' But you managed to take a group of what I thought were fairly 'straight-laced consultants' and bring out a bit of the childish creativity which we often forget about in our day-to-day drone. This will be an outstanding project, worthy of the effort already demonstrated by the URLC.

Another participant, Mike Collie, a Melbourne planner, wrote to Wendy in March 2008 offering his recollections:

They were very positive experiences.

They were valuable at the time for team building and over time for the broader thinking that they inculcated in at least those Team members who wanted to get value out of them; that is, they were valuable if you were open minded about their potential – which I think was the case for all or the majority of the people involved.

They were particularly valuable in these two cases because the client decision-makers attended or empowered them.

The good relations to this day among those key consultants who attended the sessions, I am sure have a lot to do with participation in those workshops and thus there is a spin-off value whenever those consultants work together on new projects because of what they bring from those experiences.

Conclusions

We describe another component of this workshop in Chapter 7. But for now, what can we make of this initial exercise for creative community engagement? I have a few thoughts. First, it's worth remembering that this workshop was held in 2001 and (in Australia, at least) things have changed dramatically in the professions and with professional education and training since then. There is now much wider acknowledgement of concepts such as emotional intelligence. Second, I am convinced that professionals *do* want to have fun and be creative in professional settings. They love it, in fact, so long as they can see the direct relevance to their work. Third, *we* need to do this work – those of us who are community engagement facilitators and planners. *We* need to have opportunities to dream it up, make it happen and sit back and marvel at the results. And then tell the stories about how it went, who said what and how we were transformed in the process...

It keeps our spirits up.

It reminds us, as Graeme Dunstan says in the Preface to this book, that:

> *You need a good effort, patience and plenty of time... What we did 20 years ago – at the frontier – is now a sign of good practice... Good energy is never wasted. But you need patience. I say, 'Just do it!'*

Embodying the Vision: Kinetic Community Engagement Practices

7

The Aurora Project Team: Creation of the Nonhuman Being as a team member[1]

For Wendy, by far the most dramatic part of the Aurora Project Team workshop was the creation of the Nonhuman Being as a team member. She shares her recollections:

Essentially, we were asking our colleagues to collect beautiful

Invitation:
Wendy invites you to include nonhuman (or greater than human) beings in your engagement processes (using more examples from the Melbourne Aurora team workshop), have fun creating and acting out scripts from the Greek Gods and create affinities with an embodied adaptation of the Japanese Affinity Diagram.

objects from the surrounding habitat and design, construct and welcome a representation of nonhuman Nature to accompany them throughout ten years of the planning and development process for the Aurora development.[2]

After dinner, I presented an illustrated lecture on my PhD research about nurturing an ethic of caring for Nature and important implications for planning practice.[3] Following the lecture, the creation exercise began.

We also asked the Team to design and conduct a ceremony to introduce our new member to the rest of the Team at the completion of the design and construction session, presenting it in a specially designed carrying vessel using 'found' materials. We provided a wide variety of supplementary materials such as wire, balsa, glue guns, paint, staples and so forth. The aim was that this representation would sit with the Team at all Team meetings and provide guidance throughout the next ten years on the needs of nonhuman Nature in the planning and design processes for this new suburban development. A teamwork objective was to work collaboratively in the design, construction and welcoming of the representation.

To our delight, our colleagues entered into the exercise with unabashed enthusiasm. Professor Peter Newman, who had delivered a lecture on cities and sustainability the previous evening, was probably the most enthusiastic participant. Facilitators Kelvin, Wendy and Angela stood back and marvelled at everyone's enthusiasm and dedication. That is not to say that they observed the brief or even followed it. But then, they were consultants (so were we)

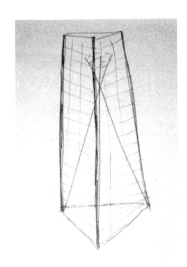

and we were used to adapting to the fluidity of the creative moment. Working diligently for several hours, the teams created the Being and the vessel (as one entity) and a somewhat self-conscious but touching and effective welcoming ceremony.

The design rationale

In the words of team members, this was the design rationale:

> *Three voices are not readily heard in many spheres of human activity. Two of these, Zak and Lee, have been 'named' for the project and symbolize adolescents and young children in urban society. The representation of the Nonhuman Being is the third of these voices.*

The Being stands for all other forms of material and life, upon which people rely (knowingly or unknowingly) for basic necessities and in many instances for more complex spiritual and social needs.

The representation of the Being consists of two elements. These are the Being itself and the vessel in which the being 'resides'. The two elements are integrated. The symbolic representation of the Being is the nest of a forest-dwelling bird. The nest in its form and substance symbolizes new life, nurturing and transformation. It is supported within the vessel by a tripod, which is a profoundly simple and stable support structure, both for the vessel and the Being.

The vessel makes use of many found and gathered elements from Nature. Plant textiles provide enclosure and protection. Mosses, lichens, feathers and stones provide diversity, decoration and carrying handles. The whole composition reveals a desire in the creative team to use natural materials. Manufactured elements have been used sparingly to make joins and connections.[4]

The welcoming ceremony

The welcoming team explained the ceremony in the following words:

> *The inspiration for the welcoming ceremony was the fundamental tenets of most spiritual belief systems: earth, water and fire. These basic elements are evident in Aboriginal storytelling and are a major focus of most religions and spiritual belief systems. The incorporation of the 'smoking ceremony' was taken specifically from the Australian Aboriginal belief system.*

The designers and builders were asked to bring the Nonhuman Being forward. Outside, a circle of fire (the 'fire ring') had been built, symbolizing the continuity of Nature. The Nonhuman Being was placed in the centre. Team members were then asked to form a circle with the 'fire ring', with the Nonhuman Being forming part of the circle. Each member then passed through the 'fire ring' and a special smoke as an act of rebirth through fire, to enable the team members to take on new thoughts, including those of the silent voices and Nature, as represented by the Nonhuman Being.

The ash from the smoking ceremony was used to mark each Team member's hand – the hand that would guide the creation of the project. Each member made a conscious decision as to which hand would be marked, depending upon which hemisphere of the brain might dominate in creating the project.

Each Team member was then given a vessel filled with water from a common source. The drinking of water from a common source signified the formation of a common bond for the group and the nurturing of new ideas.

All Team members were then asked to collect a piece of material (not used in the building of the Nonhuman Being). The burning of those materials was symbolic of the discarding of old ways. This fuel added to the fire, providing the light by which the Team could see the future, to take the project to new heights.

Each member of the Team then shook hands with each other as a gesture of mutual welcome to the Team. The ceremony concluded with acclamation.

This gentle and somewhat self-conscious ritual brought a full day to a close and members went inside for a well-earned beer. The facilitators were heartened to see Team members deferring to the Being, Lee and Zak the following day. Kelvin was quick to point out in the morning session, however, that the much loved Being had been left out in the rain all night.

The stone ritual: A silent closing

In the riverbed during the gathering process on Monday afternoon, Frank Hanson found a beautiful stone containing the shape of a heart. This precious stone was kept aside during the process of creating the Being and used for the final workshop ritual.

I employed an ancient ritual, *the stone ritual*, to complete the workshop and symbolize the feelings of connectedness within the Team.[6] We sat in a circle and said our farewells. We gave thanks and acknowledged the support of many people. Then I held the stone in two hands, modelling what was expected. I asked that the stone be passed slowly around the circle, with each person who received it pouring into the stone their disappointments and sad memories of projects gone wrong and failed teamwork processes. The stone became heavy as we poured out silent disappointments and regrets into it.

When the stone reached me, I washed it in a bowl of water (which I then carefully discarded). I dried it with a fine linen towel and then poured into it my optimism and hopes for the future of the Team and this project. Everyone in the circle followed in silence, the stone becoming warm with our hopefulness and good wishes. I then gently placed it in a bird's nest in a box decorated with leaves and feathers found on the site. We presented it to Jill (the Project Manager) on behalf of the Team.

We suggested that when the first sod was turned on the Aurora site, the Team could bury the stone. It would represent the heart of the Team living in the soil of the new development. The silent closing ritual reminded me of the value of communal silence in listening to each other, to the soft and silent voices of our disappointments and hopefulness and to the voice of the living Earth.

Making sense of this exercise

In general, our colleagues felt that the session – and the whole workshop – worked well, offering insights into individual working styles and the benefits of collaborative work. They identified some valuable lessons, including:

- being mindful of preconceived ideas and the necessity to challenge them;
- understanding individual strengths;
- realizing that skills are complementary;
- considering (respecting) other members' perspectives and approaches;
- communicating on equal levels;
- recognizing the importance of completing a task within the allotted time frame;
- celebrating the freedom to try a task that would not usually be a strength (but which was different and rewarding);
- bringing life experience, as well as skills, to activities;
- remembering to listen, not just hear;
- creating a collaborative approach where multiple ideas are contributed and developed;
- experiencing coming together as a team with many hands making light work; and
- accepting to drop something if it doesn't work and try something else without being precious about it.

Initial participant feedback was positive about the innovative process. Early in the planning process, colleagues reported successful working relationships and a good understanding of the project. They expressed only cautious optimism, however, about the promise of achieving true sustainability, creativity and innovation at Aurora. Some questioned the strength of the URLC's commitment to innovation and creativity. Others recalled past disappointments where initial permission to be creative and innovative was not reflected in continued client support.

Later in 2001, after the three-month evaluation, I wrote to my client that the Team would have to work hard to maintain the collaborative working approach established in the workshop. I identified dangers associated with slipping back into old (and ineffective) habits. They'd need careful attention to ensure that the 'silent voices' of team members were encouraged, listened to, heard and acted upon. In particular, vigilance would be required to listen for the voices of Lee and Zak (representing children and young people) and of nonhuman Nature. Further, the team would need to ensure that members listened carefully to the voices of all its human members. Some might be excluded or marginalized. A student working for the client organization commented:

> In contrast to Lee and Zak, I think that the Nonhuman Being and all that it represents is being heard. I think the ideas behind the 'Being' do in fact always enter our discussions and do inform our directions and decisions.

As one participant explained in 2001:

> I think the fact that it is in a Perspex case defeats the purpose of the original idea somewhat – it was supposed to last for ten to fifteen years![5] (Maybe we need to re-engineer it at some time!) Again, we need more reminders about how we are considering the nonhuman elements in the project.

Seven years later, additional feedback arrived from our generous colleague, Melbourne planner, Mike Collie:

> The continuing value has been more mixed due I think largely to the changing dynamics of the team and client decision-makers coupled with the lack of repeat or review sessions with key new team members. The client decision-makers all moved on, the team changed from its original key players to many newcomers (including new key consultants) and the ideals were not known, valued, considered and/or adopted by many who came into the organization.

> The client approach also changed significantly and thus much of the 'ownership' from the session was lost or marginalized. To continue to gain value from such sessions, I believe there is a need for commitment from the client to repeat them when there are significant changes in the team make-up and client decision-makers.

I couldn't agree more.

With the organization disbanded and the senior managers taking jobs else-where, it was impossible to maintain the energy of the workshop. I've been told that the two dolls were lost and that the Being, which sat in a Perspex box in Jill Lim's office for several years (too large, heavy and awkward to attend team meetings), has also been lost. I hope that the memory of the deep work of the workshop remains in the hearts of participants.

The Gods Must Be Crazy

Introduction

We've dedicated this book to community artist and activist, Graeme Dunstan, because he's the best there is. Wendy and Graeme have worked together since 1989 and chronicled some of their community engagement adventures in chapters in *Community Participation in Practice: Casebook* (Sarkissian and Walsh, 1994) and in other publications. The role play, 'The Gods Must Be Crazy', was conducted in what might have seemed an unlikely setting: a conference on safe communities in Sydney in 2004. For this project, we were blessed with client representatives who held radical views about community safety and were eager to highlight the schisms in that complex and continually changing field. Further, they were willing to take on roles themselves, as our clients had done in the original 'Gods Must Be Crazy' role play in Melbourne in 1990.[7]

The event was promoted in the conference program in the following way:

> Dramatic archetypal role play and 'fishbowl' highlighting the politics of collaboration and consensus building in relation to injury prevention, violence prevention and suicide prevention. Commentary by Professor John Forester. Great stars to be revealed on the day.

Our research revealed that community safety in New South Wales was shot through with disagreements and schisms (all of which could easily be drama-tized). We identified many 'voices' and apparently polarized views, including:

- pro- and anti-suicide activists;
- homophobia;
- right-wing churches;
- community-based activists;
- violence against women lobbies: feminist and other views;
- activists working in elder abuse;
- 'risk-control people' and 'control of the environment' (behavioural vs. environmental control);
- social responsibility vs. individual responsibility;
- economic outputs and growth vs. social capital and social benefits;
- social welfare vs. industry-driven development;
- outcome indictors vs. input indicators (another version of the criteria-driven approach or the evidence-based approach);
- capacity development vs. getting input from 'whoever is off the street';
- asset-based community development vs. 'exploitation';
- short-term economic funding cycles vs. a more longitudinal approach; and
- silos vs. whole-of-government, joined-up government approaches.

We were told of bureaucrats who were 'typical ass-coverers' worried about what 'shock-jock' radio personalities would say – or, more commonly, 'What would my Minister think?' All these considerations contributed to the final design of the role play. We were dealing with strong emotions. Additionally, in planning, in particular, many professionals appear to have an aversion to expressing emotion, as planning educator, Maged Senbel's research has revealed: 'Recognizing the presence of emotions in the exchanges and communications undertaken in planning work is the first step, but having the capacity to address emotions and manage them takes planners outside of their areas of expertise'.[8]

In the planning stages, our client, Pete Whitecross, then Director of Health Promotions for North Sydney Health (and about to embody 'far-seeing Zeus'), challenged us with a hypothetical crisis for the role play:

The classical Gods find themselves transported into Norse mythology by some cosmological phase shift thingo just at the moment of Gotterdammerung/Ragnarok where the problem is that humans have stopped believing in them because they are doing such a lousy job protecting them.

They have failed to meet their covenant to protect humankind from injury, threat and hazard.

Zeus says:

'I want to know how and when you guys are going to lift your game.

Like pull together as a team? Some humans think that some of us make matters worse and they might be right.

I have no problem with my brother Helios driving around the sky in an open chariot with no seat restraint or helmet, but maaate, we can't let humans do that.[9]

The *safe communities* scenario

Graeme Dunstan, who designed the role play, described it in the following words:

This is a story about safe communities. It happened long ago and not too long ago in a place far and not very far from here. The Gods on Mt Olympus are deeply concerned. Hestia, ancient goddess of the hearth, protector of children, nurturer of families, is worried about the needless suffering she is witnessing. So concerned is she that she leaves her hearth and prevails upon her brother Zeus, the big boss in the sky, thrower of thunderbolts, to do something about it. Far-seeing Zeus calls a crisis meeting of his divine Safe Community Council. Distracted from his creative sex life, he is wrathful. He wants to know why the Council is failing and he has his 'bulls**t detector' turned on and his punishing thunderbolt at hand. It is an open Council meeting and all the Gods are there: Major Gods and Minor Gods; Gods of Big Things and Gods of small things. The Major Gods, members of the Council, sit at a table over which Zeus presides, Hestia by his side. The lesser Gods gather about to witness.

Zeus calls them to account. These Gods, though immortal, are more like humans than like Buddhas: they are full of pride, deceit, passion, frailty and delusion. On Mt Olympus, squabbling is what makes the eternal life interesting for them.

Zeus calls the Council to order and Hestia to speak first. Then he demands account from the Major Gods about safe communities on Earth. They prevaricate, gloss over, pass the blame and suggest new courses of action according to their powers, their perceptions of the world and their hidden agendas. They interrupt each other, talk back, banter and counter-accuse.

Zeus moderates best he can with thunderbolts and asks, 'Are we missing something here? Are there voices we are not heeding?' And so he calls forth comment from the lesser Gods. He asks each of them to introduce themselves before speaking. As before, the Major Gods respond when they feel attacked, slighted or ignored.

The aim is to be provocative and funny. The object is to draw out spontaneity, laughter and insight. The role play will last for about 20 minutes. As Director, I will call a halt to it, turn up the house lights and begin the process of de-roling by introducing the session Chair. He will move participants into the theatre seating for a short debriefing. He will ask some of the most outspoken players (particularly those who are still in excitation from the experience): 'How was that for you?'

The session finishes with the Chair inviting the conference keynote speaker, Professor John Forester, to sum with his impressions and the insights he gained.

My recollections of the role play

The role play was a fractious event, with Gods squabbling as only Gods do. I have no report to refer to, only my memories. One of the most powerful incidents had an ironic twist not lost on participants or the audience. Athena, Goddess of Wisdom, a Major God played by Australian Indigenous leader and activist, Winsome Matthews, gave up her seat in response to agitated complaints by the Minor Indigenous God (Dispossessedus), that he was denied a seat at the head table.

As with the 1990 role play that dramatized interests related to Melbourne's arterial roads, this one represented the wide and deep chasms and differences among different sectors. In that respect, it was a consciousness-raising exercise. Listening to the squabbling Gods and seeing Zeus failing to bring them under control achieved our objectives and reminded me of our research findings: community safety is a very complex matter.

We also achieved a lightening-up of a very sombre topic. John Forester, who made a huge contribution to the conference, has written about the benefit of humour in planning. His words rang true for the crazy Gods:

A potentially powerful form of ironic practice, humor can work deliberately, but indirectly, intentionally but non-argumentatively. What's actually said matters, but often to convey the recognition of complexity and the legitimacy of multiple perspectives… This responsive and ironic humor has been both funny and serious at once, a source of relief and a source of insight, a peculiarly non-reductive source of recognition, revelation and hope as well.[11]

Athena gives up her seat to Dispossessedus

Part 3

Stories from the Edge:
Pushing Professional Practice

poetry | planning code-filter: all
HU: (Graham McGarva)[1]

File: [C:\Scientific Software\]
Edited by: Super

nativelanguage
mathematicpoetry
ideagraph

value spirit words
with a third eye on the street
the community feels landscape

pre-cognitive thought
stops circling bird fright
notices the poetic everyday
in circumstance

an architectural tightrope
:mass light
:private open windows
:paradox spectrum

jumbled specifics of form

                    – dh

Learning at the Margins: Margo Fryer and Pamela Ponic on Deconstructing Power and Privilege

8

An epic story for our time

In his 2007 Massey Lectures, Alberto Manguel introduces the ancient, mythic, epic story of the superhuman Gilgamesh, a king who violently abuses his power.[1] In response to the people's cry for help, the Gods create a counterpart to moderate Gilgamesh's desires and actions: a creature that is King Gilgamesh's opposite. Whereas Gilgamesh is two-thirds divine and one-third human, the 'monster' Enkidu is two parts animal and one part human. Although Enkidu is gentle, he is different and evokes fear in those who encounter him:

Invitation:
By means of an epic poem and stories from two inspirational practitioners, we invite you to join us at the edge of your comfort. Reflecting on what Paulo Freire calls the 'subject–object–dialect', we join Pamela Ponic and Margo Fryer in exploring ways to be part of promoting everyone's role as a social actor in community.

The double is human and yet not entirely so; of flesh and blood but with an element of unreality because we fail to recognize or identify every one of his actions.... He is our neighbour, our equal, but also the foreigner, the one who does things differently, has a different colour, or speaks a different language. To better differentiate us from him, we exaggerate his superficial characteristics. [2]

In this poem, replete with ominous dreams, heroic journeys, myth, visions, floods and prayers, the metaphor of the 'double' or the 'other' is a poignant representation of anyone or any group of people that societies either actively or passively exclude via real or invented psychological barriers. Manguel reminds us that we falsely separate ourselves from some humans (not to mention from nonhuman Nature) to banish 'the other' from our lives and our perceptions. The Gilgamesh poem illustrates a common reaction to 'the other'. To validate unfamiliar ways of knowing is to acknowledge the stranger's existence and their rights. However, like the mythical Gilgamesh, we are beset by fears and ominous forebodings when it comes to embracing unfamiliar ways of working. This story and Manguel's interpretations have resonances for community engagement.

Manguel claims that we use distancing from 'the other' as a sort of self-preservation. It's a way to construct our own identities, reminding ourselves who we think we are *not* rather than who we are: 'Alone, we have no name and no face, no one to call out to us and no reflection in which to recognize our features'. [3] With Enkidu's passing and Gilgamesh's eternal anguish, the city over which Gilgamesh reigns is restored to peace and greatness. Manguel's many other stories suggest that, as a culture, we believe that we must banish the 'other' from the city because we believe peace is possible only within a monoculture.

There is another option, however. This book is about that option. Turning again to the ancient poem, Manguel proposes 'a healing of these fears, a recalling of that which we are afraid to acknowledge, in order to work and live in its presence'. [4] Gilgamesh becomes a full individual only by joining with the wild Enkidu. The egotistical ambitions of civilized society become tempered by the wisdom of the uncivilized one. Thus, for us, 'the city, the place of social interactions, acquires its identity by defining itself through a sort of conglom-erate individuality'.[5] This chapter is about finding ways to avoid banishing 'the other' and instead reaching out and embracing 'otherness' in creative and challenging modes of engaging in community.

Power and the 'other'

Often in community engagement, we speak about empowerment. And we distinguish (using a variety of ladders, spectra, wheels and other tools), among information-giving, consultation, partnership or true community control.[6] Thus, it's valuable briefly to unpack notions of empowerment and participation. Critical analysis of power and powerlessness and how others are excluded can offer insights into our roles in this persistent (and largely unconscious) process of 'othering' in engagement. Through deepening self-consciousness, we can recognize how our professions' 'core stories' restrict us from engaging in creative processes (seen by some as 'emotional' or 'soft').[7] We can resist the urge to become 'split personalities': one (rational) person at work and another (creative) person in our personal lives. We can find ways to align our personal, professional, creative and rational selves. And, facing the sources of our confusion, fear and guilt, we may identify and embrace ways of knowing and being we would not have imagined. Then we can truly listen 'across difference' to find new ways of being as professionals.[8]

Through creative and genuinely inclusive engagement processes, we can come to understand that, while our agency may be influenced by the structures in which we are embedded, ultimately these structures are not in charge. They are part of a big and very old constructed story that we are trying to unravel, reframe and retell. As professionals, we can awaken from our unconscious-ness and understand our professional realities and why things are as they are. That's where dreaming and visioning come in. With self-awareness (or, as Paulo Freire called it, *conscientization*), we may dream of greater and more expansive possibilities than our current realities.[9]

It's possible that some professionals working in community planning may find some approaches in this book daunting. For some, it may be downright terrifying. That is not surprising. As professionals, our reputations and even our self-identities rely on perpetuating the myths of *good* professional practice. We reify distance, objectivity and calm rationality. We must 'sell' ourselves as the 'expert'. Engaging our creative sides – allowing room for myth, archetype, poetry, art and full self-expression – does not fit this image. Nor does an approach grounded in the reality that we are all engaged in processes of social learning. Yet, we are all learning as we go, learning from our experiences and from one another.

The first steps in engagement – venturing beyond our comfort zones – can be profoundly challenging. Once engaged, we find ourselves in uncharted territories with no markers, trying to decode complex and shifting power relationships. These unfamiliar dynamics can be very confusing. In engagement and research processes that are truly 'at the edge' (such as the ones described in this chapter), participants must grapple with emotions unfamiliar (or at least unacknowledged) in most planning contexts: power, guilt, privilege and oppression. It's common to feel discomfort. In fact, it's healthy. Rather than dismissing these uncomfortable emotions, we should embrace them as opportunities for reflective practice and expanded self-awareness.

This is a challenging process – not for the fainthearted.

Margo Fryer and Pamela Ponic: Working at the Edge

Christine spoke with two experienced community practitioners in Vancouver: Margo Fryer[10] and Pamela Ponic.[11] Working with paradigms of Community Service Learning (CSL) and Feminist Participatory Action Research (FPAR) respectively, Margo and Pamela engage with communities across vast differences.[12] Each believes that new possibilities can emerge from creative approaches that foster previously unfamiliar or unlikely relationships and understandings. Both admit that navigating power differences in these partnerships is not easy. Each offers insights into how to begin. Pamela and Margo explain how our society tends to define power in simplistic, default terms – power as a dominant, oppressive force. Although power can certainly be destructive when it is used to assert one's interest *over* another, power can also be used for creative, progressive purposes.

That's the power that compelled us to write this book. It need not be considered as a finite object but rather as a fluid and dynamic phenomenon that can be infinitely created.

Focusing on positive power

Margo Fryer is the founding Director of the Learning Exchange at the University of British Columbia (UBC). In her efforts to foster experiential learning and remodel the 'ivory tower' to value iterative, collaborative and accessible knowledge production, Margo forges relationships and partnerships with community organizations throughout the Metro Vancouver Region. In particular, her practice has brought her into the heart of the Downtown Eastside – an inner city Vancouver community more commonly associated with poverty, addiction and mental health issues than for its vibrancy, diversity and grassroots organizing. Thanks to the partnerships supported by the Learning Exchange, more than a thousand UBC students annually undertake coursework in community-based partnerships, participating in projects that provide a service to the community and offer unique opportunities for experiential learning.[13]

In the CSL facilitated by Margo, students critically analyse their internalization of societal biases and challenge their assumptions. Positive power never fails to be created through the partnerships among students, faculty, community organizers and community members formed by community service learning projects.

> **Margo**: I think it is important for us as practitioners of this kind of activity to engage with each other because of the belief that the engagement will generate more power than would be generated through the actors acting independently. And what I am saying probably applies to any kind of engagement between the university and the community or between actors who have different degrees of power with one another.

That is the premise. If we are collaborating, we are doing so presumably because we believe that we are creating more power through the synergy of the two partners. Inevitably, in any given moment there is the potential for one of the two actors to have more power than the other. So I think that part of the discourse on power is based in conceptions of power that are quite old and that view power as a thing that there is only a limited amount of and a bad thing because one player has power to dominate the other player.

There is truth and legitimacy to that perspective. But it is not very helpful to view the situation only in that way. I like the way Foucault talks about power as being more of an emergent property and a fluid dynamic.

The way we tend to think about power is not very helpful, mostly because it tends to view power as something you either win or lose – if you don't have it you are suffering in some way. It is not that easy; it is not that simple. I think it is more fruitful for people involved in these kinds of relationships to be viewing power as something that we can generate together. Because really, as we work with organizations and faculty, what we are doing implicitly is saying, 'Let's create power together, let's create an opportunity, let's create a project, let's create some learning experiences'. For me *that* is power.

Margo's commentary highlights the multiple understandings of power that we as practitioners can consider. While it is important not to disregard the potential of power to dominate in harmful ways (thus requiring constant reflection about how oppression and power are constantly reinforced within traditional planning practice), we can also allow ourselves to realize what is possible through creating truly inclusive processes.[14]

Margo uses the word *synergy* to describe what is possible through collaboration across difference, something Booher and Innes (2002) describe as *network power*.[15] We can engage this form of power if we are able to engage in genuinely inclusive processes, potentially with poetic outcomes:

Carnegie Community Centre, Downtown Eastside, Vancouver

transformative possibilities emerge for growing self-awareness and increased mutual understanding through human stories that dance with one another – illuminating our interconnected experiences and identities.

CSL engagement practices embody the power of networks, collaboration, understanding and the ability to overcome restrictive assumptions and oppressive fears. Facilitated by Margo, students critically analyse their own internalized societal biases and challenge their assumptions. In 2008, Christine participated in a CSL project as project leader, facilitating the learning experiences of a group of undergraduate engineering students who would implement a project in collaboration with a community organization in Vancouver's Downtown Eastside. Vancouverites often refer with fear to the corner of Main and Hastings Streets, the marginalized neighbourhood's epicentre, where the Carnegie Community Centre (a community outreach centre) is a focal point. Christine had past experience working in contexts of extreme poverty and marginalization and felt confident in her own understanding of the structural reasons for perpetuated poverty and social exclusion. She was genuinely looking forward to helping the students increase their understanding of such factors.

During the students' second day working in the community centre, the organization's Director suggested that they have lunch at Carnegie (the notorious building at Main and Hastings Streets). Although Christine initially tried to hide it, her surprise echoed the shock on the students' faces.

Really?

You could go into that place?

The lesson was a welcome reminder to Christine of the need for careful reflection and openness in engagement practices. The Carnegie Centre is one of Vancouver's oldest and most remarkable historic buildings, built in 1903 as Vancouver's Central Library. A spiral staircase ascends a stain-glassed dome, leading to a cafeteria offering healthy and affordable fresh fare in a congenial atmosphere. The atmosphere in the room was lively with a diversity of community members and friendly chatter. It was one of the strongest community atmospheres Christine had experienced in Vancouver.

What had happened? What often happens. Without critical analysis, Christine had internalized a societal assumption of the building's character and use. In her mind, the centre was a facility only for her invented 'other', thus excluding her. Her internalized limitations would have prevented her from entering that space – just as similar assumptions and fears prevent us from engaging with people who seem too 'different' from ourselves. Community engagement, practised bravely and creatively, is very powerful because it forces us – through new contexts, genuine listening and creative media – to come into close contact with people we think are different from us and help us to see our points of intersection rather than our exaggerated differences. Creative engagement is how we will find ways to highlight the strengths of plurality that Manguel and Sandercock describe. By breaking through the limitations of our fears, guilt, assumptions and intolerance, collectively we will create power.

Pamela Ponic: Negotiating discomfort

The discomfort we feel working in marginalized communities can take many forms. Pamela Ponic is a feminist participatory action researcher with diverse experiences in community engagement activities. She has worked on health, recreation, gender, violence and housing issues. Christine interviewed her in Vancouver in May of 2008. She focused on research for her PhD dissertation, collaborating with a Vancouver-based organization, Women Organizing Activities for Women (WOAW, pronounced 'whoa').[16] The group consisted of service providers and low-income community members, all women, who aimed to make their recreation opportunities accessible, inclusive and democratic.

While exploring power relations is not the primary focus of this book, it is nevertheless one of its concerns. As we, as authors, framed our book, we realized that we faced a daunting task: how can we act ethically and effectively while acknowledging the gaping inequities of our communities? Our professional experiences and the literature from practice and academia provide few answers. Our feelings echo Pamela's words:

> **Pamela**: I don't think it is ever resolvable for me. I came to think and to write in my dissertation that discomfort of it is really important. You don't want to be sidestepping it. The discomfort is actually evidence that power relations are shifting; it is so subtle, but the subtle shifting shows up in the discomfort. If you are comfortable in a situation going into that level of power difference with a community, then you are probably blind to the power difference.

Nevertheless, mindful reflection and sensitive action can help keep our hearts and minds open to our ultimate goal in community planning: decreasing inequities and nurturing inclusion. If we are to navigate the complexities of oppression and privilege, we must enter into relationships with others in a spirit of humility. Then we can discover the jewel: engagement processes bring value and knowledge through multiple ways of knowing, learning and communicating. It's also helpful to remember that our identities are constructed within the broader society. As our dialogue deepens, we can reflect on increasing people's access to power through shared education, growing self-awareness, new partnerships and collective action.

Opening doors – creating opportunities for inclusion

Throughout this book, we, and the practitioners whose stories we share, often speak of transformation and empowerment. Engagement processes offer opportunities for empowerment because and *only if* they create spaces for shared agency – opportunities for everyone to share at once the roles of learner and educator, thinker and doer. Paulo Freire, referring to this as the 'subject–object dialectic',[17] emphasizes the importance of every person being active in her or his learning, rather than passive receptacles of information. Pamela identifies the importance of agency in community engagement and warns that agency can be easily co-opted and rendered ineffective:

> **Pamela**: I'm careful around the word 'empowerment' because it can be used in a really unilateral direction: I am going to empower you. I have power so I can empower you. But that is not the way that I see it unfolding whatsoever. I may have access to resources where I can help facilitate a situation where you can find your own power or feel empowered but I can't empower other people.
>
> … I don't believe Participatory Action Research (PAR) or any kind of community-based research is empowering in and of itself. It is the way that everyone engages in the process that has possibilities for empowerment if you are going to use that word. I am careful about that, though, because of the way it can be misconstrued. Women in particular can be further victimized because of the sense that I can empower them or someone with privilege can empower someone without. I think it just deepens the victimization tendency.

Pamela also warns of the dangers of aiming to *help* rather than to *understand*: we cannot intervene in oppressive circumstances without understanding (or at least questioning) the sources of the oppression. Seen in this light, our role as community engagement practitioners is not to empower, but to open doors to opportunities for empowerment. We must understand the reasons why some voices are silenced and how exclusion is fostered, resulting – for some – in feelings of isolation.

> **Pamela**: The primary ways that people talked about isolation were being in prison, living in a box with no doors and that WOAW opened doors for them. There was a lot of impact to hearing those stories and the difference that WOAW made. A lot of women said it really changed their lives. For some it saved their lives.

In our work, we want to open doors. But how did these doors become closed in the first place? There are many reasons: dominant modes of language, limited access to resources and literacy skills, among others. Pamela writes:

Enactments of power are both facilitated and hindered by what I term the 'power tools' of society.[18] For example, knowledge, discourse and material resources are not power per se; rather they are socially constructed structures that privilege the power of some individuals over others.[19]

Working creatively does not mean abandoning our social justice principles. Quite the contrary! We must understand the context and question how institutions, assumptions and dominant ideologies interact to create inequalities. Lily Walker, an Australian Aboriginal organizer, recognizes that our liberation is bound up with one another and that all of humanity is restricted by oppressive forces. She says, 'If you are here to help me, then you are wasting my time. But if you come because your liberation is bound up in mine, then let us begin'.[20] Thus, we must be vigilant to avoid dualistic thinking and question dichotomies between dominant and oppressed, privileged and poor. Graeme Dunstan's role play of the Gods of Safe Communities in Chapter 7 and in Gilt-edged Resource 3 reveals that both forces live within us. When we seek to use creative approaches with disadvantaged communities, we must be careful not to 'colour' an entire community or even an individual as 'the oppressed' or 'the oppressor'.

Through the explicit use of creativity, our dream is to create safe places and invite all to participate, finding gentle alternatives to some of the more restrictive 'professional' modes of engagement that privilege some voices at the expense of others. We are aware that creativity alone, without consciousness of the exclusionary factors that close doors in the first place, can be little more than tokenism. This book seeks to find ways to reach the 'detached' practitioner and confront head-on the implicit professional expectations of this so-called 'objectivity', this 'Cartesian anxiety', as Leonie Sandercock would say.[21]

Our stories from practitioners reveal many ways that innovative approaches help us to question our assumptions and fears – forces that make us deaf to another's story or blind to their perspectives. Leonie recognizes the potential of making new understandings and meanings in this parallel process:

> *Fully participating requires an openness that exposes us to other beliefs*
> *and ways of being in the world that we must consider alongside our*
> *own, not by transcending difference but by acknowledging and fully*
> *engaging with it. In such a process, we may become more aware*
> *of ourselves as well as with the unfamiliar 'Other' resulting in the*
> *possibility of mutual creation of new understandings and meanings.*[22]

In engaging with our imagined 'others' through inclusive practice, we create spaces where all participants can act, create and show emotion openly with one another. This is what is needed to create new and sustainable living environments. By communicating our stories to one another through narrative, art, song, theatre, poetry and ways we cannot even imagine, we may discover our role of power in our privilege and disadvantage. Through that understanding, enlightened and lightened by the creative powers we invoke, we may find agency through inclusion, liberation by recognizing our agency and power by collectively envisaging new possibilities.

'And Action!' New Roles for Film in Engagement: Leonie Sandercock and Jonathan Franz

9

Introduction: Going off the map

Film is emerging as an experimental method to present new languages of multiplicity – a practice that enables us to 'listen to the city murmurs, to catch stories, to read signs and spatial poetics'.[1] In form, film has the potential to co-present multiple and conflicting voices

Invitation:
See how communities become dialogic sets for engaging with sensitive social issues. Leonie Sandercock, Giovanni Attili and Jonathan Frantz are practitioners and academics experimenting with film both for engagement and as engagement.

with more conventional types of planning information and data; voices, text, image and data can coexist on the same screen, simultaneously offering multiple versions of a story.[2] Inevitably, the complexities of using film influence how we as engagement practitioners think about listening to and presenting stories of difference, growth and change – and how we think about how we ourselves are part of the story.

Experiments, delights and cautions: In conversation with Leonie Sandercock

Leonie Sandercock – planning educator, theorist and film practitioner – uses film as part of her planning pedagogy and practice.[3] In conversation with Dianna, Leonie talks about two films she has made with Giovanni Attili, Italian planning academic and filmmaker, and one film project she has collaboratively coordinated and supervised.[4] Her stories illustrate how film in planning can be used in two ways: as a tool *for engagement,* to share the stories of one community as a dialogic catalyst in other communities; and *as engagement,* to involve community 'storytellers' in the process of creating the film and shaping their stories. Leonie also shares some of her concerns in thinking lightly about film in planning and community engagement.

Dianna and Leonie met for coffee at a favourite café in Vancouver. It was February and, atypically, the winter sun lit bright. Over croissants and the perfect cup, they began talking about cutting-edge uses of film in planning.

Leonie began with reflections from the Carrall Street Participatory Video Project (CSPVP) in Vancouver to illustrate why it's important to begin by identifying the film's objectives:

> **Leonie**: There are so many different ways of using story and film as a story medium in planning. Some of it's experimental and some of it's more directly functional. There are examples like the participatory video – or so-called participatory video – project in Vancouver's low-income Downtown Eastside, which had multiple objectives, and that's always a problem. In targeting youth who were assumed to be marginalized, working with video is a good way to attract them into a process because it's assumed that it's their natural medium. It's assumed that it's a medium that they're comfortable with and enjoy playing with and therefore that this is a good technique or tool for soliciting views about otherwise marginalized youth. That was one objective – to get a response from both youth and planners' ideas about Carrall Street for the Carrall Street Greenway.[5]

Another objective was a capacity-building objective with youth; the whole process was meant to train youth to learn how to make and use video. In this example, in very quick succession, they're actually making a short video. That example presented a number of challenges. Yes, video is a medium that youth enjoy playing with but the medium itself requires quite a lot of learning – especially the editing part of it. *Especially* the editing. Basically, anyone can take the camera and shoot for the interviews. But putting these together in some way requires a lot more thought and a lot of skill.

Dianna: Giovanni talks about introducing a whole new skill set to planners when they use this medium: how film calls more for a sensitive analytical approach than a technical objective one.

Leonie: This approach to film assumes that you can work with other people, that even the person with the power – the most technically skilled person, like Giovanni (in our working relationship) – has the ultimate power to manipulate everything on the computer. So if that person – as part of a team that's working on a project – is not a truly collaborative person, they can end up running away with the project.

You can, however, build in collaborative practices. It was possible for me to work with Giovanni through the editing process (the really technical stuff) by sitting with him at the computer. So we shape the story together by going through our footage and choosing how to put the story together. And my voice is equal to his voice and anyone else in the team we wanted to include in that process. And yet, there is a size limit to how many can fit at an editing console. If this sort of project is really meant to be participatory and to express more than your own interpretation, you have to do whole other iterations of the product. You have to work for a long time with a 'rough cut' version and take it back to the community whose story it's supposed to be telling. As an example, what happened to Giovanni and my Collingwood film was that we edited out many interviews. The ones we didn't use were where people were not articulate or where they literally would not be animated: where they were 'wooden'.

Dianna: What happens when certain stories are left out?

Leonie: You run the risk of offending people whose footage you do not use. This is inevitable, especially when you say you want a one-hour interview and you might use only ten seconds. But the other two hours is part of the research process and may end up in the voiceover or as part of what informs the film and its interpretation. So there's this issue of representation and who ends up appearing. This could be seen as bias. It could be seen as a new form of exclusion – film is excluding people that don't come over as articulate on the screen. So how do we defend that? Because on the surface, it's not really defensible.

Dianna: In thinking about film as a sort of research tool, where do we begin?

Leonie: When you start, you have a preconceived idea of what you're going to get or how you might use it. Giovanni and I start with certain assumptions about digital ethnography and its potential as an action research tool. But still there's a whole research period where we're going around without the camera and getting to know people, interviewing or having conversations with them before we film. Then there's the process of deciding whom to interview (which is always a selection process). So the story's already starting to take shape.

There's no getting away from the 'authorial' perspective. As much as you want to think of film as an expansive tool (in that it's able to bring in more voices than would normally participate, and so on), ultimately it's still a very author-driven tool.

Dianna: Right. But there's something else perhaps. Why is film important as a new approach? What does it bring and offer to planning?

Leonie: It's the multiplicity of languages that film opens up simultaneously. And again, the more sophisticated the technical skills, the more multiple languages are possible. So with film, you can combine individual biographies, or more traditional oral histories, into visual form. You can then complement these visuals with a technical data presentation, which can pop up in all kinds of lovely looking charts with voiceovers, adding an interpretative voice. At the same time, a whole bunch of, literally, conflicting voices will present themselves in the film.

And you can go beyond voice; you can go beyond the old-fashioned interviews and transcribing interviews. You know, it's not just a high-tech form of the standard interview in the researcher's realm. It's really the way that you can put all of these layers together to tell what doesn't have to be a linear narrative with only one interpretation. There's also the power of the visual language within film, the suggestive power of that and the power of images – still images as well as those that are actual film. The motion picture aspect seems to be able to convey a lot more richness about whatever the subject is: a neighbourhood, a history.

Dianna: And this idea of having many languages and interpretations, in turn enabling a notion of ambiguity to exist. It's interesting because it seems that a lot of the past and current tools in planning are used to categorize and code. Do you think planning in film is revolutionary?

Leonie: I'd like to think that it keeps auspice to the possibility of ambiguity, of revealing the real ambiguity and paradoxes of situations. But in film, just as in 'real world' planning, in the end decisions have to be made. So, in real world planning, you can only maintain the conflict and contradictions for so long until there's a moment – a political moment – when decisions have to be made. There has to be resolution.

I think there's a tension in the making of the film. There's a tension for the filmmaker because, if you think about the whole notion of narratives in Aristotle, it's a highly structured thing – it has a beginning, middle and an end. All the writing schools teach you about dramatic resolution, having creative conflict and maintaining tension for a certain amount of time. There comes a point where the story has to end, has to be resolved. People hate unresolved endings.

We know, however, that in real life, things are messy and there's never a clear moment where you can say, 'That's over – the pain is over now' or 'Now I'm going to live happily ever after'. It's all a matter of the moment where you end the story. And that's always a choice.

With the Burns Lake project, Giovanni and I are struggling with, on the one hand, the desire to tell a story of hope, but on the other hand, not to bring what would really be a 'false closure' to something that's still a very 'open' situation. Just by the nature of the medium, our story has to end. What note do you end it on? Do you end it on a note of ambiguity? There's still major racism present there and while there have been these little seeds of change, it's an unfinished story.

Dianna: So in this project, the Burns Lake project, what role does film play? It seems like it plays many roles. What made you interested in using film in that particular project?

Leonie: A few things. One was that a person in Burns Lake, who had seen the Collingwood Neighbourhood House film, had a dream to have a film made about the struggles happening in Burns Lake, to show the shift in the last decade. So there was this local desire among community leaders (leaders of change) to capture that on film. Then we were invited to come and see for ourselves if we thought there was a story worth telling. That was how I initially went there.

Then there was our experience with the Collingwood story, which I now describe as a three-stage research project. I would love to say that was all envisioned in the beginning, but of course it wasn't. It started off as a very experiential film – an attempt to make a film in a neighbourhood and to organize a whole class of planning students in a neighbourhood. The main purpose was to tell a story that might help the Collingwood Neighbourhood House with its funding, and secondarily to tell a story that would inspire other neighbourhoods.

Once we made the film and saw its impact on people and we started showing it to audiences and saw the excitement and discussions that it provoked, I had the idea of the second stage of the project (which came from the reflection of the first stage). On the one hand, we were really excited that we had this film that we were taking to audiences. People in the audiences were getting excited and they had many, many, many questions that they would direct at us. Literally, the discussions would go on for hours.

It was then that we started to realize what the film did and what it could not do. What the film could *not* do was to get bogged down by all of the information. In fact, parts of the film do get bogged down. That was a problem for us at the time. There was a choice between incorporating the information and recognizing that it totally bogged down the narrative line. At the time, thinking about the purpose of making the film, we needed to put in information about programs and services. But we felt at the time that it was a bit 'heavy', like a report with bullet points.

Through our conversations with audiences, we realized that there were so many things that people wanted to know. If there were, say, eight or so different stories within the local story, for every one of them different parts of the audience wanted to know: 'How did that happen? How come the people who were building the skytrain were prepared to have these neighbourhood meetings about the impact of the skytrain? How did that even happen? It doesn't happen anywhere else in the world'.

A whole big can of worms opened up. It certainly opened up in Australia when transportation and land-use planners watched the film. This was something we completely skipped over, we assumed as a given. But there is one kind of audience that just wants to know that whole story, which requires you to know about the whole planning culture. Other people want to know about funding: How did you go about that? Other people want to know about conflict. They said: 'There's not much conflict in this film. Is that because you didn't want to put it in?' Yes, actually, it was and because people wouldn't tell us on camera.

So then we had this idea of writing the manual to go with the film: the 'how-to' – how strangers become neighbours. [6] But the manual is also story-based, based on the stories of the different workers and volunteers. So again it's a story, rather than: 'if you want to get funding, here's what you do: you go on the internet and visit the site of Heritage Canada …' It's not like that. We realized we needed to provide a lot more information to complement the film. Once we had that, we could then show the film to targeted audiences and give them the manual. So the second phase of the project became writing the manual, presenting information about what was done by the Neighbourhood House. That was perfect; Paula Carr (the Neighbourhood House Director) could talk about the film without wasting people's time talking about how she got the funding. She could give them the manual and they could just be happy to talk with her.

So we had the manual. We took it on the road and did a couple of workshops in bigger cities. We used the Metropolis research network to target an audience: those who work in the immigrant, refugee and social services sectors. The audiences ended up being everyone from federal to provincial to municipal government to members of city planning departments, all the faith-based organizations working in the sector, artists, often immigrants themselves and all the different non-governmental organizations. It was a wide range of people.

We showed the film and ran three-hour workshops that used the film as a catalyst for engaging dialogue. With targeted audiences, it also worked well. We improvised or co-facilitated discussions accordingly, some of which were question-and-answer sessions. We also undertook evaluations and received stunning evaluations of the power of the film (that became the catalyst for the workshop).

All sorts of things happen when you get a group of people in a room together who are from the same city but don't necessarily know each other and what they're all doing. It starts all sorts of conversations in the city, which starts to create networks that you assumed were always there but weren't. This has happened to me all my life. You go and tell a story somewhere in some part of the city and they don't know what people in another part of the city are doing. It's fascinating.

Let's say it was the success of that second stage that made me think we could do a similar thing in Burns Lake. We would take film as engagement process – and we would be conscious of this from the beginning – to other communities, non-cosmopolitan communities. So from its beginning, the film has an 'action' component that assumes there was a story that was inspiring and could be used in another community struggling to move beyond racism and ingrained hostility. At the same time there was this complete segregation in Burns Lake: *two solitudes* – using the metaphor of the two solitudes to refer to non-Native and Native spaces and interaction.

So that's been our intention. Once you have that intention, it starts to affect the way you shape the narrative because you want to tell an inspiring story. On the other hand, it can't be so inspiring that they say: 'Oh, but we could never do that'. There is a really unusual bunch of people there in Burns Lake. You have to try to bring out the struggle they've been through.

Dianna: It seems there is a desire to get to the part of the story where everybody relates to a certain piece of it. And also to find a common language that can be interpreted in different locations. I was also thinking about the role of the ethnographer and the community as audience, how that relationship works. I think that's what you're talking about. Film is made by a story collector as a catalyst to engage us in or commit us to the stories. And it keeps transforming or evolving in different communities. It doesn't end; it's always moving and continuously being shaped and interpreted in different ways.

Leonie: There's another dimension: the community where you make the film. You have to recognize that the very fact that you're making the film in that community is going to have immediate and long-term impacts in that community. And you have to be quite careful. In situations where it's an 'unfinished' story and there's still a lot of conflict, it's inevitable that you become a player in the field that you walk into. It's unavoidable: the very fact that someone's coming from outside to make a film puts some people on edge; it makes some people nervous. So you have to be careful not to alienate people. You have to convey that you're open-minded.

For example, there was a real danger when we had our photo taken and a story written in the local newspaper the first time I and the whole crew were there. It so happened that the day and the hour that the photographer wanted to take the photo was when we were meeting with the Chief of the Burns Lake Band. We were sitting in the sun outside the Band office and the photographer came up and said, 'Why don't we just photograph you all together?' Without thinking about it, I said, 'Yeah, sure'.

Subsequently, when our photo appeared with the Chief of the Burns Lake Band, I thought that was, politically, a really bad move. I realized it could seem (and some people interpreted it this way) that if we weren't in the pay of the Burns Lake Band, we were certainly in cahoots with them. That would automatically – given that they were at one extreme of a polarized situation versus the white municipal council – close certain doors. The photo was taken before I had enough time to reflect. I could sense how our presence in the community had certain people on guard, had certain people on their best behaviour and had some people saying things we wanted to hear. So you really have to sort through all that. You have to be good interviewers to get people off their guard so they will say what they think.

But you have to be careful, too.

The presence of filmmakers in a situation that is highly politicized: there is a lot of responsibility. You know that, when people get a sense of the story you're telling, you can influence the direction of the town by legitimizing one particular story and making the expression of a certain set of beliefs not okay, just as behavioural norms start to get shifted. So, for example, people begin to think it's no longer okay to make blatant racist comments in the town even though people will continue to make them in private or among mates in the bar or in other situations. But they will no longer make them face to face, non-Native to Native. So as behavioural shifts start to happen because of this shift, in the same way, the filmmaker's presence says, 'Well, we think there are really interesting changes here and we want to convey that'. It's important for us to communicate that we're not here to do a 'dump job' on the town, which people were afraid of.

In that very process of legitimizing the story of change, you make it 'not okay' for the opponents of change to be so aggressively against change. This means you're having an influence in the town whether you want to or not. When you've finished the film and take it to other towns, you want to have – you hope to have – that same influence.

Dianna: This idea of responsibility is big in terms of speaking about other practitioners or planners potentially using this approach. I'm thinking about this with poetry: Should we be experts in the craft and have a lot of experience and thinking around it before we use it? Because you're looking at relationships and communities and responsibility with storylines.

Leonie: Actually, that's one of the points I wanted to make when I went into the Downtown Eastside story – precisely that. There is this superficial idea that we can use film and very quickly give people the skills to use the camera and do a bit of editing. The problem is one of ethical and interpretive complexity.

One of the things that I reflected on after the participatory video student project is that there was so much more education needed. And this was a critical reflection on my own role. I had said from the beginning that I was there to legitimize the project. In retrospect, I should have been much more active in providing some planning context. Not formal lectures but it should be a learning situation. It's not about people running around pointing cameras. That's not enough. If I'd been involved at the rough-cut stage and seen what they'd done (using a speeded technique essentially to ridicule some of the city planners), I would have not just vetoed it but opened up a discussion, asking: 'What are you doing here?' and 'Who are you doing it to?'

Some of the students also didn't take the footage back to all the interviewee participants. They just held screenings and notified people of the screenings. That's not good enough. Inevitably, there will be people who can't make it to the screenings. If you're doing anything controversial with people's footage, you have to show it and give people an opportunity to withdraw their permission. So it's not a simple medium to use.

I don't have a problem with thinking about making things one-sided. I think that's another use – for a particular constituency to show their point of view powerfully, especially if the constituency has been invisible or marginalized. That's okay, but it has to be seen as one input – seen very clearly as *their* voice.

Dianna: Giovanni talks about film not being a parallel planning technology to design or digital photography, where there is a reality placed on the page or cartographically charted. Film actively evolves and layers upon itself within the lives of communities. There is a lot of selection and thinking initially about how the story is put together.

Leonie: I think you can work in a team where only one person has to be highly skilled. It is not always necessary for everyone to learn editing and other technical aspects. It depends on the context. There may be an empowerment goal in the project – that part of this process is about imparting technical skills. But if it's not a goal, then it's sometimes a waste of time to try to get everyone up to speed on the editing. If you've got a good editor who's a really collaborative person, then everyone can sit down and shape the story. It's just that there will be only *one* sitting down at the computer doing the actual edits.

Dianna: Right. And that there will be several occasions for inclusions and exclusions within our editorial decisions.

An 'ear to the ground': Jonathan Frantz on the Carrall Street Participatory Video Project (CSPVP)

Jonathan Frantz, a planning instructor and film practitioner, also shared his experience of using film as participatory action research. While still a student at the University of British Columbia School of Community and Regional Planning (SCARP), Jonathan was involved in the Carrall Street Participatory Video Project (CSPVP) Leonie was supervising. Christine spoke to him from the film planning agency he co-founded in Vancouver, Ear to the Ground Planning.[7] The range of work Jonathan is currently doing both locally and internationally suggests this *avant-garde* method of engagement and story-telling is finding its way into mainstream urban planning practices.

> **Jonathan**: The project was made possible through a partnership with a Vancouver group called Projections, a project arm of the Portland Hotel Society (PHS). They work with at-risk youth to develop skills in film and video as a way to provide mentorship and eventually to involve them with the Vancouver job market for video and film. So they have a good relationship with the youth and did the pre-screening and came up with the interview process. We wanted to get people who were interested in the project and – we were hoping – willing to commit and stay with the project. Producing a participatory film is very time-consuming and it is difficult to keep people interested, especially people in certain population groups who are particularly mobile. We did provide a little bit of money for transportation, food and housing. We also tried to connect some of the youth with other services if need be – different kinds of counselling and help to find suitable housing – so they were supported in other aspects of the project.
>
> There was one youth in the Carrall Street project who was battling some mental illness and addiction problems. He said a few times, 'Thank you so much for working on this project'. He was grateful for an outlet to express himself and to keep busy because otherwise he wasn't sure what he would be doing. That was a really powerful moment for me in that project. Over the course of the project, I got to know him a little better and how his mental states and moods would ebb and flow. Sometimes he couldn't deal with it and would have to walk out. We would always welcome him back. He was a really creative individual – really, really intelligent – but didn't quite fit in with the standard way that education is taught. Or he didn't fit in with how people are expected to behave in the city.
>
> The youth and the students who were involved had some really interesting perspectives on Vancouver's Downtown Eastside and

how development is occurring. If you look at some of the 'normal' ways that planners solicit information from the public, they don't allow nearly the amount of expression or creativity or any of the individual catering that this kind of work does. That is what we are trying to show: the importance of that idea of multiplicity where there are different ways of getting information and seeking feedback and understanding the topic than simply responding to predefined questions. Ticking off on a scale of 1 to 5 doesn't really express the full story and the depth that certain planning processes evoke with people.

The results that you get might not always be desirable. You have to step back and say, 'Whatever you come up with is OK'. Or maybe you set boundaries and parameters that you try to come up with collectively and reach certain goals and audiences. But still you have to let the participants create essentially whatever message they are interested in telling. In a group setting, they tend to feed off of one another – so one idea will spawn another and another. It will spiral into a succession of ideas and thoughts that likely wouldn't have happened if it were just one person.

Beginning with questions: Learning through action

Film debuts in planning with a distinctive role both as a catalyst for community engagement and as an engagement process. Giovanni suggests that new technologies such as film have not entered the planning conversation by accident.[8] Film helps us to think about the multiplicity of voices in our communities from a new perspective. We may already have maps but sometimes we need to go off the path to re-imagine, retell and overlay stories. Through their reflections on experimental film as planning media, Leonie and Jonathan invite us to reflect further on some key questions throughout the various stages of the filming process:

- What are the objectives of the engagement process? How will film processes achieve all or a part of these objectives?

- Which ethical framework are we working from?
- What are some of the political consequences of working in this community?
- Where are the points and intersections of conflict?
- Who do we want to learn from? Whose stories have we traditionally listened to and not listened to? Are we including a diversity of voices in the process?
- How are we going to engage and learn in terms of collaboration, education and training or other resources?
- How much time does the project allow? How much funding is allotted?
- What kinds of technical skills do we have on our team? Do we need to hire a professional facilitator or film editor? How will different voices be part of the 'technical' process?
- What sort of long-term impacts do we think we will have on various people and relationships in the community?

Reflecting on their experiences and exploring some of these questions may help us to think about how film and other newer forms of media might be used in existing or future engagement processes, depending on the scope of the project and the resources available.

Websites as Engagement Site and Story: Aileen Penner and Think Salmon

10

Introduction

Thomas King begins each chapter of his book on storytelling, *The Truth about Stories, A Native Narrative*, with the same beginning:

> There is a story I know. It's about the earth and how it floats in space
> on the back of a turtle. I've heard this story many times and each time
> someone tells the story, it changes. Sometimes the change is simply
> in the voice of the storyteller. Sometimes the change is in the details.
> Sometimes in the order of events. Other times it's the dialogue or the
> response of the audience. But in all the tellings of all the tellers, the
> world never leaves the turtle's back. And the turtle never swims away.[1]

Each story then becomes different and yet the beginnings link us to a common starting place. The beginning also assures us that the world will never leave the back of the turtle no matter what happens in the rest of the story. We might interpret this (as listeners) to take special care of the world on the turtle's back, for us to honour the turtle that 'never swims away'.

The structure of *The Truth about Stories* suggests that many versions of a story can be told and that each version would be told differently, depending

Invitation:

Pop into another café to discover how Think Salmon (an interactive website) acts as a place for engagement. Through the sharing of salmon stories and other topical resources, Think Salmon inspires hopeful environmental actions. It links our personal and community stories across communities, connecting and interconnecting our daily experiences with rivers, people and the nonhuman species to facilitate social change.

on the voice of the storytelller, the intended audience and the variation in details. It provides a variety of entry points into a diversity of stories and extends an invitation to us as individuals to join in on the creation of story, to draw our own experiences and imaginations.

As planners, we are perpetual storytellers.[2] We craft stories when we speak of projects and project managers, housing plans and activists and policies and government officials. In so doing, we compose intersections of narrative that identify both in conventional and informal venues: public meetings, office board rooms, social events or even casual lunch hours shared with a colleague in the park. Using a variety of media such as emails and telephones, meeting minutes and informal conversations, brochures and reports, maps and policies, we inevitably evoke and layer stories together both to understand ourselves and act within the theatrical realm we collectively imagine as city, neighbourhood or community. Although stories are never in short supply, interactive venues are changing how we connect with them.

Entering into a conversation about technology is always tricky, especially considering how quickly our world in the age of technology is changing. But at the same time, we felt we couldn't neglect the fact that a large majority of us in the western world are 'online' and that this has dramatically changed many of the ways we engage with people and how we connect with stories and with information. The majority of us use virtual relationships and etiquettes in daily conversations and resource sharing. As practitioners, we might have our own website for our practice or project (such as *Creative Community Planning*) and some of us keep weblogs or 'blogs' to share photos, keep information up to the minute and allow our readers to discuss a topic or event.[3]

Many municipal governments and departments use blogs to engage creatively with multiple audiences about specific issues, such as climate change, Peak Oil, transport and water conservation. Websites and blogs offer a multimedia space to expand a topic, 'house' resources and link to other sites for further information. These interactive online 'forums' are a recent application in community engagement used to dialogue within websites or as a linked but separate entity. We know that many other innovative uses of websites, blogs and other social technology exist in engagement practice, too numerous to count.[4]

The story of Think Salmon offers a starting place for us to explore how websites and blogs work to 'house' our collective stories and connect us to ourselves, each other and our environments.

The Think Salmon tale: Reframing how we engage with ourselves, each other, salmon and stream habitat through story

Dianna spent a day with Aileen Penner, a Canadian environmentalist, visual artist, writer and community developer in 2007. Aileen was helping to co-create and manage a community engagement project for Pacific Salmon Foundation (PSF) called Think Salmon. Think Salmon is a website, sponsored by PSF and the Fraser Basin Council and designed and conceptualized to collect individual stories of salmon. Members of various communities throughout British Columbia (BC) use text, video, recipes, photographs and visual arts to tell their 'salmon story' and then send them to the PSF website development team to be edited and published online. The developers of Think Salmon are conscious of the power of storytelling. Stories on the website reflect the belief that there are many starting points or histories of the stories being told, including First Nations people, immigrants, young people and grandmothers.

At a café, Aileen brainstormed with James and Kiley – two members of the website development team – about how to improve the website:

> **Aileen**: We could do that salmon glossary.
> **Kiley**: Yeah, and maybe a walking tour for lost salmon streams in False Creek?
> **James**: What about a map of salmon names?
> **Aileen**: And I still want to do the salmon haiku poetry contest.

One of the main goals of this brainstorming session was to create ways to divert more traffic to the website. James and Aileen had recently returned from a trip to Adams River in BC, where they participated in a community event celebrating the salmon spawning season. Think Salmon T-shirts, ball caps and other merchandise were traded for salmon stories. It was here that they collected several salmon drawings and stories from kids. James mentioned the user stats and the webpage with the kids' drawings had the highest number of visits. At Adams River, kids played a significant part in the festival, learning about the salmon habitat as it relates to the history of their small town and to the health of the community as a whole.

The Think Salmon website was designed to act as a site for participatory action. Through the many diverse and personal story contributions, the website evolves, develops and shapes itself into one collaborative and ever-changing story. It asks: *How do* you *Think Salmon?* Over time, this one question evokes a dialogic approach to meaning.

Aileen believes that meeting and talking with people 'where they are at' is a growing trend within environmental engagement practice – an 'outreach' approach as opposed to 'preaching from the pulpit'. As part of her master's thesis in the environmental education–communications field, she combined a diverse understanding of literary and arts interpretation with stories and education theory. She was interested in how visual art and writing could lead to social transformation. As Aileen suggests, 'Stories have a way of interpreting larger social issues that we aren't hit over the head with and we allow them into our hearts because they are stories'.[5]

Part of her thesis involved producing a set of short stories and a visual art installation. Aileen says:

> The success of the arts installation proves to me the success of trying to argue that point, because … it was about people contributing their own stories as much as it was interpretation of our salmon stories that was the highlight of that exhibit. So people would come and draw or leave a photo or write down their salmon story. I think people want to feel that they are part of something.
>
> **Dianna**: And you referenced that to radical democracy?

Aileen: In a way. I feel that the visual arts installation (along with the short stories) contributes to a green public culture, which is about trying to fuel cultural production for the environmental movement, which then somehow relates to radical democracy about participating, not just standing by on the sidelines. People take an active role in democracy and people take an active role in creating what they see.

Dianna: You also spoke about that in terms of how it acts as an evolving or changing exhibit: how the story as the installation itself changes each time.

Aileen: That's right, because we installed it in four different places by the end of last summer and at every installation we included new stories. So it was always new; in some cases we invited other artists and their interpretations. It was always changing.

Aileen then explains how the Think Salmon project spawned from the central concepts in her thesis:

The website was based on the idea of people participating with their own stories as a way to contribute to the critical mass of the website. We're just housing these stories; we're just facilitating other people talking to each other. That's the whole premise of it. We're not telling you what to think; we're just facilitating the stories of people. These stories may include salmon-farming stories; they may include catching fish; they may include recipes. Eating salmon is a huge part of our culture.

Dianna: It's interesting to think about how societal transformation happens through a website or an installation that's always changing and incorporating personal experiences.

Aileen: Yes. And I won't be so naïve to think that one website will change how people behave or change their harmful practices around salmon. I don't believe that. But I *do* think it's a space for people to come and dialogue and debate those issues and find out what other people are doing. It's about what James was talking about earlier: the new movement in social technology. How technology can facilitate social change. I don't know if this will be the platform to *solve* some of these issues, but it certainly is a tool.

Maintaining effectiveness of the tool: Relevancy, diversity and intimacy

Aileen: The main planning goal or outcome is to make the online space where people come to share stories and dialogue and debate the most effective it can be. 'Effective' means a relevant, up-to-date, dynamic and diverse space where lots of different voices can be found – First Nations voices, as well as the traditional actors.

Dianna: It's interesting, too, to have children's voices on the site.

Aileen: That's a really important part of social change, I think. Someone at work told me once that the climate change situation is so grave that we don't have time to talk to children; we need to be in corporate boardrooms. I really disagree with that. I think it's a really short-sighted view of the world. By focusing on children, you're going to raise a generation that's more aware than their parents.

Aileen then made reference to the success of the recycling program in Canada: 'We all know from the recycling program that it's kids that make it happen, not necessarily the adults'. Again the theme of children as leaders and instructors in social transformation returns, reminding us of the importance of involving their creativity and action in all our creative community planning contexts.

As a public engagement site, Think Salmon facilitates thinking, learning and action 'to promote and conserve the rivers and places where salmon and people live'. Besides storytelling, the site offers opportunities for learning through news of community events and projects – a place for local stream stewardship groups to post and discuss issues in their community and a place to gather resources and ask questions.

The processes of writing and speaking stories through different media – such as text, visual art, photography and video – also allow individuals to reflect on values and action before sharing them on the blog or website. In other words, the act of producing the story invites us to pause to reflect on ourselves, on how we affect or interact with others and our local landscape.

Aileen wrote her own environmental narrative about growing up in rural communities, where both her parents were involved in the construction of mega-dams in the 1970s and 1980s. Aileen wanted to discuss issues from her own life that she may have philosophically disagreed with, without blaming people she loves. Rather, she felt that writing about a wild river turning into a lake, for example, provided a literal and metaphoric starting place for readers to begin thoughtful discussion.[5] In this way, stories allow intimacy. You may include many diverse experiences – and some of the values in the stories you may not agree with – but the story establishes openness around difference. These are 'hospitable' stories. They invite the listener in.[6]

Creativity and Moving Beyond Conflict: Michelle LeBaron, Norma-Jean McLaren and Nathan Edelson

11

Introduction: Creativity in cross-cultural territories of conflict

The causes for conflict are endless in our work. Multiple sources of misunderstanding, emotion, injustice and grievance are common in community relationships. These relationships are becoming increasingly more complex in cross-cultural environments, requiring imaginative methods to co-create unexpected opportunities for living and working together. In some countries, conflicts may be as old as European invasion, while others may arise out of fear of losing a particular

Invitation:
Take an incremental step or two with three experienced practitioners. Michelle LeBaron talks about moving outside our norms into realms of beauty and transformation and Norma-Jean McLaren and Nathan Edelson share how they use creativity in relationship-building processes as story carriers, matchmakers and facilitators of local leadership.

community asset in a newly proposed development plan. Michelle LeBaron, Norma-Jean McLaren and Nathan Edelson are three well-respected practitioners with many years of experience. Dianna spoke with each about creativity in practice and seeking moments for community transformation.

On beauty, play and falling in love: A conversation with Michelle LeBaron

Conjuring beauty, embracing play and falling in love are not typical in conflict rhetoric. But Michelle LeBaron acknowledges that these themes are at the heart of conflict – in relationships. Currently a professor in the Faculty of Law at the University of British Columbia, Vancouver, and internationally renowned for infusing conflict resolution with the creative arts, Michelle began this work by reigniting her creative self within her professional practice.

> **Dianna**: Michelle, there is a lovely quotation in your book, *Bridging Troubled Waters:* 'Creativity is the process of bringing something new into being'. This quotation becomes an anchor for us as we work with communities to re-imagine planning practices as more culturally diverse. Why did art become a practical way for you to bring something new into being with communities in conflict?

> **Michelle**: In one way, it's obvious because conflict resolution is really an interdisciplinary field. You cannot fully know human or social conflict through any discipline you can name. And so, broadening out, especially into expressive disciplines, seems so important because there is a conduit outside the rational mind and the kinds of logic that sometimes keep us confined. That's one answer.

> And the other personal answer is that I'm a musician. So I really cared about finding a way to infuse or integrate my love of music into my work. For me to be able to bring music and movement and multiple creative modes into my work was such a relief because it makes everything more connected, rather than having all these disconnected episodes in my life. It connects the passions.

By infusing her professional work with her creative passions, Michelle experiences synergies in her creative work. Wendy and Michelle have both found that when we 'embody' our work through artistic processes, we open up spaces for transformation.

Finding ways to work with mystery

Dianna: You write about how each context has its own culture – whether it be different disciplines, different community organizations or different groups. How did you begin to use art both to bridge those groups and to encourage diversity in the process?

Michelle: I guess what I had seen, over maybe 15 years of mediating and trying to help people come together in commercial, community or international situations – it doesn't matter; to me the line runs through all of those – was that conflict is mysterious. We don't understand it. If you think about the terrible conflict going on right now in Gaza, you can't get the Palestinians and Israelis together and use some sort of cultural mapping tool. It's just insulting because it's so much deeper than that. So we have to find ways to work with mystery and ways to tell new stories. If we are going to tell new stories, we are going to have to get out of our cognitive habits. That is what led me to start focusing on this work.

Breaking office rituals to incorporate 'play' and 'beauty' in our professional workplace

Through weaving artistic and traditional office rituals, we redefine professional practice. Introducing play and personal expression into settings dominated by routine professional conduct seems a particularly brave move. Through her practice, Michelle realized that people love to play. When we play at work, the love of play re-energizes our work, our relationships with ourselves and others and inspires new ideas and strategies. Seen as a form of ritual, play need not be such a vast and untenable stretch from current practice.

Michelle: Play involves my definition of ritual, which is 'a time out of ordinary time' when you are stepping out of business-as-usual, where thought and analysis are less in your awareness than feeling and sensing. You're not thinking and analysing. So maybe play is a way to get people out of our heads and out of those loops in our heads that keep us stuck, the way we have of thinking A leads to B to C. We have our own individual and group loops. These keep us in the same rhythms and patterns even when they are very destructive.

I think play is a way of shaking it up, loosening it up a bit for ourselves, whether you sit by yourself playing music or if we're playing together. I'm just thinking of this as we talk: If you look at child development and Piaget, he says, first, a child begins to play by itself. And then it learns to play in parallel. Only after that do they start playing together.[1] So maybe when people are in conflict – if you could get them to play in parallel even if they won't play with each other – that would be a way of playing together.

It makes sense in another way too. If you look at studies of proxemics (human behaviour in space) and communication, one of the things we know, strangely enough, is if you and I are in conflict and we sit as we're told, facing each other, it begins to escalate conflict. This happens because I'm seeing your face and body language and how right you think you are. And I am communicating to you that I am clearly in the right. So we know, for example, that couples or friends tend to resolve things best in the car when they're sitting side by side or they're side by side on a walk together. They're not fixated with each other and they don't have to be squarely engaged. Maybe play does the same thing.

As the majority of planning institutes may not take play seriously, we are likely to encounter challenges in incorporating play in our work environments. Michelle believes it is a question of translating play into the work environment, framing and packaging play as part of the work, rather than its opposite. Depending on the existing work environment, this translation can be subtle.

Michelle: One of my favourite stories is a story of a colleague in Alberta who was sent in to mediate a planning dispute. There was this huge dispute outside Calgary about the siting of a road near a school. Indigenous people, parents, the school personnel, the regional district, people with various resources and interests and all these people in the neighbourhood were involved in the process. There were over a dozen parties who had been fighting with each other in court for three years and they'd spent heaven knows how many thousands of dollars on expensive lawyers.

So they were told to get together and mediate. Now, you can imagine, if you have $500-per-hour Calgary lawyers and you come in and say: 'Let's sing first'. You can't. You can't – because you would be fired! So this friend of mine did a very smart thing. He wore the proper uniform: he wore a suit. He brought an agenda, brought his briefcase. You can't signal to people, 'I'm really a weirdo'. You have to act the part in some way and what he did was, I think, brilliant, because he managed to infuse some creative expression into a very conventional process without anyone even noticing.

What he did was he said: 'OK, welcome. I've talked with many of you. I'm glad to be here, I've got the agenda and I know we have a very busy day. We have until 4:30 to get this done and I know from talking to you this is a hard problem. It's been going on for three years; it's complex'.

So he acknowledged all of this. He said, 'Just before we get started, before we get into the agenda, I'm thinking that most of you know each other. But we haven't been in the same room together before. So I would like to do a quick round of introductions and I'd like you to introduce yourself by talking about your connection to this place'.

And people kind of went, 'Huh?' You know, because that's strange. You wouldn't normally ask that. But it's not too far outside what they are expecting in terms of introductions. Normally they would say, 'I'm so-and-so, I've come from this firm and I represent this side'.

My colleague didn't want to redefine *those* identities. So he asked them another question. And they started saying things like: 'See that mountain over there? That's where I proposed to my wife'.

So what happened? Their identities, which had formally been more monolithic with each other, became more complex. And they became more human and enlivened. One person said, 'Well, I'm from the Provincial Ministry in Edmonton and I don't have any connection to this place, but it's certainly beautiful'. So now you have people talking about beauty, which normally they never do. Lawyers do not talk about beauty.

My friend told me that the entire atmosphere in the room changed. They quickly did the introductions and the atmosphere was different from when they started. Then he went into the agenda and went right through it. And the whole lawsuit settled in one day. He thinks it would not have settled without this process.

Michelle concluded by explaining that settlement in one day was a feat that she and her colleague believe was possible only because participants were given the opportunity to know one another more intimately than is usually possible. Michelle says we have to ask: 'What is the culture?' and 'How can I fit in the culture and just take one little step?' We don't want to take a huge leap outside the culture because people won't follow us.

As engagement practitioners, our first (and ongoing) step is to assess the existing culture and to enter the scene 'dressed appropriately'. Then we can let the method emerge – a method that will introduce the first increment of change. Before taking these first steps, we must ensure that participants feel safe and comfortable enough to disrupt what they might perceive to be process norms. In the Alberta mediation example, people introducing themselves differently and 'speaking beauty' were integral to moving beyond conflict's destructive rhythms or loops.

The Alberta introductions invited beauty because they invited participants in conflict to acknowledge their connections with each other. In another example, Michelle recounts how a bus trip played a practical and spiritual role in an engagement process.

> **Michelle**: Back in 1993, I went to Dublin with a group of diplomats from around the world. And there we were. We were supposed to be illuminating the Israeli–Palestinian conflict. What a surprise! Some things have not changed. And nothing was happening because people kept saying, 'The position of the Government of France is... The position of the Government of Venezuela is...' even though we said this is off the record and you don't have to represent your own government. That's what diplomats do.
>
> They're not going to speak from some radically different place from what their governments want them to. So it wasn't until we went on this bus trip that things started opening up. Then people met each other spiritually. They met each other holistically. They started seeing something more complex than common ground.
>
> This is about a kind of connection, a kind of alignment, that people experienced with each other like the sparks they experience when falling in love. But I don't mean in a 'romantic' sense. I think we can fall in love with each other when we see each other's essence – just through a conversation like this. And it doesn't mean a 'sorted' kind of thing. It's an acknowledgement of the other, like the greeting, *Namaste*. Which is to salute the eternal in the other or the spiritual in the other. I think that happened on the bus trip.
>
> **Dianna**: A kind of seeing?
>
> **Michelle**: Yes, seeing. Aligning. There's physicality to it. You feel different. Did it fix everything? Did it change anything? No. Did they solve the Israeli–Palestinian conflict? Obviously, no. But they had a lot more fun with each other. And some productive things came out of

it. And, believe me, nothing productive would have come out of it if not for that bus trip.

Michelle returns to the question of translation when we speak of spirituality and art in the work place. In *Bridging Cultural Conflicts* (2003a), she chose to talk about spirituality as 'connected ways of knowing' so as not to alienate people from the essence of the work: to connect us in spirit, thereby collectively transforming us. This transformation transports us beyond conflict to a place where we can align or connect with others, enjoy their presence and seek a deeper understanding of different perspectives. Creative methodologies create new spaces for these perspectives by embodying passion and breaking the loops of stolid thinking.

Listening, leadership and connection through conflict: A conversation with Norma-Jean McLaren and Nathan Edelson

Canadians Norma-Jean McLaren and Nathan Edelson work to promote cross-cultural understanding and connection in both planning practice and education by using creativity to navigate and bridge relationships. They have both been active in community work for many years – Norma-Jean as a community development facilitator and practitioner working in rural communities, and Nathan as a senior planner with the City of Vancouver. Recently, they have begun to work together on projects dedicated to community transformation through listening, leadership and personal connection.[2]

Creating a culture of deep listening: 'It's not about agreement; it's about being heard'

Norma-Jean translates into her work the belief that a significant component of the healing process for communities in conflict is to give people the opportunity to share their stories – maybe even for the first time – and to really listen to these stories.

Norma-Jean: Where our work has been moving for the past few years is much more towards trying to bring groups together that have always been in conflict, whether it's the left and right politically, Natives and non-Natives, or business groups and the poor, police and the underdogs. What's difficult is that in our society we confuse *listening* to the story with *agreeing* with the story. That's the place where we are working now, trying to bring people (or both sides if there are sides present) to an understanding that it's not about agreement. It's about being heard.

When they started the truth and reconciliation process across Canada for the residential school survivors, Michael Ignatieff said that it was a way of creating a new history, which is the history of *all* the stories rather than the history of one side. So when it's spoken and said: 'This is what happened', it becomes part of the record.

Planner as 'story carrier': Locating leadership in communities

Nathan has worked for years in a neighbourhood with the lowest income bracket in Canada. To encourage listening among different people or groups, he tries to meet initially with key people on a one-to-one basis. He speaks of taking on the cautious role of 'story carrier', going back and forth from person to person and, at first, intensely listening to each story. Listening requires a commitment to better understand the roots and implications of a person's emotions, thoughts, concerns and hopes. Sometimes being a story carrier involves listening to individuals typically isolated from decision-making processes, people who may think of us as 'the other'.

Nathan: In Vancouver's Chinatown, one of the business people has been very concerned about almost every initiative the City has undertaken. So it's very easy to marginalize his concern because everything the City does is wrong in his opinion. There are a lot of problems in the way he presents his concerns because there is so much anger and he's not always listening to other people.

On the other hand, he's done a number of really powerful things to promote Chinatown. I spent quite a bit of time with him and found out many things about him. I had assumed because of his accent he had grown up in China but he actually grew up on Vancouver Island in a very large Chinese community there. The mine was closed down and his parent's general store was eventually closed because the first people fired were Chinese.

Then he came over to Vancouver and became involved in real estate. But the whole story – the levels of racism and discrimination he faced, the powerlessness of watching a whole community die in front of him – made much more sense with respect to what he feared was going to happen to Vancouver's Chinatown. He had deep cultural roots within the Canadian Chinese society. It was still very challenging to work with him, but I could let other people know so that when he was frustrating to them, they could also see another side of him.

Norma-Jean feels that in North American society, people no longer know how to use story effectively. When we disagree with what someone is saying or classify someone as 'not worth listening to', we shut down possibilities. Story carrying is the responsibility of communicating people's ideas about other people and realizing there is more than one truth in any circumstance. Norma-Jean expands the conversation about story carrying, suggesting how to identify key individuals who can lead the process of listening.

Norma-Jean: If we are doing work between police and Aboriginal communities in BC, we take people who are ready for a discussion. So we have two or three of the police community who think of themselves as moving through transformations and learning processes. We also have Aboriginal leaders who are into understanding the process of healing and building across communities. And then we have them talk to each other about what the pathway looks like.

In a way that is similar to story carriers, these kinds of people may be understood as 'process carriers'. They break the ice between each other to build a wee bridge so we will have something to stand on when building the actual bridge. This is because if you just start leaping in, especially as someone in the middle who's trying to negotiate some sort of process, you have to have some sort of idea of what's going to hit the fan, what's going to work and what's not going to work.

After individuals' stories have been shared and listened to, Nathan and Norma-Jean act as a kind of 'matchmaker', arranging meetings between individuals who may see the world very differently but who share common concerns or goals. Nathan uses small meetings to go back and forth between the two individuals or groups for a while to get a sense of what will work.

Depending on the issue, meetings are held on as neutral territory as possible. Meeting spaces are particularly 'political' spaces, especially for individuals or organizations that have been 'ancient enemies'. But this can change once openness to listening has been demonstrated and the 'tone' of the relationship goes from one of opposition to one of working together on a common project. Building the relationship happens slowly: increment by increment, conversation by conversation, meeting by meeting.

> **Nathan**: What's important is allowing people the time to talk to one another – talk a bit on the issue they are concerned about – but as much as possible find out a bit about each other. We all live complicated lives. So we need to create more opportunities to see some of the things people have in common – whether it's families, or that they grew up in the same place, or they shop in the same place. Or other things about each other that they might not know. These discoveries start to weave together the kinds of initial connections that become important to moving forward.
>
> Another important aspect is providing opportunities for groups or individuals – who don't usually get the opportunity to work together

on a project – to work together on it. When groups who normally oppose each other come together to present a common idea it becomes my 'talking dog' theory: it doesn't matter what it says, it's interesting.

Nathan encourages us to seek out opportunities to facilitate groups working together on a project, no matter how small or seemingly irrelevant. What is most important, he emphasizes, is the chance to create a 'common history' of working together for a project and an example for themselves and for others with whom they share common ground and a capacity for cooperation. This does not mean the parties have fully reconciled or that they agree with how the other is operating. Nathan argues that even the smallest increment of trust and cooperation is important, including the decision to remain silent on a project one group brings forward that another would normally oppose.

Working in parallel: When working together doesn't work

Realistically, parties with a long history of conflict may not always find an opportunity to work together towards a common goal. As Nathan confides, this does not necessarily indicate the demise of a potential project. The planner may become the only common bond, so it is important to continue working on establishing and maintaining trust separately within each group. The key is to ensure that your actions are careful and do not to harm anyone's interests.

> **Nathan**: There's a general assumption that you can get people who disagree talking together relatively easily or quickly. On some issues I've worked on, we may have tried to get people talking but realized it's not going to be too productive because the differences are too great. But you don't need a consensus of everybody to do *something*, even for significant things.

When working *together* is not feasible, working *in parallel* might be. Nathan's experiences remind us of some of Michelle's observations: two people in conflict resolve issues by walking side by side. So, too, parallel action might be a path towards agreement and future cooperation.

In other contexts, groups may be able to work together but they need a neutral facilitator to encourage the possibility. A fundamental premise of Norma-Jean and Nathan's work is to invite individuals and groups to be change agents in their own communities. This asks people to be leaders, turning the focus from 'What are you – the planner, the City, the facilitator – going to do?' to 'What can I do to make the community a better place and with whom do I need to work?'

Nathan recently resisted the impulse to visit the site of a non-profit service-provider proposing expansion to judge for himself whether neighbours' complaints were justified. For him, the most important thing for community members was for their stories to be heard. So the non-profit agency was sent out into the community.

> **Nathan**: We insisted that they go out and meet people in the neighbourhood, to visit various organizations and let us know what those organizations and individuals thought. And, of course, they had a lot of supporters but they were also hearing people who opposed.
>
> Their first reaction when they heard opposition was to think, 'Well, those people are NIMBY' or just gentrifying the neighbourhood or they didn't care about the poor. [3] So a lot of work was put into encouraging the agency to hear what people were actually saying.

The communication that Nathan encouraged not only resulted in meaningful changes to the proposed site designs but also fostered understanding and shared goals among the two community groups. The non-profit agency ensured that the building was constructed with sufficient space to minimize line-ups (queues) and agreed about how to handle unexpected line-ups. They also approached the conversation constructively, asking how street-level retail space could best be used to contribute to their client services and to the neighbourhood as a whole.

Listening to stories, identifying common goals and forming partnerships in action: *this is creative community engagement* – engagement that is as much about learning as doing. This is engagement that sees a project to its end *and* builds a stronger community by bridging differences, humanizing the other and creating spaces for all involved to imagine their own futures under their own leadership.

One of Norma-Jean and Nathan's current projects, the Safety for All Campaign, is attempting to transform an ancient community conflict among sex trade workers, business owners and residents. Instead of inflicting measures to force the sex trade workers to move to another neighbourhood, Nathan and Norma-Jean are facilitating a process that helps pull apart what it means to be in community, to be a sex trade worker and to be a resident. They speak about challenges in the beginning phases of this project.

> **Nathan**: In terms of developing the Safety for All Campaign, we're not sure what it's going to look like. We know that it needs to be resourced to have considerable community dialogue and to set up the things that the community feels it could do. We don't want a big facilitated process, initially. We want small groups of people being able to talk to one another in safe circumstances. And to start to build the consensus or channels of agreement with a better understanding of what people think is realistic. This is because it's very easy to go from an interesting vision to something that's just delusional, that doesn't have practical grounding. It has to be in the vocabulary of the kinds of people you want to work together and who can see it in their interests.
>
> It's also about hearing the stories of safety issues and having people take time to talk about that, rather than: 'Oh, it's terrible here!' or, 'I phoned the police and nothing happened' or, 'The City didn't do this or that'. What is the real issue? 'I've gotta clean up condoms in front of my store every day. My customers can't get in here ...'

Norma-Jean: '... because people are sleeping in the doorways until after I open my store'.

Nathan: They say: 'What are you going to do?' I say, try to transform that into: 'What are we/you going to do together to try to change that?' We try to create the common story by giving as many people as possible the opportunity to contribute to the solution and build a stronger community through the process.

When community members replace 'pointing fingers' with listening, they are able to envisage working with 'ancient enemies' and working towards collaborative solutions. Creativity then works its transformative magic.

Nathan: When people can break through the stiltedness of disagreement to a point where they have the beginnings of a common project, the possibility of new ideas can occur.

Nathan's words echo Michelle LeBaron's: 'Creativity is the process of bringing something new into being': new relationships, new understandings, new possibilities and new hope for our communities.

Part 4

The Growing Edge:
Creative Engagement Processes
for Children and Young People

the song will continue

            in our branches for the young
and we're crossing our fingers for the songbirds
we're closing our eyes and wishing the best for
the songbirds we are not just wishing but planning
for the forests and for us

we've got a listening room we have a haiku room
no need for microphones we sit in circle tones so
we might hear so we will always hear:

        silent map songs written in our chests

                             – dh

But They're Only Kids! Why Engage with Children and Young People?

12

In this next century,
we will have the chance to save the world, or to destroy it. By involving
young people in the solution, the dream of sustainability may be one
step closer to reality.

James B. Moody (2000)[1]

Introduction

When it comes to creativity, children and young people challenge all our preconceptions about community engagement. Attending one of Wendy's lectures on urban design and engagement with children, Dianna remembers feeling surprised that she had never considered children's involvement in planning and decision making. The topic is difficult to find in mainstream 'adult' engagement literature, although many practitioners focus specifically on children and young people's engagement. Children and young people already know a lot about their environments – what makes them fun, safe and practical for learning, playing and commuting. Young people also have a unique ability to tap into creativity and dream about the future without many of the

Invitation:

We are constantly making decisions in our communities that will affect our common future. And we feel a particular responsibility to work closely with children and young people. Wendy presents the *Savvy Cities* argument to include children and young people in our decision making, Arthur Orsini opens up a fun space for young people to provide creative leadership and Norma-Jean McLaren and Nathan Edelson talk about intergenerational learning with Elder and Youth Councils.

inhibitions adults often have. In this chapter, we talk about how (and why) we can honour and value the knowledge of children and young people through engagement processes. We have also included some examples for children and youth engagement in the Gilt-edge Resources (Resources 3 and 4).

Wendy begins by sharing some of her passion for including children in community engagement processes.

Engagement with children: What we've been missing

In October 2004, I co-authored a paper at the first *Creating Child-friendly Cities* symposium in Brisbane with my Malaysian planner colleague, Elyssa Ludher. The symposium aimed to assess whether Australian and New Zealand cities are 'child-friendly' and to identify what can be done and what is being done to improve their liveability for children. Our paper was entitled, 'Are We Shutting Kids Out: A Review of Government Community Engagement Advisory Material?' Elyssa undertook much of the research and we were both alarmed by the results.[2]

Working in a small social-planning firm, we always try to include children and young people in our engagement processes (although with young people we often seem to fail). We'd been refining processes for these groups for some time and nevertheless wondered why we seemed to be shutting children and young people out of engagement processes – and the engagement discourse generally. Our hypotheses in undertaking the research were that government engagement manuals were ignoring children and young people as groups to involve in participatory processes related to planning and design and probably other aspects of civic life. We were correct.[3]

As Gilt-edged Resource 5, we've included the *Week with a Camera* method. It is a way of helping planners and designers understand the 'mental maps' children hold in their heads about their neighbourhoods. It enables children as young as 10 or 11 to document use of environments and articulate their wishes for that environment. They can also identify significant landmarks, play circuits, focal points and 'sacred places'. This method is best used when you want photographic documentation of children's use of their built and natural environments. It can be used alone or in conjunction with other methods. We have seen a variation of this method used with adults and have used it with great success with children in both urban and remote rural locations.

Collage making and facilitation, Kennedy Bay, Western Australia, 2003

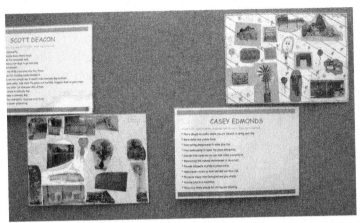

The collages and the comments displayed at the public event

After seeing the results of the *Week with a Camera*, Brian Borlini, Principal of Port Kennedy Primary School in Western Australia, said:

> It was great that you actually gave kids a chance to have a say... They felt like they'd been consulted and that was good. I was surprised how much the kids came up with which was the same as what was being put forward by the [adult] community. We've been involved with local community groups and sports groups – but nothing like that ... no one has ever come in and actually asked the kids for their opinion... I was a bit unsure what the finished product would be like... But when I saw the pictures and what the kids had actually said about them, that made it meaningful. I thought it was interwoven really well.

In debriefing sessions, we have found it essential for adult participants of any simultaneous workshop to be fully involved. This involvement ensures that all information is shared and that the children's participation is not treated as a token. So that the report accurately reflects the children's views, facilitators, recorders and animators must be fully trained and briefed.

Working with young people: Some guiding principles

Children and young people are different groups with different engagement needs. One way of looking at the engagement needs of young people is to consider ways of increasing their representation in decision-making forums. Adults who have embraced youth engagement as a guiding vision have generated a flurry of activities – ranging from placing young people on governing boards, establishing community service programs, establishing youth leadership programs, forming national youth forums, supporting youth-initiated activities to convening international youth conferences. Regrettably, we have not matched this enthusiasm with an equivalent effort to build a coherent conceptual framework to inform policy and practice.

Young people from, say, ages 12 to 20 are not easy to reach, as they are a heterogeneous, complex, individualistic, busy and media-savvy group. They are open to a variety of engagement methods but are most likely to respond to small-group face-to-face situations. They are looking for a sense of trust in the engagement process, as well as a serious commitment from organizers to listen to, respect and value their views. To maximize young people's involvement in participatory processes, planners and others should ensure that young people:

- are fully informed about opportunities and invited to be involved;
- understand why they need to be involved;
- believe that getting involved will benefit them personally; and
- hope to help others as much as themselves.

Good ways of working with young people are not very different from good ways of working with adults. Respect and autonomy are key requirements. We've found it best to be direct and candid, authentic in our message and to provide opportunities for them to make decisions and find out more about the process or project. Establishing a creative and supportive atmosphere, developing options that allow flexibility in levels of involvement and preparing a communications plan with frequent and open communication are also useful. Anything we can do to avoid wasting young people's valuable time will send a strong message that we care about them and understand their needs.

Community engagement with young people:
The *Savvy Cities* argument[4]

Wendy explains:

Working with Melbourne community planner, Andrea Cook, I have been developing an approach to engagement with young people that we call *Savvy Cities*. The first premise – or argument – of this work is based on David Driskell's path-breaking *Creating Better Cities with Children and Youth* (2002): all young people have a need to discover and experiment in communities. The second is that young people are our future 'civil society', responsible for our communities. However, in reality, we confer little responsibility on adults who make up the current 'civil society'. Further, we offer few opportunities for involvement for this group of future adults.

So why, we ask, should we involve young people? There are many answers and the answers change, for democracy and citizenship are constantly changing. Essentially, people want more involvement in public life than they did over the past few decades. However, many adults see young people as problematic in participatory democracy and shy away from involving them in decision making. Why is that? Well, young people have 'multiple personas' (because adults label them in ambiguous ways: *invisible/visible, victim/criminal* and *naïve/knowing,* and so forth). Many of us see kids as 'messy' or not worthy of engagement.

Often when we approach engagement, we are thinking about risk, not care. However, if we are to nurture creativity and an engaged citizenry and accept our responsibilities as adults, we have to work harder than we have in the past.

Many presumptions about young people inhibit us from listening to what they have to say. Over the years, Andrea Cook and I have heard the following:[5]

Adults are here to take care of young people. We should not expect young people to shoulder our responsibilities. We argue that young people's participation should complement adults' participation. It is not a replacement. Adults are not giving up their responsibilities. Rather, adults are taking their responsibilities more seriously when they seek to discover what is truly in the best interests of young people in their communities.

Young people are unreliable and tend to change their minds often. They are too immature and naïve to make decisions. Well, it's true that some young people show these limitations, but so do some adults. There are methods to involve young people with varied skills and maturity levels. People who work in participatory projects with young people are continually amazed at how mature, insightful and creative they can be. And, if we recall, the same arguments were used for many years against the participation of women.

Young people cannot foresee the long-term consequences of their actions. Many adults cannot either! In fact, education is an important part of any participatory process. Young people need to understand the potential consequences of their recommendations and actions, for, if anyone has a stake in the future and a concern about long-term consequences, it is young people. Their voices are critical to the decisions that will affect the future.

I was young once, so I know what young people want. Adult experts have the information and knowledge to make the best decisions in the interests of young people. Things have changed since adults were young. Truly, nobody knows better than today's youth what it is like to be young today. Young people themselves are most knowledgeable about their own lives. Outside 'experts' should facilitate, not dominate, democracy.

Some *Savvy Cities* principles

We seek to help young people to escape from the 'bubble wrap' of adult control into engaged citizenship. This means:

- getting authentic representation: a range of young people – not just the 'good ones' (so not just selecting the ones the principal chooses for the workshop);

- working at 'kid level': directly with young people – from their perspectives, not adults' perspectives (actively listening to their stories and not using questions we framed beforehand);
- developing skills and assets: engaging in 'two-way learning' – learning from young people, passing on skills and developing assets; and
- celebrating youth 'savviness': acknowledging and celebrating their experience – validating their contributions to public life.

Young people are a heterogeneous group with a lot of difference, just as adults are different from one another. In community engagement practice, we often tend to work with easily accessible ones – those who can 'operate' in adult structures. But what about all the other sorts of young people: girls, boys, 'homebodies', 'carers', 'roamers', 'groupies', culturally and linguistically diverse kids, children and teenagers, for example? We know that young people have unique perspectives, culturally and physically, of the world.

With *Savvy Cities*, our advice is to get down on our knees, get out on our bike, into the dirt, take a ride on the swing, get down to the shopping centre or skate park and get a sense of the socio-physical sensations of public spaces from a young person's perspective. These young people need to be supported in their development (gaining skills to participate in community life). Professional development (helping designers and planners understand their social needs) also requires support and facilitation. Helping young people to express their 'culture' in their own ways and in their own words will validate their experiences and empower them as they move into adulthood. Empowered people are savvy people, able to negotiate the world with confidence and contribute to a better public life.

Barefoot Mapping is one example of an embodied method for young people (see Gilt-edged Resource 4). Without a great deal of experience in working with young people, Wendy and John Murray pioneered a 'barefoot mapping' approach in a community engagement project in 1997 in Airds, Sydney. The results were highly successful and led to the use of the model for adults, children and young people in a variety of settings in the intervening years. The

model is particularly useful for working with people for whom English is not their first language.

Sustainable cities and the 'cool' edge of engagement: A conversation with Arthur Orsini in Vancouver

Arthur Orsini, Director of Programs at Urbanthinkers in Vancouver, is a highly skilled and innovative practitioner, who works to engage young people in elementary and high schools by first finding a way to begin a creative conversation.[6] Sometimes he brings a toy box full of planes, trains and automobiles into the classroom. Other times he asks kids to map out their way to school, to talk collectively about where they cross the road and why and to notice where the bike racks are located, to wonder about sidewalks built only on one side of the street. He invites engineers into the discussion to hear what kids know about the inappropriately placed (and dangerous) sidewalk and why their parents discourage them from riding their bike to school.

From experience working with older kids, Arthur says youth will make any engagement process 'cooler' than we possibly can as adults. In one process, he presents the context using an image like an altered car advertisement (one of his many collected images).

Arthur then invites teenagers to decode car culture in terms of their own experience of the environment. Other times he presents a film or shows photos or projects other teens have worked on to provide ideas and to begin transforming a 'room of shy teenagers' into a 'room of enthused questioners', examining the habits and routines around them. Youth add 'bike culture' into 'multicultural', dress up for 'bike fashion' shows and create dramas, rap songs, bike slogans and zines to present their ideas.

Here is an excerpt from Dianna's conversation with Arthur on his approaches and methods for working with young people.

Arthur: With the youth themselves, I don't want the dynamic of teacher–student. I think in terms of our approach to things, we aren't following a text book, we're not going from Chapter 1 to Chapter ten, so to shake up their mindset, I like to ask what other things are going on in your life, what clubs or teams are you in? Volleyball team? Job at McDonald's? Or the cafeteria or something. And I turn it around to: 'How does that role in your life make you better?' Being on the volleyball team, what can we learn from that? And then hearing the responses they give because it also allows for their outside experience, which compared to someone who's been working for ten years in the field, they might ask, 'What do I have to offer?' But they have a lot to offer. And their perspective is quite important.

Dianna: That reminds me. One of the things we are thinking about in community engagement is how to involve the spirit of play. How do you think we can support youth to share their knowledge on topics like transportation in a way that isn't boring or dull?

Arthur: The first two things that come to mind are drama and rap and hearing stories from a different perspective. Also I think in terms of satire for the drama side. That's valuable.

Dianna: And do you use those in your practice?

Arthur: Yeah. They definitely come up. We make zines…

Dianna: Wow!

Arthur: Oh, that's probably what we do the most. There's a lot I like to do in terms of creativity. I believe a lot of what I do is in that realm of creativity.

One of the things I do is I quickly rip out strips of paper and get them to write bike slogans for bike stickers. Then we sit around the table and we pass it around and people can read it and say, 'Oh, well, that reminds me of this'. Then it keeps going around, so you're not just writing your own ideas but it's building on that idea; those are the wordplays.

The zines are two-dimensional art. The satire is drama and the rap is again words, but conveyed with emotion. And the other activity I have is walking haiku. I ask them to write several *haiku* based on the weather. I ask: 'What was it like that day?' 'Did you walk?' 'Were you in a rush?' Then I ask them to reflect back on the *haiku*.

Arthur also talked about the importance of 'spontaneous interactions' to interconnect issues within young people's learning environments. He told a story about the cancellation of one of his workshops and how he took the opportunity to go into the staff room and begin a conversation with the economics teacher about using learning examples from transportation. Arthur says that keeping on the lookout for these kinds of conversations is a necessary part of working with young people, that these are 'new spontaneous interactions [which] I believe are the soil for creativity'.

Intergenerational imaginings: Using *Talking Circles* with elders and youth

In Chapter 11, Norma-Jean McLaren and Nathan Edelson described how they use creativity to shift relationships and find common goals. In this conversation, Norma-Jean and Nathan explain their use of *Talking Circles* to promote intergenerational learning. The structure of a *Talking Circle*, developed by North American Aboriginal people, allows those sitting in the circle to speak without interruption.[7] Others may observe outside the circle to witness the sharing of stories, but they cannot speak. This method creates space for people – who might not be typically heard in other types of processes – to speak and be listened to.

Norma-Jean and Nathan share the story of *Talking Circles* in a Vancouver suburb with distinctly separate communities.

> **Norma-Jean**: The elders wanted to hear what the youth were saying. Nathan was saying earlier that, in this community, it was the largest number of commuting parents to work...

> **Nathan**: They had a lot of young people whose parents were not available to them for many hours during the day; there were many two-income commuting parents. We also found a lot of seniors living in a sense of isolation.

> **Norma-Jean**: The committee we were working with to coordinate the program said: 'These are the two communities that we are most concerned about. They are most cut-off, most at-risk'. There was

very limited transit at any point; in the evening it shuts down. We knew that some of these kids were learning how to drive and needed someone to teach them. Others had a licence but no car. And the seniors needed someone to drive them. So it was a 'win–win' to go in the direction of talking about car-pooling or car-sharing.

This particular community consists of four very distinct districts separated from each other by agricultural land and by a huge abyss. One of them is a Native (First Nations) reserve; one has become a very, very wealthy community of people who have left the city; one is a hundred-year-old fishing community; and the fourth community, some distance up on the bluff, is largely a South Asian community. So they're four very, very different communities.

We wanted four or five elders for the Council of Elders, people who were active from those four communities. We brought those people together. It was the first time they had been brought together for a project and there was some success. Some of the early success was not all that great. But it was a beginning point. And I think it would have continued. These elders wanted to have contact with the youth and to hear what the youth had to say. They wanted to meet them and to talk with them under these same sorts of circumstances.

But the unusual thing we did there, which I think is tremendously important, is that we asked the same kinds of questions in both circles. It wasn't as successful with the kids (as with the adults) because history is not quite the same with them. But with the elders, we went around for as long as they needed to talk, asking them to be mindful of how many people were present. We had the whole day together that first time. Again we asked them the questions: 'What was in this community? What is now? What could be?' The important question is the last one: 'What's your role in it?' The other thing we said was, the only words you *cannot* use are: 'They should', or 'You should'. Using this limitation as a ground rule gets people to take personal responsibility for doing something about past issues and dreams for the future of their community.

The experience of sharing reflections in the circles was pretty powerful. Everyone wanted to hear from the youth. And in each case, in the Council of Elders and the Council of Youth, people could stand outside and listen, but they couldn't speak until it was over (at the very end there was a go-around to find out what they learned). That was most powerful in the Council of Youth. There were school teachers and police officers and the elders sitting outside listening to 20 youth from four different high schools and four different communities talking about the separation between their schools, the fights, their limited positive contact and how it could change. And, of course, with the kids, their immediacy and their solutions were not like: 'Well maybe we should think about'. It was like: 'Now!'

Some of the things they talked about included mentorship (with all the skills these seniors had in this community). It was just phenomenal. It was all there! The adults were really shaken by listening to these kids.

With *Talking Circles*, the form of speaking and listening allows us to receive each other differently. Norma-Jean emphasizes that it is not the kind of meeting where someone could 'drop in'. Rather, it is a series of very personal offerings of personal experiences in the community. When people participate in the *Talking Circle*, experiences can be honoured in a unique way. There is time for each person in the Circle to recount their version of the past, to describe what they see now, to dream of a future and to voice how they wish to be a participant in bringing changes to fruition.[8]

Honouring the savvy knowledge of young people in our engagement processes

Challenging our assumptions about children and young people and honouring their voice and leadership in community engagement processes opens the door to a unique discourse. As Wendy and Elyssa discovered, relatively few resources are available for engaging with young people. When we neglect their experiences, ideas and feelings, we miss out on creative solutions to future dilemmas. We can risk being guilty of creative negligence. Wendy, Arthur, Norma-Jean and Nathan inspire us to help young people share their ideas through creating and supporting spaces for listening, thinking and presenting in their own voices and their own styles.

Part 5

Blurring the Edges:
A Call for an Integration
of Transformative Processes

!open up! (sound of   :wall blast)

planner as: polyglot

meeting place: market place. week
days. cafés. community acts.
spoken words.
          poetry speaks
          a new
          shape.

a new stage. a dance hall. a
lantern parade.

bridging forward   forward   forward
relationships with the past

          – dh

New Languages for Community Engagement: Translation, Language and Polyphony

13

Introduction

In early spring, 2009, Wendy and Dianna stepped out to the fragrance of cherry blossoms and fresh rain on concrete in the West End streets of Vancouver. They were walking to a Korean fusion restaurant to celebrate the completion and success of Dianna's recently defended master's thesis and to continue a discussion on the important role of language in community engagement.[1] Dianna's research stemmed from Leonie Sandercock's call for planners to gain literacy in artistic expression. In her book, *Cosmopolis II: Mongrel Cities of the 21st Century* (2003a), Leonie emphasizes that gaining literacy is not only learning to read artistic expression in both traditional and contemporary forms of poetry, visual

Invitation:

Planner as translator? Poetry and planning? Jump into this conversation between Dianna and Wendy as they discuss how language can cultivate a more meaningful place for creativity, interconnecting the multifaceted voices of ourselves, our communities, our neighbourhoods, our bioregions, our cultures, our languages and our relationships.

art, music and theatre, but also learning to speak and act these languages within the planning field itself.[2]

Wendy: So Dianna, when we talk about literacy, creativity and building new relationships in planning, what sorts of roles do you feel that language plays?

Dianna: There was an important moment for me about ten years ago where I felt something was very wrong with our community literacy as planners. In the city centre, I was attending a panel discussion on Vancouver's homelessness and affordable housing. A research report I had co-written was being disseminated and discussed. During the question period, a young Aboriginal woman from a local community organization stood up and asked if there were any way to 'translate' these reports into something understandable. She asked if community groups could hire someone to rewrite these reports into something they could use. In that moment I felt something shift in me physically: a skin-crawling realization that the report was useless to her.

The woman's questions were astute observations on language, literacy and the current relationship of exclusion. As policy researchers, we were employed by a regional governmental agency to gather qualitative interview material and translate people's thoughts and ideas into languages – languages they could apparently no longer recognize as their own. People were asking for their own ideas and experiences to be translated back to them. How problematic! To me, that experience reinforces that our engagement work in communities – talking with people, writing up reports on what was said and presenting our materials – requires a lot of careful attention.

Wendy: Ah, yes. This story resonates with Leonie's assertion that policy reports are most often 'dry as dust. Life's juices have been squeezed from them. Emotion has been rigorously purged, as if there were no such things as joy, tranquility, anger, resentment, fear, hope, memory and forgetting at stake'.[3]

Dianna: Exactly. As planners, we are politically employed as translators of processes, bylaws, hopes, trees, land use, materials, emotions – an endless list, really. We have all these codes in our language to analyse and streamline everything into formal reports. Our work looks very 'official'. But do we have the languages to include everything we hear in community engagement?

The multiplicity of languages in the community is so colourful, imaginative and full of passion. But I would say we are still predominantly speaking 'pseudo-rationally'. I think we regularly feign objectivity. Most of the time our norms accept a homogeneous product written in one voice. How can this represent the musical tongues of the communities we listen to?

Wendy: Impossible! I so agree with you! This is why I pay such close attention to transcription and reporting in engagement processes such as the SpeakOut. It's important for multiple voices to be present in the actual words used when they were spoken.

Dianna: Right. And this refers to what Meg Holden describes in sustainability planning when she says one of the things we need to pursue is integration 'without making unrealistic demands for comprehensive knowledge, and so that personal experiences are recognized as valid and necessary tests and contexts'.[4]

Working in the field of affordable housing, I've had more than a couple of experiences where personal experiences were negated as invalid. Do you remember my telling you about how, a few years ago, I was in a meeting with the research director of a government housing agency? She was telling me that the government agency required more 'hard-and-fast' statistics to tell us what kind of affordable housing was needed in the Province. All we had now, she said, were anecdotes from the community – nothing 'substantial' or 'proven'. Even though I happened to think that we did need more quantitative research in this area, the statement, 'all we have now are anecdotes', shocked me. I felt that it assumed that the knowledge tenants and housing providers were sharing with us was not factual. That somehow the 'facts' had been blown out of proportion. And furthermore, that somehow statistics are apolitical and truthful. Statistics can offer us a part of what's happening in a community, but I feel that what's really going on in any community is also colourful, imaginative and full of passions and fears. We need a variety of both direct and indirect 'translations' to show the depth of this.

Wendy: Certainly, in writing this book, we have found some ways to expand language…

Dianna: Yes. Leonie Sandercock's work (with Giovanni Attili) using film in conjunction with imaginative report writing, for instance, looks at how to expand language in planning, collaborate artistically on projects and share stories of what people are doing creatively in the community. Arthur Orsini's work with youth is another example, creating 'zines' with youth as a report to the funding agency. And the example of Think Salmon challenges us to think about ways to share stories in our own words, drawings and photographs through weblogs.

The Vancouver Public Space Network (VPSN) is also drawing our attention to public space in the city, organizing creative dialogues, design competitions for public gathering spaces and guerilla gardening initiatives.

David Diamond of Headlines Theatre is also doing interesting work in terms of the translation of social policy.[5] In March 2004, I attended a production of *Practicing Democracy* – a play about poverty, co-written and acted by people who themselves experienced homelessness or were at risk of being homeless in Vancouver. As the audience, you watch the entire play once through. You get to know the characters and their struggles. For example, a homeless couple is sleeping in a dumpster and a lonely senior woman is uncertain about the security of her housing.

When the play has finished, there is an intermission. And then (this is so surprising), the actors begin the play again from the beginning. Only this time, you as an audience member can interrupt the actors at any point and 'jump in', taking the place of the character to alter the script of the play. I saw members in the audience eager to jump in and address underlying issues that would prevent the violence that occurs in one of the scenes. This process of interaction and interruption allows a multitude of ideas to interact or play themselves out in a dialogue on stage. In this case, one of the main objectives was to document these interactions as public contributions in the reform of municipal legislation.[6] A person with legal expertise was hired to translate the actions into a report to be presented to the City Council.[7] And certainly, there would be other participatory options for 'translating' these actions, depending on the objective.

Wendy: As a poet, you reflect deeply on language. Why do you think we need to integrate poetry into our practices?

Dianna: To me, poetry investigates a unique set of truths or meanings in our lives. Poetry in the midst of our daily lives: these are the moments that move us. That pause to welcome and acknowledge us. Poet Betsy Warland says: 'Poetry is change in the act of. Like beauty, its fluidity surprises and transforms us. As with species' survival, poem embodies resilient inventiveness'.[8] Practicing poetry is the intimate practice of noticing – noticing with intensity and with a spirit of play that both you and Michelle LeBaron describe. Kate Braid also says that we need poetry to help us to play so that we can participate in the languages of our community. We need to play with language, to pick it up and roll it down a grassy hill. We need to taste it, experience it. Otherwise, how can it be of any real relevance or interest to us?

Returning to the example of the young woman who stood up and asked if the reports could be translated into something she could understand, I feel we also must be committed to opening up poetic spaces for people in the community to pick up and 'translate' our professional language into something meaningful. Translation is a local and continuous act. This act makes language beautiful and alive. Living language breathes and enables us to hear the breathing of others.

Wendy: Then, what do you think is the relationship between 'planner as translator' and 'planner as poet'?

Dianna: We are all translating – all the time. The Canadian poet, Steve McCaffery, talks about the idea of 'homolinguistic translation'.[9] This means to translate something within the same language so that traces of the original source are preserved although the meaning may be interpreted in new ways. For me as a poet and a planner, this is fascinating.

Oana Avasilichioaei, poet and translator (Romanian and French), says that the poet is:

…*acting as translator of the present, a present which necessarily implicates the past, a past that is partly knowable, but mostly unknowable and invented. Further, this present not only holds within it the ways in which its past has been historicized (which largely affect what is possible to know of that past), but also what is possible in the future (and what we know or don't know of the past partly affects what we can make possible in the future). Land/landscape/ environment is fluid, always holds within it possibilities of what is has been and not been and what could be.*[10]

Oana's ideas refer back to the importance of visioning and dreaming forward as a community, bringing forward something we know from the past to see what is possible for the future.

In the essay, 'What is Found in Translation', poet and linguist, Robert Bringhurst, says that without poetry in our professions all is likely to go awry for our institutions because we are not listening properly to the world around us. We close the door to the art of making, to the practice of creativity. Bringhurst says, 'Poetry and thinking are vocations, not professions'.[11] So I take on poetry as a calling and a responsibility.

He goes on to say: 'The translator, trafficking in poetry, trafficking in meaning, must smuggle *that which makes and breaks and twists the rules* from one set of rules to the next'.[12] Planners practicing the vocation of poetry are presented with the tender job of translating not just rules, but contexts and meanings. We take what is said, try to understand the meanings of what is said and decide how to bring it forward to make decisions, policies, recommendations and so forth. Bringhurst says that this job as translator is full of cautions and social obligations to:

1   keep our links with the past;
2   keep us informed of our neighbours' achievements; and
3   reveal the unknown – a neighbour we did not know, a past of which we were not conscious, or one we had undervalued or misunderstood.[13]

I believe a planner's social obligations as translator are to do the same, while bearing in mind what Oana says about the past and our environment being fluid, unknowable and invented. We are to stay connected and aware of how we translate people's stories and emotions into a report narrative because even if their direct words are used, we are translating the context in which they speak – the process, the venue, and so on.

Wendy: As planners, we often have the job of engaging with community residents and working for developers or governments with an already established style or 'template' for reporting. How do we shift this style? What skills do we need to enhance?

Dianna: Building on Steve McCaffery's idea, we, as planners, are really talking about learning the skill of polylinguistic translation. If we learn how to make 'reporting' a series of polylinguistic translations, we can seek spaces for more voices to enter. We would then continue assessing who is speaking and how they speak differently both in language and in form – for example, through theatre or photography or spoken word or graffiti. For me, language in planning is also about *how* we speak what we know and what we love and what we believe.

Wendy: What about *how* we listen?

Dianna: Ah, yes. I remember doing one of Norma-Jean's diversity-training/listening exercises, working in partners. One of the partners is assigned the role of listener and the other is assigned a 'pause time'. So when the listener asks a question or makes a comment, the person with a 'pause time' waits from one to seven seconds to respond or doesn't wait for the listener to finish speaking before jumping right in.

I remember being assigned the listener role and realizing I had a 'no-second' pause time. My partner was assigned a 'five-second' pause time and it seemed like several minutes before she responded to my inquiries. If I had not asked a question and was talking about a topic, I discovered that I wanted to fill the silence to encourage or invite her to jump into the conversation. It was fascinating!

Norma-Jean suggests that our ways of speaking in conversation have much to do with our family culture.

Wendy: Yes, that's interesting in terms of how we listen deeply to people in engagement processes. Let's talk more about polyphony. It's a new concept to me. How does this fit into our discussion of poetry and community engagement?

Dianna: Well, as you know, in the (northern) summer of 2008, I was living on a boat in and around Paris. I was commuting by metro to the Centre Pompidou to work on this book during the week. What a building! Besides being a library, it is a fascinating 'house' of modern and contemporary art and architecture. The whole structure is an example of artistic engineering genius. All the building's systems are infinitely traceable because they have, in effect, been turned inside-out. Every pipe for every system is colour-coded for heating, cooling or providing energy or whatever. Instead of these systems being hidden in the exterior walls of the building, they are visible. It is an extremely 'rational' and beautiful building – the creative twist of colour coding and making visible these functioning systems makes it extraordinary and beautiful.

This building, as metaphor, is polyphony.[14] One independent system carries on with its function while showing it is interrelated with, and interconnected to, several other systems operating on independent lines. Polyphonic thinking in planning seems implicitly present because the planner is always acting within a multitude of voices, relationships and priorities. But often it seems that planners understand voices as 'competing' rather than 'complementary'. Adapting polyphony as a metaphor for planning in diverse and cross-cultural contexts allows us to secure a place for more than one idea or way of being, rather than assuming that there are only dominant or monophonic voices that compete 'against' each other.[15]

Wendy: And what about using poetry in our professional work?

Dianna: Some very practical applications of poetry in planning come to mind – from poetry in a broad 'practice of noticing' sense to hearing it spoken on the street, to the actual writing of it on paper. In my thesis research, I interviewed poets and used my own poetry practice to see what poetry might bring to planning practice. Many different insights or transferable learnings suggested, to me, what planners might gain through interacting with poetry. I summarized these learnings in the following ways.[16]

Language is local

Each city, each neighbourhood, each street, will have its own distinctive languages. A city like Vancouver will 'speak' very differently from a city like Paris because the cultural and linguistic lineages are different. If we don't listen to all the languages, or to as many as we can, our policies and bylaws will inevitably be harmful.[17] Older European cities often experience a distinct challenge in welcoming new people into old cultures, whereas Canada (and I expect it's true for your adopted country, Australia, too) seems to have more trouble honouring its Aboriginal heritage. The segregation of cultural groups is visible in blank blocks of suburban housing structures for North Africans in France or the fringes of poorly serviced Native reserves for First Nations people in Canada. A dominant political tune is played in our urban landscapes that exist to exclude these 'other' languages in our environments.

Local poets and their work offer unique and diverse information sources for understanding place, forms of language, histories and cultures. Vancouver poet, Wayde Compton, spoke about how the 'lineage of the locality' works to create identities within our cultural contexts. His work alarms us to the 'erasure' of people in neighbourhoods (specifically through the design and building of the Georgia Viaduct displacing Vancouver's Black community in Hogan's Alley).[18] Wayde also spoke about researching poetry written by Black pioneers in British Columbia as a historical resource.[19] His work picks up these lineages to experiment and hybridize forms that reflect a local context. [20]

Poetry offers a parallel construction of text to the built environment

Graham McGarva, Vancouver architect and poet, uses Bringhurst's social obligations as a translator of poetry in architecture. He uses poetry first as part of his personal reflection to connect to the history of a site, then to engage with community members and colleagues as a clear communicative device and, finally, to present the project to clients and city councils. Mathematics and poetry counterbalance each other throughout the design and implementation of each project. He uses poetry when ideas and relationships require construction (or cultural associations with materiality require deconstruction). He uses mathematics in parallel to realize manifestations of these ideas and relationships in the environment. Graham's presentations and architectural drawings are created as a kind of visual poem that translates what he's observed on the site and heard from developers, community voices, and from listening to his own poet's voice.[21]

Planners, like architects, are involved in many decisions that will not only affect the current social world and landscape, but will also affect the future. Poetry is a language that allows planners to reflect on land use and comes to their aid at a time when the entire context of planning has changed. Poetry also offers a form to alter course in the context of report presentation – a form that will personally connect with people in local communities, including those in decision-making bodies.

Poetry brings intimacy to place

Oana Avasilichioaei says, 'Poetry which responds and is created out of a community has a special relationship with and awareness of that community. In fact the poet/citizen in this case might be said to have a particular sensitivity to that environment, because they cannot write out of it unless they spend a great deal of time trying to sense, understand and interact with it in every way that they can'.[22]

In their intimate and self-reflexive relationships with place, poets use various approaches, forms and lineages to construct place with text, sound and image, to place intimacy in event, relationships and environment.

Kate Braid also tells a story about her poetry students reading their work aloud at the end of the semester. She said that they actually *felt* the transformation in the room, in their bodies.[23] I experience this working in writing workshops. My hope is that people leaving good community engagement practices would be able to *feel* it working. Poetry offers planning the intensity and intimacy required for such transformative processes.

Poetry is a critic

Poetry understood as 'resistance' or 'oppositional' poetry, which tends to experiment with form using a more openly political and intellectual approach than a lyrical or emotional approach, presents a different line of engagement. Many poets offer a critical discourse for us to engage with issues of displacement, gentrification and power (for example).[24] Other forms of poetry, such as graffiti and spoken word poetry, are texts that offer commentary and insight into who is excluded from current planning practices and processes.[25] Planners could engage more fully with these texts as a form of global–local discourse, one that offers viewpoints to climb and survey the inter-connected landscape of even the tiniest detail of a planning decision. This discourse also provides clues for engaging directly with citizens most affected by transnationalism, in effect, mapping areas most in need of support and protection.[26]

Planners require a critical approach to poetry

Just as we as planners require a reflexive and critical approach to planning, we also require a critical approach to poetry. As with any language, poetry can work to exclude. So we need to ask: What are we using it for? How do planners enter the conversations already occurring in the local (or locals of a) community without attempting to synthesize a vision for the community? Who is it excluding? What is it resisting? Where is it moving us? How do we feel it in our minds, in our bodies, in our selves? How are the many experiences of a community made visible in text? In presentation?

I believe that we need to keep asking questions: to remain reflexive and critical in our approaches, leading us into greater insight and opportunities for – as well as limitations on – the use of poetry.

Poetry is a layering of multiple interactions – multiple multiples

I adapted polyphony to emphasize the rethinking we need to do to incorporate multiple voices into our planning processes and our products (such as presentations and reports). The emphasis on multiplicity is, of course, what Leonie has spoken of extensively in regard to the role of film in planning. Oana says, 'Poetry, at its root is an oral art, one that necessarily implies both poet and audience and thus community. Poetry does not get made in a vacuum but in a community of listeners and speakers, it is a give and take, a dialogue'.[27] In ways that are similar to film, a dialogue using poetry seeks to expand, enhance and beautify planning approaches and to relieve them from the urge to dominate other community narratives. Finding the beauty in the layering of language, culture, sound, nature and the built environment is part of understanding poetry's communal voice in planning. I believe that using a layered approach communicates the true complexity and multiplicity of voices in any planning discourse.

Poetry may allow for universal understanding and active interpretation

Poet Kate Braid had an interesting thing to say, not so much about connecting via a common language, but rather about a shared rhythm. She spoke about being *in utero*, listening to our mother's heartbeat. So perhaps the common language is the heartbeat or the rhythms of our humanity, which is quite like what you describe in using embodied processes – that the one thing we have in common is our physical reality, our bodies. Our languages remain multiple and polyphonic, but our hearts beat the same music. We are first-most rhythm. When we come together robed in our own language, we ignite our senses, rhythms and counter-rhythms. And we become capable in our music.

Poetry requires practice; practice requires poetry

Poetry is one of the languages used to understand struggle and solidarity across localities.[28] As we cultivate the practice of seeing, knowing and experiencing our environments – our soundscapes, our landscapes, our biospheres, our visual and our tactile cues – we will connect with each other and ourselves quite differently. I believe our practice will expand and connect into other arts, fields and languages. Poetry, as an art, offers multiple points of intersection, interaction and interconnectivity. These points are the veins by which we connect to each other.

Wendy: This typology for poetry in planning gives us several points to think about in terms of community engagement: How we engage, whom we engage with... What thoughts do you want to leave us with?

Dianna: A couple of months ago, Christine lent me her copy of Alberto Manguel's *The City of Words*.[29] As I was reading, this quotation continued to haunt me:

> *Language is a form of loving others.*
>
> Alfred Döblin[30]

Manguel's highlight of Döblin seemed to be an intimate and enlightened application for language in planning. I feel that to love well takes a lot of inquiry into who we are and a lot of acceptance of who we are. If we apply this to a community context, we need to do a phenomenal amount of work. We must work with practitioners, such as those mentioned in this book, to find a language to love each other. For me, this is poetry because it invites conscientious translation, multiple interpretation, play and imagination. Poetry invites us to reflect and to bring our thoughts forward, not at the expense of erasing any other idea. As Graham McGarva found in his architectural work, poetry invites people into the work on a visceral level.

And, as Kate Braid reminds us, the beauty of poetry, as in the structure of buildings, must be functional. Beauty and function are not separate.[31] So perhaps we can say that poetry is an expansive project in beauty and function: to evoke the past and to envisage the future in ways in which all of our beliefs potentially have a place. Alberto Manguel, speaking of Kafka, says: 'the language in which we formulate our beliefs, in order to be effective, must carry us forward to something not yet accomplished'.[32] I believe that language is an essential vehicle of creativity that we use every day to construct new thoughts and ideas and to infuse a kind of love into planning and community engagement.

On the Edge of Utopia: Stories from *The Great Turning*

14

Introduction

With all our talk about creativity and visioning, it makes sense to conclude with dreaming an ideal future. Influenced by the utopian tradition, Wendy wrote 'Stories from *The Great Turning*', a prayer for our cities, from her tiny rural village in New South Wales (pop. 350). Sir Thomas More wrote what is considered the first utopian novel in 1516 (*Utopia*) and was followed by more contemporary authors of speculative fiction, including Ursula K. Le Guin (*Always Coming Home*), Marge Piercy (*Woman on the Edge of Time*), Starhawk (*The Fifth Sacred Thing*) and Ernest Callenbach (*Ecotopia*).

Invitation:
Sit with us and become part of a future story where we are more fully interconnected with ourselves and eachother in cities and nature.

Not surprisingly, given that she's educated in environmental ethics, Wendy's story has ecotopian underpinnings. Ecotopian stories invite us to visit a utopian future that reflects more grounded and connected relationships with the Earth and all life.

And so Wendy begins…

Stories from *The Great Turning*

> *So… here we are and there we were… once upon a time… or below a time, or under a time or beside a time. It doesn't really matter – in a place far and not so far from here… in a time long ago… and not so long ago… our grandmother was calling us – to hear a story.*

Gran's story, as my story, was about the time of *The Great Turning*. My grandmother's Nana was living in a large city like this one and she saw and heard all these things herself. And these changes were not just happening in the cities, though they started and spread from the cities to multitudes of communities all over the Earth.

The first time I heard this story, us children were sitting with my Gran around the campfire in a little community garden just like this one full of pea shoots and berry bushes. Old as the hills, my Gran leaned forward with that look I loved in her tanned, lined face. And she whispered the same words I say to you now. These things I am about to tell you…

My children. What a time it was!

In those days, people in the cities had lost touch with the living Earth and all the important things – things like their place in the local and global community, and even the inner scared parts of themselves. It sounds ridiculous, after all of us here and those before us have been through, but that's how it was in those days. Cities were contradictory and confusing places, with really rich people and really poor people. Many people felt isolated, though they lived right next door to someone.

People were really separated from the land, too. They depended for their lives on the living Earth around them but gave nothing back. They had forgotten that the Earth was alive or where they came from or who and what they were connected to. They were frightened by the Earth Changes and many of them refused to believe they were happening. It took the *Time of the Great Storms* to convince some of them.

My Nan told me that part of *The Great Turning* was about bringing sacredness back to the city. Do you know what that word means? It's a word they didn't use enough in the Old Times but if you listen closely to my story, perhaps it will make more sense to you. To make that happen, the people did not have to learn anything new; they just had to learn how to remember. Like you remembering the story I am telling you right now – and passing it on to your children and grandchildren.

In the Old Times, cities were centres of advanced scientific, technical and intellectual development. They were also places where individuals, rather than the community, flourished. People who were concerned about that problem were writing books and articles about the 'good city'. They wrote about these kinds of things: social justice, community identity, emancipation, the commons and the common good, justice and fairness, rules and responsibilities. Some put forward lists of the conditions that would support human flourishing, with ideas about housing, health care, creativity, work and social supports.

Sadly, they also got bogged down in their own words. They succumbed to despair and apathy. They told stories about cities riddled with anxiety and depression, full of people who were disconnected and excluded. It made some people feel fearful, guilty or hopeless about the problems in their own communities. Everyone was saying such bad things about the cities but my Nana felt that the cities could make a big difference – if people just looked at them in a different way.

People wanted their public spaces – their everyday public spaces – to be magical, beautiful, comfortable and creative places. Small, special places were essential to people's everyday lives. They had special rituals attached to them. One of the new creative types described a process that he called 'eco-revelatory design': ways of making the life of a place manifest in the city. People could really understand what he said.

There was no time for delay at the time of *The Great Turning*, which was what they called that time when the Great Storms came and the people had finally lost their faith in the ways things were 'supposed to be' in the Old Times. In those days, there was a great yearning among people to be whole and to reconnect with everything that had been lost. This story is about how people went from being isolated from each other and the Earth, to reconnecting.

At that time, people grew to relearn skills they had forgotten: listening with the ears of others, even listening with their hearts. The chattering mind grew quieter so that the heart and spirit could flourish. Balance was really what was required. More and more people began questioning what was real and looking more carefully at what was already in their cities. They held lively and boisterous public meetings that overflowed local halls, school gymnasiums and all the online social networks. People were speaking their hearts.

Although it took a longer time for the universities to welcome the new ideas, planning students started learning about concepts like 'right livelihood' and 'skilful means' and about 'working from the heart' on practical and intelligent solutions to the most urgent challenges facing the cities and the Earth. New courses, even on subjects like 'heart politics', were proposed. Local people started coming into university classrooms to help teach these important topics. Some of the more influential contributors challenged the students and their teachers to be part of the changes, not to resist them. They implored city planners to become actively engaged social-change workers and told them that 'teachers' and 'lessons' were everywhere in the world. They argued that their planning work should express their interconnectedness.

And you can imagine ... before long, the cities began to look different – and to feel different – more like what we have today. People came out of their houses and met in cafés and parks and held meetings and social events and gatherings to organise themselves to work together. As people spent more time with people they saw as different from their 'own kind', some of the tensions between different groups released.

The Indigenous people and the poets assumed new creative leadership roles in all city planning projects. Before too long, city building processes began to change. Architects began to embrace spiritual principles that were becoming popular before the Turning, breathing new life into buildings and giving them what they called *The Quality without a Name*. People began to talk about 'the timeless way of building' and architects and builders became much more respected members of the community.

The wider community of all ages became deeply involved in the process of city imagining, city dreaming and city building. Visioning, they called it – or creative visualization. In workshops in the community centres, people would sit together and decide how the cities should be planned. Their voices sounded like Tibetan bells: so many different languages, softly spoken at the same time – people dreaming together about their cities. The adults and children listened with their eyes closed.

There were great outpourings of love and reverence, as people flocked to public meetings, events and ceremonies to work out ways to save and repair and protect the Earth so it could be passed on to the future generations. There were gatherings and activities everywhere: vegetation and food-planting events and days devoted just to collecting and saving seeds, and others where people built small shade structures and benches so that they could sit alone or together in the parks. Other people made paths so you could stroll through these places and then sit and just reflect on things. In these places, they sensed spiritual inspiration, in feelings of peace, oneness and connectedness and a sense of freedom, reverence and humility. Gradually, people came to understand the restorative qualities of Nature – that it could restore mind, body and spirit.

There were places in the city that already had significance to people and, with the help of the planners and the artists, their stories were woven into the wider community story. The environment of stories changed, as well as the physical environment. People started talking differently about things like stigma and failure. They found brighter words to fit their new optimism. They talked about imagining, flourishing, strengthening, resilience, reclaiming and community partnerships.

Probably the most marvellous thing that happened during the Great Turning was that the distinctions between the separate and defended territories of the formal religions and alternative (often older) wisdom traditions began to melt away. It was not necessary to have one definition of 'spiritual'. People spoke about spiritual ecology and spiritual geography. My Nan remembers that talk of the creative spirit was present and easily evoked in these new and rediscovered city places – places that held special sacredness.

In the newly sacred places in the cities, groups of children and teenagers often gathered and played. They loved the vitality and aliveness of those places and preferred the wilder places. The adults slowly grew to accept that this was natural and tried not to be fearful when the children went there. These places were initially the undeveloped lots and places that had been flooded or bombed or damaged in other ways by earthquakes and cyclones. Many of these places, though spoiled, were once again yielding to the forces of Nature. Colonising plants rambled over old structures and pushed through the cracks in the old concrete below; colourful insects hid in humusy undergrowth or buzzed in the sharp, hot stillness of desertified lands. In the riverbeds there were fossils to find – and rocks of extraordinary shape and colour. This was the *ecotone*, the edgeplace of healing between the old way and the new.

All of these wild spaces were alive, but for many, the favourite wild places were the natural wooded areas left alone by development. The children gathered in these newly consecrated places and were at the forefront of the community activities to renew them. With so many children playing in places that were natural and wild, consecrated to the work of community building and spiritual development, a new breed of young people emerged. They came to love Nature with a great fierceness. These spiritual warriors gave birth to new children, who – as children and adults – reaffirmed the sacred place of Nature in the city and worked to preserve all aspects of the living Earth.

And so, today we have everywhere precious natural places – deeply nourishing and spiritual places – that were saved and cherished and handed down by those courageous people at the time of the Great Turning. In their quest for spiritual nourishment, they rediscovered something vitally important.

Everyday spirituality they called it.

Some just called it love.[1]

Gilt-edged Resources

Gilt-edged Resources 1
A Visioning Example:
Our Bonnyrigg Dream

This is a guided visualization written by Wendy, Yollana Shore and Sophia van Ruth for the 'Our Bonnyrigg Dream' workshop in Sydney in 2005. We had been working in this community for six months when we held this workshop so we had an understanding of how the participants were likely to respond. The main issue of concern was the renewal of the predominantly public housing estate via a private–public partnership.[1] A week in advance, we made the visioning script available to eight interpreters who then translated it for their community members who would sit at language-based tables in the workshop of about 90 people.

Sophia read each part of the script and then paused so that it could be interpreted at each table of non-English speakers. The interpreters at each table read their pre-prepared translations.

Here's our script:

Preframe the Power of Visualization (2 minutes)

Visualization allows us to bypass our normal logical way of thinking about things and become more creative. If you really enter into this visualization with an open mind, the results may surprise you. You may discover solutions that you never would have 'thought of'.

The best way to get the most out of this visualization exercise is to imagine you are actually there, doing it.

The interpreters at each table have translated the script I am about to read and the various translations will be read in your own language at your tables.

Introduction

Before we start, I'd like to do some silly laughs with you.

Explain to the group why you are doing them and guide them through the laughs: 1-metre laugh, silent laugh, clam laugh.[2]

When conducting guided visualizations, Sophia has experienced that some people find it hard to get beyond visions of a negative future (especially when visualizing a sustainable future). In response to this, she began to develop 'pre-visioning' exercises to promote creativity and a positive outlook.

Sitting down again, settling yourself, closing your eyes, just become aware of your bodyweight on the chair below you.

Notice if you are scrunching the skin around your eyes and allow it to spread and soften.

Notice if you are clenching your jaw and allow the lower jaw to be free.

Allow your shoulder blades to slide down over your back ribs a little to open your chest.

And as you relax now, see if you can let something different happen…

Start to listen to your own hopes for your community – here, where nobody will judge you.

Let your mind be free and playful to enjoy this journey.

I wonder what it would be like if you were to transport yourself into the year 2020?

What if you could imagine Bonnyrigg as the best place to live, a healthy place, a place where you belong, a place you had a say in shaping?

Feel yourself now standing on a local street and see that a good friend is walking towards you. Her name is Kim and you have arranged to meet her to look around Bonnyrigg today.

Kim has grown up in Bonnyrigg since the renewal process began.

THE STREET

You smile because Kim is full of enthusiasm and when you are ready, you and Kim can begin to walk down a typical street in Bonnyrigg in the year 2020…

As you walk, notice what different kinds of houses are here now? Can you see some front doors and yards?

PAUSE

How many storeys are the highest ones? How close together are they?

PAUSE

Notice how many people are on the streets? Who is around? And what are they doing?

PAUSE

What kinds of sounds do you hear from the neighbourhood and from the natural surroundings?

PAUSE

You may also notice that there is a better sense of safety in the neighbour-hood now... What has changed to make the streets so safe?

PAUSE

A PLACE FOR GATHERING

You keep walking and find Kim is leading you to a place that is special to her. What kind of place does she lead you to where young people like to go in Bonnyrigg?

PAUSE

What if you could turn around in a full circle, what kinds of things would you see?

PAUSE

What kinds of scents do you smell? And what sounds do you hear?

PAUSE

How does it make you feel to be in this place? What kinds of feelings come up for you now?

PAUSE

Hear Kim telling you what makes this place so wonderful for her. What do you hear her say?

PAUSE

A LOCAL PARK

Now that Kim has told you all about her favourite place, you make your way to a local park to sit for a while and watch.

Can you see how many people are there using the park?

PAUSE

And what ages do you think they are?

PAUSE

How do they interact with one another, can you hear what people are saying to each other?

PAUSE

Notice how you feel as you are sitting in this park.

PAUSE

A BALLOON RIDE

As you rest here, taking in the surroundings, Kim announces that she has a surprise for you and you see her pointing to a huge hot-air balloon.

You arrive and climb aboard. Allow yourself to feel safe and excited while the balloon rises into the sky.

Looking down you may see the Bonnyrigg Plaza shopping centre and familiar streets. And see how different it has become in 2020 from the way it used to be.

Notice the open space and green areas. How many are there? Where are they?

PAUSE

You can see the roads and pathways from up here. How do you see people moving around down below? Are they on foot, bike, train, car or bus?

PAUSE

And now you start to notice the buildings. What is the mix of houses and other buildings? Where are the taller buildings and the taller housing buildings located now?

PAUSE

And can you see how the housing areas are linked with other parts of the neighbourhood – like transport, recreation, schools, mosques, temples and churches and shopping centres?

PAUSE

COMING HOME

The balloon begins to come back down. As it lands, you return to the present – to the year 2005.

You step out of the balloon and with your eyes still closed, you come back to the present moment … here in this room.

Now with your eyes still closed and still in silence, gently go back over the most powerful aspects of your journey in your mind. Which images are the most important to you?

PAUSE

Only when your inner journey is clear in your mind, you can open your eyes and record your images on the paper provided IN SILENCE for a few minutes. Then you will share your images with the people at your tables.

Gilt-edged Resources 2
The Embodied
Affinity Diagram

By allowing participants to engage in an *active* conversation with one another, while sorting and analysing issues or lessons thematically, the 'Embodied Affinity Diagram' ensures everyone will get involved, listen to others and express their opinion – not by voicing it but by showing it. In silence, participants brainstorm issues (or lessons) on individual notes that are tied to balloons and then sort them. Only later, once much has already been silently said, does vocal dialogue begin.

This exercise can be successfully undertaken with 20 to 200 people.

These instructions are designed for an exercise with approximately 100 people.

The Embodied Affinity Diagram has excellent process and outcome results. It is excellent for team building and gives participants an opportunity to learn about each other's values.

The 'product' is a set of lessons, values or ideas that are grouped in categories. They can later be transferred to a document and sent to participants as a memento of their experience.

Requirements

- at least ten staff;
- a large open space / seminar room with walls/display boards for posters;
- a place to hide 100 balloons;
- 100 balloons with cups, sticks and string;
- 100 *lesson cards* with the words, 'The most valuable lesson I learned was...';
- ten bins/stands to hold the balloons;
- 11 A0-sized sheets of paper with the words printed on them: 'Who are we? What is our main lesson? What are our individual lessons?';
- 11 blank A0-sized sheets to place behind the ones on the wall (to prevent damaging wall);
- lots of staplers and staples;
- Blue-tak, Velcro dots and pins;
- 50 wedge-tipped pens (black);
- ten boxes to put them in; and
- a camera and photographer for all the great photo opportunities in this exercise.

Creating 'lesson cards'

Just before a break in a workshop or conference, each participant writes down one lesson that they learned at this conference or seminar on a pre-printed lesson card and hands their lesson card to staff as they leave.

Balloons set-up

This is best done quickly when participants are on a break – so it can be a surprise. Secretly bring balloons in place around spacious area in bins (you may need lots of helpers).

Affinity framework set-up

Stick ten A0-sized framework sheets around the walls. Place a small plastic box next to each one, with at least five wedge-tipped marker pens in it.

Beginning the activity

The Facilitator welcomes people back from the break as they filter in and says:

> Come in, take a balloon. Please remain IN SILENCE. Each balloon has been affixed with a lesson that was recorded earlier by a participant. Please accept whichever lesson you receive. Take it to heart. It has come from someone else's heart. Please REMAIN STANDING and then begin to WALK AROUND THE ROOM. (5 minutes)

When everyone has a balloon, the Facilitator says:

> Keep walking around the room, slowly and read each other's lessons... What are they saying to you? Do you agree? How does their lesson relate to the lesson you are holding?

Please REMAIN IN SILENCE. (10 minutes)

The Facilitator says:

> You may start to notice that some lessons are in tune with the lesson that you are carrying. Perhaps they 'go well together'; perhaps they have the same flavour or are about the same topic. Notice which other lessons resonate with your lesson. Now, when you find a lesson that you think resonates, just give that person a nod, then stay together, REMAIN IN SILENCE and look together for another person whose lesson resonates with the lesson you are holding. STAY TOGETHER with lessons that resonate with yours. You can leave a group ONLY if you find a group that resonates more. (10 minutes)

The Facilitator says:

> Now that you have found some AFFINITIES, some lessons that resonate with each other, please walk together with your group towards ONE LARGE SHEET OF PAPER. There are only ten sheets in the Framework, so the number of groups is limited to ten or less. If you haven't found a group, keep looking or stay in the middle of the room until you find one...
>
> Anyone who is not 'resonating' with the lessons around them should go to the middle of the room and survey the process until they find somewhere where they might fit. (10 minutes)

The Facilitator asks the groups to check that they all feel like they belong together. Each lesson is the responsibility of the person carrying it. No one else can tell that person whether or not they belong.

Everyone stands near each other beside their blank category on the Framework.

Everyone reviews the lessons on their balloons.

The Facilitator instructs the groups that they can now come out of being 'in silence' and asks them to think: 'Who are you? What is your main lesson?'

Together, the group discusses the main lesson that they represent and writes it with the wedge-tipped pen on their A0 sheet.

Anyone who is in the middle of the room and has not found a group may choose to enter at this point as the group categories emerge. If, at the end, anyone really feels they cannot go into one of the categories, they can use the spare A0 sheet.

The Facilitator also asks participants to write the individual lessons from their balloons onto their large sheet.

Concluding

The exercise can conclude in several ways:

1   Groups can visit each 'station' and read what is written on their paper and their balloon cards
2   Groups read out their summary sheets
3   The facilitator can simply collect the material for analysis and reporting (and feedback), especially if time is short
4   Participants can provide reflective comments on process and content.

Gilt-edged Resources 3
The Gods Must Be Crazy:
Script and Instructions
from the
Safe Communities
Scenario, Sydney

Graeme Dunstan's instructions

Graeme's instructions to his helpers reflected the playful nature of the role play. He instructed that during afternoon tea, the main 'Gods' would be robed and Nymphs would serve Greek sweets. Nymphs were also to serve 'roles' to randomly selected people to take a minor part. All delegates congregate at the theatre door for Graeme to brief them and then delegates are ushered into the theatre that has been 'dressed' for the Council of Gods in session. Graeme Dunstan would direct the role play and allow it to run for approximately 20 minutes. He would then call a close and introduce the Chair, who would manage the debriefing. The session would conclude with Professor John Forester invited to sum up.[10]

Scripts for players

Scripts for Major Gods

The artistry of the role play was in the design of the roles for the Major and Minor Gods, which are presented below.

Note for role players: The following sentences are offered as a guide to the role. Please DO NOT read them. Either learn and remember them or find your own words for expressing the same or similar sentiments. Let me suggest you rehearse your lines; that is, give them voice at least once, delivered in front of a mirror or to a friend. You are Gods. Be grand of speech and gesture. Be outrageous in the extreme. And then marvel at what comes up and what comes out.

Hestia, Goddess of the Hearth

Dear brother, Zeus, thank you for calling this Council. Thank you too to all the Gods who have gathered here out of concern for the safety of humans. You know me as the Goddess of the Hearth, protector of children, nurturer of family and community. In fact, I am the very heat in the warmth of all nurturing. I love those humans. I love to have happy, warm and well-fed babies about me. I love to see them grow, change and become happy children, happy adults and happy grandparents. You know I am much worshipped but no one builds a temple to me and that's okay with me. Rather that I serve than be adored. I don't like to be away from my hearth and my dear humans. But I have come here because I am worried. I am noticing a lot of unhappy humans, humans depressed, humans injured, humans maimed, humans in despair, humans killing themselves. Fine young boys, once bonny babies, necking themselves; I weep! In so many homes, the only warmth is the flicking glow of the tv Ray; do something, dear brother!

Zeus, Big Boss in the Sky

Thank you, Sister Hestia. Fellow Olympians, you heard her! Enough is enough! I thought you guys had a handle on this! You have the responsibility of making it better. But the human problem is only getting worse. Pull your collective fingers out! Your incompetence is a threat to the dignity of the Gods. Indeed, it is a threat to our very existence as immortal Gods. If humans cease to believe in and honour us, we will exist only as a memory of a once-upon-a time-grandeur and power. What is going on with you guys? Explain yourself!

Apollo, God of Reason

Dear father, you know me as the God of Light and Reason. Let's step back from this a little. I fear Aunt Hestia is being a tad overemotional, for she is too close to the problems, too caught up in human emotions. If there is a problem, let us bring it into the light and apply science and reason to it. Let's take a cool, detached look at it from all angles and really get to understand it before we commit to action. My research suggests that while there are diffi-culties in some areas, we have had some major successes with some of our fixes and are making good headway in many areas. Look, for example, at the injury that has been prevented by making seat belts compulsory and drunk drivers and smokers social outcasts. So might I recommend we make provision for some research funds so that we might get the overview, the big picture? My fellow God and friend, Academicus, will no doubt have something to say about this later. And when it comes to dealing with harm, what divine being is more pre-eminent in science than my friend and fellow, Medicalscripticus.

Hermes, Messenger God

Dear father, everyone here knows me as Hermes, the God of shepherds, travellers, merchants, thieves, PR flacks and advertising agents: all who live by their wits. My brother Apollo is an illustrious God, but any credit for the successes he claims is due to me, my winning words and cunning ways. It is all in the messages that we put out to humans. And I am the man for messages. Is there really a problem? It's a problem only if it is generally believed that there is a problem, I say. It's all in the spin. But Aunt Hestia has a point about the needless and neglectful deaths. You ought to see some of those mangled and premature dead that I lead to Hades. Words fail me! Maybe it's time for another super-duper advertising campaign. My friend and fellow God, Admanus, has a lot to say and a big bucket of gold he will want to spend. I love doing deals with doers of deals. Maybe it's time to get the humans to get a fix on it for themselves. My friend and fellow God, Politicofixus, will have a lot to say about that.

Athena, Goddess of Wisdom

Dear Father, I sprang from your mind fully grown, fully wise and fully armed. My mother is Metis, Goddess of Caution. And I am Athena, Goddess of Wisdom, Strategy and Craft, Protector of Heroes. Let's not rush into solutions. Let's take a long view and be strategic about this. And let's back the heroes who are working at the coalface of human suffering: those who stand in their communities and struggle for change to bring about greater safety for humans. Only if we back the change makers will we get changes. Give me your blessings, Father, and I will bring help to all struggling heroes that they might overcome calamity and confusion and find their way back to home and hearth, like I did for the noble and resourceful Odysseus.

Ares, God of War

Bloody interfering, Athena. There she goes again. A lot of good she did for the humans of Troy. She brought calamity and death upon the lot of them. You all know me as Ares, God of War and Eruptive Male Energy; the Can-do God. Look here! Dad, if we are going to get anything done, let's just do it! Let's get on with it and crash through. If there is a problem, any problem, let's declare war on it! Look at the wonderful success of the War on Drugs. Police services are now all armed up with new weapons and new powers of surveillance, search and arrest, sniffer dogs everywhere and cannabis users put to flight! Wonderful success! Now I have a couple of excellent boys to put at your service. They follow me everywhere.

Artemis, Goddess of the Chase

My step-brother Ares is vainglorious. He disgusts me with his macho strutting. Does he never see the vicious crowd that follows him and preys on humans after his campaigns: pain, panic, famine and oblivion? I am Artemis, Moonchild, Feminist, Goddess of the Chase. I say we hunt for elegant solutions and steer clear of men and their methods. I am protector of all those legions of dedicated women working steadily, craftily and with great perseverance to make the world safer for women. Let's keep our eyes on target and hunt for the elegant solution.

Hades, God of the Underworld

Oh, Artemis, my pretty niece, my ruthless hunter of moonlight, come and hunt with me in the Land of the Dead. Lots of shadows there. Lots of shades. I am Hades, Lord of the Dead. Mortals don't like me but I welcome them all. I am the great hospitality provider. To me humans come and stay forever. Listen to my wisdom: Death wins in the end. Don't get too arrogant and try to deprive me of guests. Remember what happened to the great healer,

Asclepius? Got so rich and arrogant that he started raising the dead. What folly! You, yourself, brother Zeus, put an end to him with one of your thunder-bolts. I haven't much else to say. But I have a couple of lads who might want to speak: Thanatos, the God of the death wish in every human, and his twin, Hypnos, the God of sleep. So many humans like to be dead and asleep. You ought to listen to them and temper your do-goodism.

Selected scripts for the Minor Gods

There were many Minor Gods. Some of the key roles are summarized below.

Mediatrics, God of Advertising, Public Relations and Promotions

My Lord Hermes, he of the clever words and fast wit, has already introduced me. I am Mediatrics, God of Advertising, Public Relations and Promotions. Let's face it, the problem is all about getting the right message across and we live in a marketplace of competing messages. You need me. With my media skills, we can create new role models, correct aberrant perceptions, generate new demands, marginalize dysfunctional social behaviour, cover up old lies and invent new truths. At a cost, of course. But then it is a marketplace. Pay peanuts, get monkeys.

Politicofixus, God of the Political Fix

I don't know why I am not sitting at the high table. No safer community solu-tion is possible without my engagement and my blessing. I am Politicofixus, God of the Political Fix, patron saint of the Premier's Department A Team, Lord of Damage Control. My Lord Hermes, master of the timely word, is my guide and inspiration. I am the one who knows who to speak to and who NOT to speak to. I know what to say and what NOT to say. All media releases come by me. Act on a problem without my approval and you will discover that I am the problem. Act with my approval and all doors will open. You are at my service.

Phobus, God of Fear

My energetic Lord Ares, God of War, praises me as a great motivator. I am, and I am central to all perceptions of harm and danger. Better listen to me. I am Phobus, God of Fear, and I am very good at focusing the attention of humans and getting them to move collectively. Or not to move and become stuck, as the need may be, for I am also a great inhibitor. You see, humans are like a flock of startled sheep! When alarmed, first they stop eating and become intensely alert, all looking in the same direction. Then they run off together, safety in numbers, each hoping someone else knows best where safety lies. Look at the wonderful success my devotees have had with the Get Tough on Crime *media campaign. Now humans have more fear than crime. They fear the worst of each other and public places. But never before have we had a citizenry so compliant to the good sense of 'Big Brother' government. Mind you, we have never before had so many jails and so many men in jails. Merely, a few lambs sacrificed for a more comforting perception of greater community safety.*

Eris, God of Strife

You Gods are all pretending to be Goody Two Shoes. Get real! Humans act just like you Gods. They are full of hatred, greed, lust and delusion, too. They are always fighting, feuding and contending for scarce resources. I am Eris, God of Strife, constant companion of my Lord Ares, God of War. Hear me when I say: humans love a barney. Every human solution will generate its opposition and create conflict. You gotta be prepared to fight for what you want. I want action. Mt Olympus is full of wimps and time servers. You are not taking me seriously. I have had enough! I am out of here! (Stages a walk out. Storms out of the theatre! And then quietly creeps back in again.)

Demeter, Goddess of Crops and Grieving Mothers

Why is my grief being ignored? Hear me and help me! I am Demeter, Goddess of Crops and Grieving Mothers. I was once a bountiful benefactor of humans but now I am desolate with sorrow. My daughter, delight of my life, has been taken from me. She was gathering flowers and suddenly snatched away: taken in the Underworld. Gone! Hear me, help me! Hear me, help me! Bring my baby back!

Bureaucratis, God of Proper Procedures

Now I am just a small voice but unless you take heed of it, you will stub more than a few toes as you go forth. I will bring you unstuck. I am Bureaucratis,

God of Proper Procedures. There are ways and means of getting things done: precedent and right procedure. I may be able to help you, or I may not. Outcomes are not in my department. Right procedure is everything.

Frazzle, Goddess of Burn-out

Listen to me. I am the occupational hazard of all who tend to the vast ocean of human suffering. I am Frazzle, Goddess of Burn-out. I am the harm that harm preventers do to themselves. Care too much; try too hard; do too much; stress; lose the plot; fall apart; despair; deny and bring down the ceiling with me.

Copticus, God of Police Officers, Guardians of Good Order and Decency

How is it that the ones first called to any episode of traumatic injury, us cops, never get close to harm-prevention policy making. Why are we not being consulted? I am New Copticus, God of Police Officers, Guardians of Good Order and Decency. Police are community professionals. My devotees have university degrees now, you know.

Old Copticus, God of Direct Action Policing

I am another small voice that wants to be heard, the Ares voice, the man's voice of old-style policing. I am Old Copticus, God of Direct Action Policing. These new university-trained coppers are community theorists. Their fine theories are useless when someone is coming at you with an axe. I say, get real and engaged with the human neighbourhood. A kick in the pants may be just what a wild boy needs!

Ambo, God of Ambulance Crews

Hear my voice! Tending to human injury is my service, my daily duty. I am Ambo, God of Ambulance Crews. My devotees pick up the messes. They clean up when community safety fails. And they notice patterns of injury before others do. For example, I noticed that traumatic falls by elderly people are more common than trauma due to car accidents. But who listens to me? Like Cassandra, I am doomed to know the future and not to be heard.

Fiery, God of Fire-fighting Crews

I want to be heard too. I am Fiery, God of Fire-fighting Crews. My devotees are not just people who put wet stuff on red stuff. They are the frontline of many responses to trauma in human communities. They see stuff, like fires that appear to be random yet are not due to chance. For example, a dropped cigarette sets a chair smouldering and an isolated older person dies of smoke inhalation. Looks like suicide by neglect to me.

SES/Poseidon, God of Big Emotions and Natural Disasters[1]

The Gods must be crazy NOT to listen to me. When it comes to harmful events, I bring the big ones. I am SES/Poseidon, God of Big Emotions and Natural Disasters. My forces are so enormous; human efforts, so feeble. My devotees can prepare but they cannot predict or prevent. How frail those humans are! They sit and wait upon my mood.

WetBlanketus, God of Cynicism

You Gods make me laugh when you talk about 'community' this and 'community' that. The reality of your community task forces and your community consultation committees is that they are stacked with the wounded, the crazy, the losers, the misfits and the weirdos. You call it 'community'; I call it delusion. I am WetBlanketus, God of Cynicism. Every committee has got one. Been there. Done that!

Gaia, Goddess of the Living Earth

You Gods are missing something fundamental to human life if you do not hear me. Far-seeing Zeus seems to have his head in the clouds. Can you not see on what all human welfare depends? I am Gaia, Goddess of the Living Earth. You are gathered here to worry about a few humans lost to injury, intentional and unintentional. How does that compare with whole species of creatures becoming extinct because of actions, intentional or unintentional, by humans? From a whole-of-life approach, a few fewer humans are not such a bad thing.

Hypnos, God of Sleep and Getting Out of It

My Godly companion, Thanatos, God of the Death Wish, tells us that humans secretly workshop him and yearn of death. But what about me? I am Hypnos, God of Sleeping and Getting Out of It. Humans embrace me daily, every night and for most of the waking day. So many sleepwalkers! Humans asleep at the wheel, asleep at the office, asleep in front of the TV, asleep in consumerism, asleep on the mass medication of hypnotic drugs. Getting out of it is a recreation pastime. Humans just not there for their families and communities. Is it true, Lord Apollo, that 90 per cent of humans are 90 per cent asleep 90 per cent of the time?

Poorme, God of Old Wounds and Sad Stories

I know I am only a very Minor God and no one really cares about me or what I say. But I have a lot of followers and they pray to me at community meetings, particularly when care and safety are being discussed. I am Poorme, God of Old Wounds and Sad Stories. Oh! So often betrayed and disappointed. Sad stories have got to be told. Someone has to listen.

Incarceratus, God of the Imprisoned

Mine is a voice seldom heard. But hear me now and hear my warning. I am Incarceratus, God of the Imprisoned, God of all those made to suffer the cruelties of jails. Terrible cruelty is done when a man is taken away from his family and locked up and forgotten, in the company of mad, mean and broken men. A terrible dysfunction it is for human society to make jails and the suffering of prisoners a job creation industry. Men come out of jails either broken or angry. And where do they take their anger and brokenness? To the communities of the poor and so add to the misery there. Hear me! Jails are schools for crime. Jails are a crime against tomorrow.

Dispossessedus, God of Crushed and Overridden Indigenous People

Hey! Do white fellas ever realize why Aboriginal people go to so many funerals? Listen to me. I am Dispossessedus, God of Crushed and Overridden Indigenous People. Black fellas are dying 20 years younger than white folk. The life expectancy gap between black and white has increased over the last 50 years. Aboriginal people make up 20 per cent of the prisoner population but only 5 per cent of the population. Is Safe and Strong Communities just another code for white supremacy?

Gilt-edged Resources 4 Barefoot Mapping: Learning Through the Soles of Our Feet: A Participatory Design Workshop for Youth In Airds, Sydney, New South Wales[1]

This process aims to enable a group of 30 or so 12 to 18 year olds to articulate and record their views about the desirable and undesirable features of their neighbourhood, specifying features they would like to keep, change and add with some indication of the relative importance of different issues. This approach could be used in any physical planning exercise, providing that the territory being dealt with is seen by the young participants as their home ground and is vitally important and familiar to them. It would be effective at suburban and neighbourhood scales. It requires expert small-group facilitation by experienced local youth workers who are not seen as authority figures, but who are respected by the young people and who respect them.

Ideally, the adolescent participants are broadly representative across sex, the age range (12 to 18 years) and the ethnic profile of the community in question. They are residents of the area or, if homeless, identify with it as their base or place of origin. Thirty was an optimal number for the venue (the school library) and for the number of group facilitators and recorders available (one of each for each small group).[2]

The small-group facilitators were youth workers from various agencies active within the district of which the specific neighbourhood is a part. They need to be expert at working collaboratively with young people, familiar with the area and with local adolescent issues. The workshop convenors (a team of three in this case) need to be expert in the procedures being used. In this case, the high school staff undertook selection and registration of participants. In a non-school setting, some administrative help would be needed for this.

Steps in the process

- Within a school, participants are recruited by the school. They need written permission from their teacher and parents. The school authorities need to be advised that participation must be voluntary but that a representative cross section of student residents of the neighbourhood by sex, age, ethnicity, academic performance and any other relevant characteristics is desirable. In a non-school setting, participants could be invited by posters in places frequented by young people and through youth workers, schools and other youth organisations (e.g. sporting clubs). An article in the local newspaper and/or a circular letter to local households (perhaps distributed through the school) explaining the purpose and credentials of the workshop would be useful. Attendance would likely be estimated by youth workers and teachers.
- If the event is not held in a school, a local facility such as a youth centre or similar place accessible and familiar to local youth would be appropriate. In addition to having the appropriate space, it needs to be secured so the workshop can proceed undisturbed.
- Liaising with local youth workers before the workshop is essential. Their support and involvement will likely help to recruit participants and ensure that the approaches and localities being used are appropriate to the context.
- The workshop convenors need to arrive at least one hour before the facilitators to set up. The large paper map is laid in a central position on the floor. A table with chairs around it is arranged for each small group, maintaining as much distance as possible to

protect the acoustic privacy of each group. Each group is equipped with three ruled issue sheets headed *ADD, CHANGE* and *KEEP* on a vertical surface, an A0 or A1-sized map of the area on the table, gold stars, voting chips and coloured pens and crayons.[3] The group name or symbol should be prominently marked on each issue sheet and map.

- Ask the group facilitators to arrive half an hour before the participants to brief them by explaining the agenda. Let them pair off as group facilitators and recorders and give each pair a set of name tags for their group. Each name tag should be marked with the group symbol (we used animal stickers: sharks, fish, sheep and so forth).

- In an out-of-school setting, as the adolescent participants arrive, their names and addresses should be taken for follow-up. If working in a school, ensure that the school has a record of the participants.

- The workshop begins with a light lunch or other light refreshments for all participants. Use caterers so the food preparation and clearing up are not a distraction. This gives the facilitators a chance to mix informally with the young people and help them feel at ease and welcome. (30 minutes)

- At the appointed time, the workshop convenor calls for everyone's attention, introduces the facilitating team and briefly explains the purpose of the workshop, emphasizing the value given to contributions from young people. In a school setting, a word about this being an instance of the adults learning from the youth instead of the other way around may be helpful. (3 minutes)

- Everyone is invited to gather around the large map of the neighbourhood on paper taped to the floor. Participants are asked to find their dwelling on the map (or if the map is not that detailed, its approximate location), write their first name on it and stand on it or as near to it as room will permit. Each group facilitator will identify six young people (or whatever was the pre-arranged number for each group, less than ten) who live near one another as their group, giving each of them a name tag to put their first name on.

- While still standing by the map participants are asked to write or draw something on the map that expresses for them what it feels like to live in their neighbourhood. (15 minutes)
- Each facilitator takes their small group to its designated table. The young residents are invited to brainstorm issues that concern them about the redesigning of their neighbourhood, things they want to *KEEP*, things they want to *CHANGE* or remove and things they want to *ADD*. These will be listed on the ruled sheets in no particular order, but on the appropriate sheet, by the group recorder. Some examples of possible issues are listed in advance to help them get started. Explain brainstorming as mentioning any issue they think of without judging how important, sensible or 'correct' it is. This will be decided in the next step. (15 minutes)
- When they have listed all the issues they can think of, the group will vote on which issues are the most important, each member having a first, second and third vote. The recorder will mark first votes against the issue with a large cardboard gold star, the second votes with, say, a blue square and the third votes with a purple square. (5 minutes)
- Drawing and writing on the map on their table and referring to their issue lists, each group will identify and locate more specifically things they want to *keep*, *change* or *add* to their neighbourhood. All opinions can go on the map. There does not have to be group agreement but group discussion and exchange of ideas is to be encouraged. Ask them to use verbs and actions, e.g. 'plant trees', 'remove trees', not simply just 'trees' – so the planners who read this material later understand their wishes. (40 minutes)
- Reconvening as one group the young people, led by the workshop convenor, compare the 'Feelings' map and the 'Plans' map and make any additions or changes the comparison suggests.

Inconsistencies between the two maps may provoke further discussion and ideas. (10 minutes)

- Suggestions from the group about how young people can continue to be involved and consulted in the neighbourhood refurbishment are now recorded on butcher's paper. A method of giving the participants feedback about how the ideas expressed in this workshop influence the plans is discussed and agreed upon. (5 minutes)

- The adolescents are thanked for their participation and farewelled. The convenors and facilitators then have a debriefing session to help evaluate the workshop (20 minutes).

- After the workshop, the facilitators and anyone else who helped should be thanked in writing.

- The workshop convenors, if they are not themselves the planners, need to go through the material with the planners to ensure it is understood and does, in fact, influence the plans.

- When the plans are finalized, the agreed method of feedback to the workshop participants is implemented. Some options are another meeting of the group, a public exhibition to which they and their families are invited personally in writing, or a circulated newsletter explaining the resultant plan and identifying their contributions.

Points to remember

- Legibility and intelligibility of notations on maps are vital; neatness is not. Use only strong colours to ensure clarity and easy reproduction. Encourage creativity. Make sure each sheet and map from the small groups is identified as coming from that group.

- Vertical surfaces for lists need to be suitable for writing on – *not* paper taped to a table surface, which is awkward to use and difficult for everyone to see.

- If the large walk-on map cannot be plastic-coated or otherwise impervious to shoes, have participants remove their shoes at the start. They should be forewarned of this request (holes in socks may be embarrassing).
- Ensure that facilitators adopt a collaborative and supportive rather than authoritative relationship with the youth. An in-school workshop facilitated by teachers probably would not work.
- Be sure the workshop has the approval and support of the community, especially parents or guardians, teachers, local youth workers and the like.
- Props and supporting materials.
- Plenty of thick marker pens and crayons in a variety of strong colours (we usually remove yellow and pastels to enable photocopying).
- Issue sheets, A1 size or larger: two or three of each per group, labelled with the name or symbol of the group attached to a vertical surface suitable for writing on. (See examples below.) Butcher's paper. Blue tak or masking tape, depending on the nature of the vertical surfaces. Drawing pins are dangerous.

KEEP SHARKS	
ISSUE	VOTES

'Keep' Issue Sheet

CHANGE SHARKS	
ISSUE	VOTES

'Change' Issue Sheet

ADD SHARKS	
ISSUE	VOTES

'Add' Issue Sheet

- Table-sized (A1 or A0) plans of the neighbourhood, with streets, major facilities and features clearly marked one for each group and labelled with the group name or symbol.
- A huge broad-brush map of the neighbourhood (6m x 4m), with main roads and landmarks labelled. It can be a painted tarpaulin or a blown-up base map printed on strips of paper and taped together. A high-quality labelled orthophoto map also works well. A clear plastic covering (e.g. Contact) is desirable but not essential.
- Stick-on nametags and group identification labels (e.g., stick-on animals).
- Large cardboard gold stars and two other coloured voting chips square shaped and made from cardboard: three of each for each participant.
- A table and chairs for each group (hire them if they are not available at the venue) and vertical surface for sheets (e.g. white or black boards, partitions, blank wall).
- Background music during small-group sessions provides atmosphere and masks noise transfer between groups.

Evaluation

With skilled facilitation, this approach works well within its limitations. It is a 'one off' exercise, with the young people coming in cold. It does not explore issues in depth and is no substitute for ongoing involvement. It is only an initial registering of issues and does not, of itself, engender a sense of owner- ship, responsibility and power. It does raise expectations, however, and that is why feedback and follow-up are essential.

The time allotted for the workshop at Airds was governed by the high school timetable. The times allotted to different steps are indicative only. We were surprised, however, at how quickly the young people completed each step. A more extensive workshop would require a greater range of guided activities.

The in-school version is easy to organize given a supportive school administration (but it is impossible without this support). The school controls selection of participants and this probably limits the range of young people (and their perspectives) involved. An out-of-school workshop would probably be more interesting, raise more diverse issues and perspectives and incorporate more 'intelligence' about the area. However, it would be more difficult to attract people and to manage, although competent youth workers could easily handle it.

Comparing the 'feelings' map and the 'issues' maps did not work well at Airds, partly because of an unresolved confusion between 'feeling' and 'issue'. 'I feel we need a basketball court' is an issue more than a feeling. 'I feel bored (because we do not have a basketball court)' is a feeling. This distinction needs to be illustrated. Feelings do not necessarily need to be related to specific issues.

Using the device of pre-recording some issues on the sheets as examples was a two-edged sword. It did test the planners' preconceptions (the source of examples) and focused discussion on physical planning issues. But it may have limited the thinking of the young participants and deprived us of some of their more offbeat ideas (these are often the best starters for innovative and creative planning and design).

Gilt-edged Resources 5
A Week with a Camera

'A Week with a Camera' is one of Wendy's tried-and-true methods of engaging children and young people in planning for their communities. It's effective, informative and most importantly – it's fun! This process is a real hit with children and a wonderful tool for understanding what children value in their neighbourhoods.

By means of a structured workshop process, children are given a camera and asked to record important aspects of their neighbourhood with photographs. This method is a way of helping planners, designers and others understand the 'mental maps' children hold in their heads about their communities. It enables participants to document their use of, and wishes for, particular environments. Significant landmarks, play circuits, focal points and 'sacred places' in the children's realm can also be identified.[1] As this method requires some understanding of photography (although the disposable cameras are easy to use), it is best used with older children and young people.[2]

'A Week with a Camera' can be used alone or in conjunction with other methods. We have seen a variation used with adults and have used it with great success with children in both urban and rural locations. We have used it successfully with children as young as 10 or 11.

Our experience has shown that children are generally excited about seeing their developed photos and are often reluctant to cut them up. Thus, in the workshop it's important to emphasize that they have permission to cut the photos so that they fit onto an A3-sized sheet. Remind them that the collages will be returned (laminated) for them to keep. Also, make sure you return the laminated collages promptly. Although costly, having a second set of developed photos that children can keep will likely encourage children to be more liberal and creative when making their collage.

This method is very resource-intensive. You require the disposable cameras and film (if film cameras are used), film processing (preferably two sets), lamination, colour photocopying or other copying and/or scanning and access to a Polaroid camera, as well as other craft materials. It can also be done with disposable digital cameras, but arrangements must be made for printing the photographs.

On the activity day, each table of five or six children requires at least one facilitator. Ideally, children should work in groups of about four with an adult helper. Parents can easily do this work with minimal training and are valuable helpers in a classroom setting.

Steps in the process

- Ten days before the activity day, participating children are given film cameras with 24-exposure colour print or disposable digital cameras (disposable film or digital film cameras are a relatively inexpensive option). This is often done through their schools. A facilitator attends their class, explains the purpose of the project (a local social or environmental plan, for example) and asks them to map and photograph their favourite areas in their immediate neighbourhood ('around where you live'), as well as areas that cause them concern.
- Each child labels their camera with an adhesive label with their name, age and telephone number.
- Care is taken not to prompt the children to look for any particular features of the environment.

- Friday is a good day to distribute cameras.
- The children are also asked to take at least one photograph of themselves (while they are in the classroom, as this aids in identification if cameras or prints get confused). Their classmates or the teacher can help with this. They are then asked to go out in their neighbourhood and take photographs of their neighbourhood, as well as photographs of their friends, their family and any important people, landscapes, places or animals.
- Log sheets are distributed to enable children to explain their choices, to help in later analysis (and to communicate seriousness on the part of the researchers).
- Each child is asked to draw a 'mud map' showing where the photographs were taken.
- The cameras, log sheets and maps are collected after a week and the film is processed or the digital images printed. Two prints are made of each negative (or image) to provide a record for the researchers. One set of prints is carefully labelled with the child's name, age, sex and address and filed with a copy of the log and map for further reference.
- On the activity day, the children are given back one set of their photographs and a copy of their log and map and asked to make a collage on A3 paper. The exercise is generally conducted at tables provided with scissors, glue, paper, crayons and coloured pens.
- We explain the following 'rules':

1. Children should feel free to cut out the parts they consider most important for the collage – or use a whole photograph (though smaller parts work best).
2. The collages will be temporarily annotated with children's comments on yellow Post it™ notes, which will be removed before the collages are laminated and returned to them. (Where necessary, a facilitator will annotate, following the child's instructions.)
3. The notes are intended to clarify interpretation and provide a basis for analysis.

4   Children are also offered paper and crayons to embellish their photographs.

- This activity must be carefully facilitated. As the children cut out and glue pieces of their photographs, facilitators at each table pay close attention and inquire about their reasons for selecting that view or image and keep a general record of the issues raised at each table, as well as recording on Post-it notes on each collage.
- After the collages are completed (perhaps an hour for this exercise), the children explain the main components of their collages to their small group or, if time permits, to whole group. They may like to tell a story about how they live in their neighbourhood.
- At the end of the workshop, all collages are collected.
- Once the information is analysed, the notes are removed and the collages laminated. They are then returned to the children.

Points to remember

- Remember to label all cameras before distribution, to label film before processing and all maps and log sheets with the names, addresses, telephone numbers, ages and sex of the students.
- Some children will require instruction to use the camera. Remember to tell them to have the sun behind them, that there needs to be adequate light and that indoor photographs generally don't turn out (unless the camera has a flash).
- For flash cameras, remind students to turn on the flash.
- The number of photos taken will vary and may limit the quality of the work produced. Possible factors affecting the success include inclement weather and parental control of the child's independent mobility and/or choice of subjects to photograph. You will encounter varying degrees of freedom to take photographs. Often children will be accompanied by a parent or care giver. This can significantly influence their choice of photographic subject.

- Be prepared for the unfortunate eventuality that some child's photos may not turn out at all. Drawing materials and magazines to cut up could be used as an alternative. Select the magazines carefully, making sure that they have photographs of houses, landscapes and natural places.
- At the end of the collage workshop, some children may be disappointed when their collages are taken away. We like to send children home with something to show for their work. Thus, we often take Polaroid or digital photographs of them with their collages and give each child a photograph to take home.[3]
- The collages can be photographed, scanned and/or colour-photocopied for inclusion in reports or exhibitions.

Props and supporting materials

- disposable cameras;
- log sheets;
- pre-printed A3 sheets for drawing maps;
- A3 paper, crayons, pencils, glue and scissors;
- magazines for collage, carefully selected;
- Post-it notes, markers and note paper for documenting discussions with children;
- somewhere to laminate the A3 collages; and
- Polaroid or digital camera and film (if Polaroid).

Questions to help facilitate the collage

Once a collage is coming together, facilitators are to start asking children for more details about the images that they have put into their collages. Questions you can use:

- What is this picture of?
- Why is this picture important to you?
- What is it about that part of your neighbourhood that is so important to you?

- If the image is something that the child wants to change about the neighbourhood, ask what would they like to change it to? What would be better?
- What do you like about the picture? It is essential to understand what about the picture the child likes. For example: if a child says that they want to keep a local park and that is all the information recorded, there may be a park built with play equipment, lots of lawn, garden plots and tent-style shade structures. However, the child might have liked the original park specifically because of the trees and these might be omitted from the new park.

Tips for recording

- Stick a Post-it note on an image in the child's collage, label it with a number.
- Record the child's name on your notepad and then list the number of the Post-it note and write next to it the child's ideas, hopes and/ or concerns.
- Record what the child is saying in their own words; do not try to interpret it for yourself or suggest ideas to the child. What adults think children want is rarely what children want! Always ensure that the child's *own* ideas are recorded.
- Make sure that you use full sentences to record. If you were to write something like 'trees', this would be difficult to understand later. *Be specific* – What about the trees? Does the child want more trees, less trees, bigger trees, climbing trees? or Do they NOT like the trees?

Mud map and log sheet

The mud map and log sheet are important components of the process, as they allow the child to reflect on their reasons for taking certain photos and add an element of accountability to the process. They should be collected with the cameras. Not all children will use them but they are helpful guides.

Mud Map

Note: North is at the top of the page: ↑

Log Sheet

Photo No.	This shows ...	It's important to me because...	I want to KEEP this √	I want to CHANGE this √	Priority (from 1 to 5) 5 = highest 1 = lowest
1					
2					
3					
4					
5					
6					
7					
8					
9					
10					

11				
12				
13				
14				
15				
16				
17				
18				
19				
20				

Final tips

- *Listening is important.* Listening is much more difficult than most people realize. Much of the time when someone is talking to us, we are not really listening; we are thinking about what we are going to say in reply. When you are listening to someone, try not to evaluate what is being said immediately in terms of what it means to you. Instead, try to understand what it means from the child's perspective. Ask questions that will help you understand better what the child is thinking and feeling. Be sure to listen much more than you speak to the children.

- *Try not to assume anything that a child is thinking.* Always ask questions to determine exactly what they like or dislike about a photograph. Try not to be leading in your questions. For example, rather than asking 'Is it the swings that you like in this photograph?', ask simply 'What is it that you like in this photograph?' Children often want to please. If you suggest the swings, they may agree with you just to try and win your approval.

- *Photos of friends*: Many children become excited at having a camera and want to show it off by photographing their friends. If they have many photos of their friends, the facilitator needs to determine whether the most important thing in that child's neighbourhood is actually their friends, or whether they were just photographing their friends for fun. The best way to do this is to ask them if they had to move from their neighbourhood, what would be three things that they would miss the most. If they say three friends, you can assume that they photographed their friends as they are the things that they want to keep in their neighbourhood.

Notes

Preface

1   Sarkissian et al (2008)
2   Innes and Booher (2004)
3   We have dedicated this book to Australian activist and artist, Graeme Dunstan, as a way of acknowledging his fiery commitment to community cultural development. For more about Graeme's activities, see peacebus.com.
4   See Sarkissian et al (1994b).
5   See Chapter 7 in this book.
6   For more about Yollana Shore's work, see www.soulbusiness.com.au.

Poem *Practice is sensuous activity*

1   'Practice is sensuous activity' is a quotation from John Friedmann's experimental planning text, *The Good Society* (Friedmann, 1979).

Chapter 1 Why Traverse the Edge: Creative Underpinnings

1 From Christopher Logue's poem 'Come to the Edge' (Logue, 1969). The original version of the poem, entitled 'Apollinaire Said', was written for a poster advertising a Guillaume Apollinaire exhibition in 1961.
2 Forester (1999)
3 Pinson (2004)
4 Hopkins (2001)
5 Beauregard (2001); Birch (2001); Dalton (2001); Hopkins (2001); Sandercock (2003a); Pinson (2004); Stiftel et al, (2004); Myers and Banerjee (2005); Goldstein and Carmin (2006)
6 Holden (2008)
7 Holden (2008), p477
8 Holden (2008), p480
9 Holden (2008), p480
10 Holden (2008), p492
11 Holden (2008), p475
12 Reason and Hawkins (1988), pp78–101
13 Krall (1994)
14 Wendy's dissertation, Sarkissian (1996) is available online from Murdoch University, Western Australia. See www.lib.murdoch.edu.au/adt/browse/. view/adt-MU20051109.104544.
15 Ehrlich (1994), p94
16 Sandercock (1995), p79
17 See also Sandercock (1998a).
18 Norma-Jean McLaren is a trainer and facilitator who has worked in diversity, community development and organizational change for 20 years. In 1992, she founded 42nd Street Consulting to support inclusive community building within a diversity of contexts (including workplaces and communities in cultural conflict) and she also co-teaches cross-cultural planning at the University of British Columbia. Recently she was appointed one of the John Bousfield Distinguished Visitors in Planning at the University of Toronto.

19 Norma-Jean has adapted the Diversity Wheel, originally developed in 1990 by M. Loden and J. Rosener in their work with 'Workforce America!' to examine the complex dimensions of diversity and to help explain the layers of oppression that many people experience. See McLaren and Edelson (2007).

20 Forester (1999), p131

21 Forester (1999), p132

22 Forester (1999), p32

23 Forester (1999) uses the term 'human flourishing' to discuss the political uncertainties dominating the urban design profession within the 'always precarious possibilities of human flourishing' (p72) lurking within every imagination of space and environment.

24 Friedmann (1979), p8

25 Forester (1999), p129

26 Forester (1999), p131

Chapter 2 Practitioners Working at the Edge: Creativity in Practice

1 Scarry (2006)

2 Kane (2004). Kane's website is www.newintegrity.org.

3 See on Kane's website: www.newintegrity.org/documents/SpiritinBusiness-PlayEthicpresentation.ppt.

4 Kane (2000)

Chapter 3 The Practice of Inhabiting the Edge: Interview with Wendy Sarkissian

1 An earlier version of some of this material was presented to the Community Arts Network of Western Australia (CANWA) Forum, July 2005 in a presentation entitled, 'The Artistry of Community Consultation'. It was reported in Sarkissian (2005), pp27–32.

2   Brassard (1989). Also in the same series is *The Memory Jogger*[TM] *II: A Pocket Guide of Tools for Continuous Improvement and Effective Planning*. This spiral-bound pocket guide of tools is based on the original *Memory Jogger*. It contains the same basic tools for problem solving and continuous improvement as the original version, as well as other collaborative decision-making tools, including the 7 Management and Planning (MP) Tools and team techniques. Chapters are sequenced alphabetically by tool name, cross-referenced by subject with graphics. See also: Mizuno (ed) (1988). A good summary is at www.skymark.com/resources/tools/affinity_diagram.asp, accessed 8 May 2009.

3   See Gilt-edged Resource 2.

4   For an explanation of the *Groan Zone,* see Kaner et al (1996), p19. In the *Groan Zone,* people are struggling to understand a wide range of foreign or opposing ideas. It often is not a pleasant experience. Group members can be repetitious, insensitive, defensive, short-tempered... After a while, so much has surfaced that some in the group begin to get nervous. There can be calls for 'process check' and the facilitator may wonder if things have gotten out of hand. When people start to think about all of what they have said, it just doesn't seem likely they will be able to wrap it up. This, says Sam Kaner, could be called the 'Groan Zone', in which the group really has to grapple with all the aspects of the problem, all the parties involved, and so on. Here is where workshops can easily collapse, because facilitator and group lose their nerve. See Imagine! (2004).

5   See Hammond (2009).

Chapter 4 Community Visioning as Engagement: Why a Conversation is Merited

1   Rumi, 'Emptiness' in Barks and Moyne (1997), p27

2   See Sarkissian et al (2008) 'Chapter 2: Practical recipes for community engagement with sustainability'.

3   Senge et al (2005), p140

4   Shipley and Newkirk (1999), pp573–589

5   Shipley (2000), p234

6   Shipley (2002), p11
7   Shipley (2000), pp227–231
8   Shipley (2000), p233
9   Shipley (2002), p7
10 The chief American proponent of community visioning, Steven Ames, calls community visioning 'an adjunct and an overlay for community planning' (Ding, 2005, p91). Local municipalities in many countries have embraced Ames's straightforward five-step process. He argues that in undertaking a visioning process, a community can better understand local strengths, weaknesses and core community values; identify outside forces, trends and issues that are shaping its future; articulate a preferred vision to guide its future directions; and develop the strategic tools to achieve its vision. For Ames, a vision is *the guiding image of what a community would like to be and a vision statement is the formal expression of such a vision.* It depicts in words and images what the community seeks to become – how it would look, how it would function, how it might be different or better. A *vision statement* is the starting point for the development and implementation of a strategic action plan that can help the community mobilize to achieve its vision over time.

Five main stages characterize his updated model, the *New Oregon Model:*

1   *Community profile*: Where are we now?
2   *Trend statement*: Where are we going?
3   *Vision statement*: Where do we want to be?
4   *Action Plan:* How do we get there?
5   *Implementation and monitoring:* Are we getting there? (Ding, 2005, p91).

Ames divides his methods and techniques into *representational* ones (working with groups that are reflective of a given population or subgroup) and 'flat-out participatory techniques' such as public meetings and events (Ding, 2005, p92). He offers no guidance, however, about how to undertake the 'visionary' components of the process.
11 Shipley (2002), pp8–12

12 Walker (1994), p1
13 Ziegler (1996a), p10
14 Ziegler (1996a), p10
15 Ziegler (1996a) p26. See also: Ziegler (1995) and Ziegler (1996b).
16 The emphasis at this stage is on attunement of the vision with the spirit of the person participating. Thus, '... each envisioner [should] discover what is true to her spirit, that to which her spirit calls her *in all of its uniqueness and integrity, prior to looking for common cause, common purpose, common action*'. This means that the participant must *live in the future-present moment* before considering wider social and community issues. This is a sacred place and a generative one, as Ziegler explains, 'In that state, your images come alive to you in all of their specificity and concreteness and *you live in them and with them as if you were in their presence*' (Ziegler [1996a], pp39–45).

    Transcription of the visioning process involves recording the compelling image, its indicators, its positive and negative consequences (detailed worksheets are provided to aid this part of the process) and the one central theme. This is a summary of what the vision is about and what concerns it expresses. Following the sharing and visioning teamwork, comprehensive scenarios can be developed with the following components: a vision statement, long-term goal, central theme, indicators of the goal's actualization, positive and negative consequences, assumptions and a futures matrix.

17 Scharmer (undated), p5. See also: Senge et al (2005), Scharmer (2007) and Society for Organizational Learning (undated) www.presence.net.
18 Scharmer (undated), pp5–8
19 Floyd and Hayward (2008)
20 Scharmer's 'intelligence of the heart' echoes both Goleman's emotional intelligence (1995) and Gardner's (1993 and 1999) multiple intelligences.
21 Scharmer (undated), pp7–11
22 Senge et al (2005), p145

Chapter 5 Heartstorming:
Putting the Vision Back into Visioning

1   Although Wendy thought she'd invented the term 'heartstorming', others have beaten her to it. Mark Silver uses it in his passionate guide to soulful business, *Unveiling the Heart of Your Business*, available at www.heartofbusiness.com. Others have websites and books dedicated to similar concepts. See Ian Summers' www.heartstorming.com. Paul Keenan has written an Adobe e-book called *Heartstorming*, which purports to offer readers a revolutionary path to lasting inner peace and fulfilment linking the mind, soul and heart – a process he calls heartstorming. See www.amazon.com/Heartstorming-Purposeful-Life-Paul-Keenan/dp.
Nevertheless, in this context, we advocate *heartstorming* as an antidote to 'brainstorming', which is the dominant approach to community visioning.

2   Wilson (2004), p6

3   The depth and span of Clare Cooper Marcus' influences on my life are beyond imagining. I describe one small part of her work in this section. Yollana Shore, a Journey™ Practitioner, has guided me, co-written many visioning scripts developed by Sarkissian Associates Planners and is a visionary in her own right (see www.soulbusiness.com.au). Community advocate Christine Fraser contributed many ideas and former Redemptorist priest, Denis McNamara, offered the memorable instruction, 'Let your heart picture your world the way you would love it to be'. Sophia van Ruth introduced collaboration, calm, wisdom, laughter and body awareness. Graeme Dunstan enlisted powerful language to envisage transformative community events and then created them before my eyes. Daniel Weber embodied the practice of transmuting dreams into dance, song and poetry. Poet Dianna Hurford shows me how.

4   Cooper Marcus (1979)

5   Cooper Marcus (2006)

6   Creative visualization or guided imagery is another way to express what is going on that can build our confidence that we are growing in our experience and – at least to some extent – making sense of it. Now in its 25th-anniversary edition, Shakti Gawain's classic *Creative Visualization*

is an excellent resource for understanding the power of visualization. It includes many exercises and meditations to guide the inner journey of discovery. See Gawain (2002).

And there are many other marvellous sources available. Mark Burch suggests 'Visioning a Well World', with a guided imagery exercise that involves reconnecting with our own imaginative powers and our visions of a healthy world. See Burch (2000).

7   Rietz and Manning (1994), p112

8   See Ng (1996), p20. See also: Grogan et al (1995), pp101ff.

9   Source: New Economics Foundation (1998)

10   We always 'cleanse' the room in which we work, reminding us that community engagement is a sensory practice. The space may require nothing more than airing out; cleaning and placing flowers, a candle or a beautiful object or piece of art inside it. Or we may need to erect a small, welcoming marquee as a porch if we are working in a large, bare tent. To transmute any negative energy, I'll burn a candle or some essential oils (selected for the ambience we are seeking – like 'harmony') or I'll flick water into all the corners of the room. I always do this unobtrusively.

Music can also transform the mood of a room and create a welcoming atmosphere. If it's not appropriate to play it, it can be played at such a low volume that the effect is subconscious. The slow movements (*largos* or *adagios*) of works by Baroque composers such as Bach, Handel, Corelli and Vivaldi are ideal because they have a tempo of 60 beats per minute. A Gregorian chant, a light and airy Mozart sonata or a slow movement of a Haydn cello concerto can have a soothing effect (Hatherley (2001), p72). We synthesized Pachelbel's *Canon in D* to a human heartbeat to play silently in the background of a video on crime prevention and often play it quietly (or silently) in the background of workshops and meetings. Not surprisingly, even in high-conflict contexts, people often comment about how relaxed they feel in our workshops.

11   See Houston (1982), Houston (1987) and Houston (1992). Jean Houston, scholar, philosopher and researcher in human capacities is a founder of the Human Potential Movement. She is the author of 26 books, including: *A Passion for the Possible, Search for the Beloved, Life Force, The Possible*

Human, Public Like a Frog, A Mythic Life: Learning to Live Our Great Story and *Manual of the Peacemaker.*

12 In a Sydney conference workshop in the early 1980s, I asked participants to spend the next two days in the role of a person with a disability or their carer to identify barriers to accessibility in the conference building. As I was setting the exercise, a group of Torres Strait Islander women abruptly – and silently – left the room. During lunch, they apologized, explaining that while some cultural groups may be comfortable with role playing, it may be inappropriate or even dangerous for other people to assume or embody another person's 'spirit'. They felt it was dangerous for them to continue.

13 See Academy for Guided Imagery (2009).

14 See Rietz and Manning (1994), p115.

15 *VOJ* involves 'fear, judgment and chattering of the mind' when we begin to develop a capacity for suspension. 'Suspension requires patience and willingness not to impose pre-established frameworks or mental models on what we are seeing'. See Senge et al (2007), pp30–31. For more on the *VOJ*, see Ray and Myers (1986).

16 See Sarkissian and Walsh (1994a), Chapter 5. See also Engwicht (1993), Grogan et al (1995) and Engwicht (1999).

17 See Gardner (1993) and Gardner (1999).

18 See Infed (2002), Gardner (1999), p52 and Louv (2005), p71.

19 See Goleman (2006) and Gardner (1999).

20 See Revell and Norman (1997).

21 Senge et al (2007), pp83, 104

22 Shipley (2000), p231

23 Tip: If we are going to photocopy the drawings, we remove yellow crayons from the boxes before drawing begins. With scanning, that's not an issue.

24 Senge et al (2007), p112

25 Additional instructions can include:

- Draw only with your non-dominant hand and try to draw in the mode of a young child;
- Put a drawing of yourself in the drawing (but no stick figures);
- Identify all the important features of your drawing (you can use your dominant hand for labelling);

- Consider recording a dialogue between you and one element or feature of your vision; record this as a conversation; and
- Record the qualities of the environment in as much detail as you can (how you felt about it and what it communicated to you); consider giving a name to those qualities or to the place itself.

Chapter 6 Acting like a Child: Welcoming Spontaneity and Creativity in the Aurora Team Development Workshop

1   Kane (2000)

2   The creative genius of creativity consultant, Kashonia Carnegie, inspired the program design for Sunday afternoon's first two sessions (particularly the 'making like children' process). Her specialist expertise in recalling the qualities of Australian children's parties, favourite desserts and dinners contributed to the design of the party and the Sunday dinner. I am grateful to Kashonia for many insights expressed in this chapter. See www.kashonia.com, accessed 22 June 2009.

3   See von Oech (1973).

4   For a peek at modern-day Aurora, eight years on, see VicUrban (undated).

5   See Sarkissian with Walsh (1994b).

6   *Ecologically Sustainable Development* (ESD) was the term used in the 1990s and early 2000s in Australia for what is now generally known as 'sustainability'. See Australia Department of the Environment and Heritage (1992). Together these are a set of radical documents worked out by panels of representatives from industry, the conservation movement, unions, social-equity groups and government.

7   *The workshop program*
    This chapter describes only the first day's program, which focused on creativity and opening up to participants' 'inner child'. We describe the powerful exercise of creating the Nonhuman Being in Chapter 7.

Workshop Program
Day 1   SUNDAY

3:00pm	Bus departs from central Melbourne
4:45pm	Arrival at Warburton, check-in
5:00pm	Welcome and introductions
	Listening to the silent voices (Part 1)
6:35pm	Dinner
8:35pm	*Sustainable Cities: A Challenge for Planners and Developers*
	Professor Peter Newman, Director, Institute for Sustainability and Technology Policy, Murdoch University
10:15pm	Drinks and chat
	Close of Day 1

Day 2   MONDAY

7:30am	Breakfast
8:30am	Introduction to the Workshop Program
8:45am	Introduction to the ULC Performance Objectives Workshop: Jill Lim
9:20am	Sustainability at Aurora? Implications of Professor Newman's presentation for this project
	Sustainability Objectives Part 1: what are our main sustainability objectives?
10:45am	Morning tea
11:15am	The Team sets its performance objectives (Part 1)
	Workshop on project objectives and team's needs
1:00pm	Introduction to the evening's program and material gathering task
1:10pm	Lunch
2:00pm	Free time and materials gathering and other activities
4:30pm	Trust Games: facilitated by Paul Traynor
6:00pm	Dinner
8:00pm	*Nurturing an Ethic of Caring for Nature* (Wendy Sarkissian)
	Listening to the silent voices (Part 2)
	Group exercise and concluding ritual
10:30pm	Close of Day 2

Day 3   TUESDAY

8:00am	Breakfast
9:00am	Where are we up to? Recap of Workshop to date
	Sustainability Objectives Part 2: refining our Sustainability objectives
	Identification of further tasks to be undertaken
10:30am	Morning tea
11:00am	Listening to the silent voices (part 3)
11:45am	Best practice team processes
	What makes a good team?
	Role play and debrief
12:45pm	Working as a team (Part 1)
	Team rules and principles
	How we will work together
	Brainstorming session
1:15pm	Lunch
2:00pm	Working as a team (Part 2): Team management and process
3:00pm	Working as a team (Part 3): Teamwork actions to achieve results ... now and into the future
4:15pm	Jill Lim: Where to from here?
	Next steps and feedback
4:30pm	Close of workshop and goodbyes
	Bus leaves for Melbourne 4:45 pm

8   Goleman (1995). See also: Sarkissian et al (2008), Chapter 5.
9   See Sarkissian (1996).
10   Orr (1994), pp17, 30
11   Orr (1994), pp48–49
12   Bowers (1995), p113
13   Bowers (1995), pp72–73, 91

Chapter 7 Embodying the Vision: Kinetic Community Engagement Practices

1   The Aurora workshop (held in Melbourne in 2001) was a two-day project team development exercise packed full of team-development exercises, as well as project planning and organizational matters (as this was the first meeting of the Team). Chapter 2 described several early components of the workshop. This was a true team effort for the organizers. The brilliant and courageous co-facilitation of Kelvin Walsh (the 'tall koala') is acknowledged with many thanks, as is the great support of Angela Hirst.
The second part of Monday's program is set out below.

1:00pm	Introduction to the evening's program and material gathering
	task for the afternoon
1:10pm	Lunch
2:00pm	Free time and materials gathering and the activities
4:30pm	Trust Games facilitated by Paul Traynor
6:00pm	Dinner
8:00pm	*Nurturing an Ethic of Caring for Nature*, Dr. Wendy Sarkissian
	Listening to the silent voices (Part 2)
	Group exercise and concluding ritual
10:30pm	Close of Day 2

2   The Nonhuman Being project had four phases:
Phase 1: Materials collection from the surrounding natural habitat – done individually during free time on Monday afternoon.
Phase 2: Design of the representation of nonhuman Nature and its carrying vessel, as three tasks by three unified teams:

Task 1:	Team 1 to design the representation of nonhuman Nature.
Task 2:	Team 2 to design the vessel.
Task 3:	Team 3 to prepare a ceremony to introduce the Being to the Team members.

Phase 3:   Construction of the representation of nonhuman Nature and the carrying vessel undertaken by teams 1 and 2 working together as one collective team.

Phase 4:   Team 3 designed and conducted a welcome ceremony, which was accompanied by music and dance, poetic speech and appropriate ritual paraphernalia.

3   See Sarkissian (1996).

4   Prepared by Graeme Quin and reviewed and approved by John Prentice, 19 April 2001.

5   Perspex is a transparent thermoplastic acrylic resin used where an inexpensive, clear vessel or window is required.

6   For the origin of my use of the stone ritual, see Mariechild (1989).

7   See Sarkissian et al (1994b).

8   Senbel (2002)

9   Whitecross (2004)

10   Role plays cannot last for very long or they become boring. Participants might think they are being funny but the audience often does not – after about 20 or 30 minutes. This session ran from 3:30 to 4:00pm, followed by a debriefing conducted by the Workshop Chair. Then John Forester provided a summary, followed by a question-and-discussion session with the audience.

11   Forester (2005), in Johansson and Woodilla (eds)

Poem *Poetry | planning code-filter: all*

1   This poem is part of a series in Hurford (2008) 'Breaking the Line: Integrating poetry, polyphony and planning practice', Masters thesis, School of Community and Regional Planning, University of British Columbia, Vancouver BC, where interviews with Vancouver poets were 'coded'. They are a play on form, using the form and language of *Atlas-ti*, a qualitative software program designed primarily for coding and analysing interview data. This poem is one of three from an interview conducted with architect and poet, Graham McGarva.

Chapter 8 Learning at the Margins: Margo Fryer and Pamela Ponic on Deconstructing Power and Privilege

1   See Kovacs (trans.) (1989).

2   Manguel (2007), p36

3   Manguel (2007), p34

4   Manguel (2007), p50

5   Manguel (2007), p51

6   For discussion of the ladder of participation, see Arnstein (1969). For discussion of a wheel of participation, see Davidson (1998). For a spectrum of participation, see International Association for Public Participation (undated).

7   Dunstan et al (1994)

8   See Young (1997) and Young (2000).

9   *Conscientization* is defined as the process in which people, not as recipients, but as knowing subjects, achieve a deepening awareness both of the sociocultural reality that shapes their lives and of their capacity to transform that reality (Freire (1985), p93). For Freire, the mark of a liberating process is to help local people tell their own stories.

10 Margo Fryer is the founding director of the *Learning Exchange* at the University of British Columbia (UBC). The Learning Exchange is an institute established to foster experiential learning within the university and to forge closer working relationships between the university and the broader community.

11 Pamela Ponic continues to work with public health issues through participatory approaches in Vancouver and throughout the Province of British Columbia.

12 Both Participatory Action Research (PAR) and Community Service Learning (CSL) belong to a family of action research paradigms. Both ground practice in emphasis on the dialectic between research and action and the consequent place for continued, careful reflection. Both paradigms have roots in Critical Theory that question how power is distributed and perpetuated in society and theorize about how marginalization occurs through structural inequalities. The roots of these diverse disciplines

are so rich that we cannot cite them here. Wicks et al (2008) recently compiled the reflections of Action Research practitioners to discuss the most influential thinkers and doers in the field and the list is impressive. See Gayá Wicks et al (2008).

13   For more information on UBC's Learning Exchange and their Community Service Learning Initiative, see University of British Columbia www. learningexchange.ubc.ca/ubc-cli.html, accessed 8 May 2009.

14   Later in this chapter, Pamela Ponic shares her growing understanding of the positive potential of power, using terms from feminist work to build on Foucault's (1977) work and differentiate among 'power-to', 'power-with' and 'power-for', as opposed to 'power-over'. In her work with Women Organizing Activities for Women (WOAW), Pamela committed to distinguishing among different uses of power, asking: Is my use of power potentially preventing other women in WOAW from exercising their own agency, or could my use of power potentially manipulate their actions and decisions? Instead, she aimed to use her power only when she was confident that her access to resources could support the women to achieve *their* project objectives. For some of the formative roots of this discussion, see Foucault (1977).

15   Booher and Innes (2002), pp221–236. See also Innes and Booher (2004) pp419–436.

16   WOAW has since disbanded.

17   See Freire (1970) and Freire (1992) .

18   Ponic (2000), pp48–61, cited in Ponic (2007), p20

19   Fraser (1997) and Giddens (1984), cited in Ponic (2007), p20

20   Lavarack (2004), cited in Ponic (2007), p22

21   Sandercock's epistemological critique, which she humorously describes as 'Cartesian anxiety' (Sandercock, 1998a), focuses on the separation of fact and value, the objective of scientific understanding and what Patsy Healey calls 'the dominance of instrumentality'. See Healey (1997), p251.

22   Sandercock (2003a), p165

Chapter 9 'And Action!'
New Roles for Film in Engagement:
Leonie Sandercock and Jonathan Franz

1   Sandercock et al (2009), p88
2   Sandercock et al (2009)
3   Leonie Sandercock is a professor in the School of Community and Regional Planning at the University of British Columbia.
4   Respectively, 'Where Strangers become Neighbours: The story of the Collingwood Neighbourhood House and the Integration of Immigrants in Vancouver', the Burns Lake project (currently with the working title of: 'Finding our Way: A path to healing Native/non-Native relations in Canada'); and The Carrall Street Participatory Video Project (CSPVP).
5   The Carrall Street Participatory Video Project explored the City of Vancouver's plans for redeveloping Carrall Street in the Downtown Eastside (DTES). The project was a partnership with Projections, Ear to the Ground Planning and the School of Community and Regional Planning (SCARP) at the University of British Columbia, seeking to include the marginalized voices of the neighbourhood in the City of Vancouver public engagement process. The project resulted in several SCARP Master's projects and theses and a suite of three short videos shown at the World Urban Forum in 2006.
6   Cavers et al (November 2007)
7   Ear to the Ground Planning: www.eartothegroundplanning.com, accessed 12 May 2009
8   Sandercock et al (2009)

Chapter 10 Websites as Engagement Site and Story:
Aileen Penner and Think Salmon

1   King (2005)
2   Sandercock (2003a)
3   In 2006, the United Nations Economic Commission for Europe submitted a paper on blogs with the following definitions:

- There are as many definitions of a blog as there are 'bloggers', the people that write them. Derived from 'weblog', a blog is a particular type of website. Frequently described as a personal online journal, their most distinguishing feature is that content mainly consists of dated entries, known as posts, appearing in reverse chronological order. New posts are added regularly and often include links to other blogs and websites, forming a network of opinions and people.

- Blogs fall within the family of 'social software', along with instant messaging, internet relay chat (IRC) and other tools for online communication. Blogging systems have the optional feature to allow readers to respond to posts with their comments. This ability to interact, along with the personalized style of writing, is what sets them apart from other websites.

- Since their inception in the mid-1990s, the growth of blogs has been rapid. [In 2006, there were] nearly 50 million blogs currently in existence, with about 75,000 new ones being created every day. In 2004, United States dictionary publisher Merriam-Webster made 'blog' its word of the year, based on the number of searchers for the term.

- Blogs have made publishing on the internet easy, free and accessible to anyone with a computer and an internet connection. This has revolutionized communication and mass media, by providing a means for unbiased reporting and voicing opinions.

4   See United Nations Economic Commission for Europe (UNECE) (2006). For example:

One Day Vancouver, a City of Vancouver website and blog, designed to encourage individuals to commit to lifestyle changes, is working to meet the city's climate action plans. The site includes resources for taking action at home, work, school and in the community. Individuals, organizations and businesses are invited to share their success stories, post on message boards and receive news and event updates, including 'easy action tips'.

The site is also available in multiple languages, including English, French, Spanish, Punjabi, Vietnamese and Cantonese.

The City of Portland's Water Bureau developed The Water Blog in 2005 in order to gather public thoughts and distribute information and resources about drinking water. Since then, postings have connected the issue of drinking water to other regions, mobilizing users to action in other communities, such as New Orleans reconstruction efforts. Media includes links to YouTube™, photographs and text. Comments and posts are managed by the Interim Public Information Officer.

5   Penner (2005a)
6   Sites like Think Salmon (see Think Salmon, 2009) act as an informal 'living room' type environment for the community to enter to write stories and share photographs and events. Stories and topics are archived and referenced, 'tagged' and linked to a web of other associated sites. Software for blogs is often user-friendly and free (although resources to keep the site 'live' and monitor or facilitate online content can be time-intensive). Although young people tend to be fluent users of web-based tools, many individuals are not as literate. As more people begin using technology to engage with each other, the use of online technology such as blogs will be an important part of our creative engagement projects.

Chapter 11 Creativity and Moving Beyond Conflict: Michelle LeBaron, Norma-Jean McLaren and Nathan Edelson

1   Jean Piaget (1896–1980), biologist who studied child development through observation and speaking and listening to them. His work has been influential in educational theory.
2   Norma-Jean McLaren and Nathan Edelson developed *Community Initiatives 2007*, a series of five initiatives with modules or templates to tailor to the needs of each client. These include Living in Diverse Communities (diversity train-the-trainer workshops); the Community Healing Initiative (developing and strengthening capacity for diversity within the community);

Community Partnerships (inter-agency partnership building); Partnerships in Diversity Organizational Change (developing a framework for partnership with service delivery agencies); and Initiating Diversity Organizational Change (implementing diversity change within organizations).

3   Not in My Back Yard (NIMBY).

Chapter 12 But They're Only Kids!
Why Engage with Children and Young People

1   Moody (2000)

2   For more information on the symposium, see Griffith University (2004); Sarkissian and Ludher (2004) and communitybuilders.nsw.

3   In our preliminary research, we searched for government community engagement documents (mostly on the internet): manuals, guides, frameworks, checklists, protocols, policies, advisory materials, 'how to' materials and volumes and appendices of techniques. We defined *children* as being aged 0 to 12 years. In all, we reviewed 108 publications and documents and found only 14 mentions of United Nations Convention on the Rights of a Child, 30 mentions of children's participation techniques and little mention of young people and children in any way in an engagement context. There was also little indication of the consideration of intergenerational equity issues. Only one Australian publication focused on engagement with children and young people. See NSW Commission for Children and Young People (undated) *Participation Kit: TAKING PARTicipation Seriously*, which has 144 pages of children's engagement tools. It received the 2005 *Core Values Award for Robust Public Participation*, International Association for Public Participation (IAP2), Australasia.

4   Sarkissian and Cook (2002)

5   Adapted from Driskell (2002).

6   See Urbanthinkers (undated).

7   McLaren and Edelson (2004, unpublished)

8   Norma-Jean and Nathan passed on the *Talking Circles* documents to the United Way 'Communities in Action' Project Coordinators. They would like to make the following recommendations for future *Talking Circles*:

1 There should be a fair amount of preparation for the Circles – choosing participants who will offer thoughts and listen to others with respect.
2 There should be some training on the principles of listening prior to the start of the Circle.
3 There needs to be an agreement before the Circle ends as to the next steps and who should be present for future Circles.

Chapter 13 New Languages for Community Engagement: Translation, Language and Polyphony

1 Hurford (2008)
2 Sandercock (2003a)
3 Sandercock (2003a), p196
4 Holden (2008), p492
5 Headlines Theatre (www.headlinestheatre.com) was founded in Vancouver in 1981 and is based on Augusto Boal's 'Theatre of the Oppressed'. Boal created Forum Theatre in the 1970s as a participatory and experiential method for theatre, making both the actor and the spectator active participants in addressing social issues in the community. Headlines Theatre Director, David Diamond, uses the term 'Theatre for Living' to describe the unique role Headlines Theatre has formed in the community to create space for people to share their stories about how social issues are affecting their own lives, inviting audience members to enter into a community dialogue to seek alternative solutions. Headlines hosts Theatre for Living training sessions with several variations and adaptations on using theatre as a transformative engagement method. Sadly, Augusto Boal passed away while we were completing this book.
6 Headlines Theatre and Vancouver City Council established an agreement to use the theatre as a public engagement process and that the recommendations from the audience, 'translated' in the *Practicing Democracy* report, would be considered for policy deliberations by Vancouver City Council.
7 Gallant (2004)
8 Warland (2005)

9   McCaffery (2008)

10   Avasilichioaei (2008), cited in Hurford (2008), p72

11   Bringhurst (2007), p93

12   Bringhurst (2007), pp74–5, author's own emphasis

13   Bringhurst (2007), p75

14   Much inspiration for adapting the concept of polyphony in my thesis was found through Bringhurst (2007) and Glenn Gould's contrapuntal radio trilogy: the Solitude Trilogy, created for the Canadian Broadcasting Corporation (CBC) in the 1970s. Gould was greatly inspired by Bach's use of polyphony and applied this concept to overlaying interviews from people living in Newfoundland, the Canadian prairies and the Canadian North. The effect of each of these programs is much like the Centre Pompidou, where each voice is independent and other voices run parallel.

15   Bringhurst (2007)

16   Hurford (2008), pp100–105

17   Avasilichioaei (2008) Personal communication with Dianna Hurford, cited in Hurford (2008), p72

18   Compton (2004)

19   The first written work is a poem written by a black poet leaving San Francisco for British Columbia. The poem reveals insight into how the poet felt about leaving one city and anticipates or speculates what the new city will reveal. The starting place for this lineage is in transit, in the emotional process of imagining what lies ahead.

20   Including hybridizations of hip hop and rap, sound poetry and concrete poetry, among others.

21   McGarva (2008) Personal communication with Dianna Hurford, January, cited in Hurford (2008), pp53–66

22   Avasilichioaei (2008) Personal communication with Dianna Hurford, cited in Hurford (2008), p71

23   Braid (2008) Personal communication with Dianna Hurford, cited in Hurford (2008), pp90–91. Kate Braid expands on this by saying that up to 80 per cent of our speech is in iambic pentameter and that these students were writing in traditional structures of poetic form. Kate suggests that the connection to the music and rhythms of the poetry resonate with the biological rhythms of the human body.

24 Dersken (2006)
25 Compton (2004)
26 Derksen (2006)
27 Avasilichioaei (2008) Personal communication with Dianna Hurford, cited in Hurford (2008), p71
28 Derksen (2006)
29 Manguel (2007)
30 Manguel (2007), p8
31 Braid (2008) Personal communication with Dianna Hurford (2008), cited in Hurford (2008), p89
32 Manguel (2007), p56

Chapter 14 On the Edge of Utopia: Stories from *The Great Turning*

1   Sources: Alexander (1979); Alexander (2005); Callenbach (1975); Hester (2006); Korten (2006); Le Guin (2001); Macy and Young Brown (1998); Peavey (2000); Piercy (1976); Starhawk (1993)

Gilt-edged Resource 1: A Visioning Example: *Our Bonnyrigg Dream*

1   For more information about the Bonnyrigg community and other community engagement processes we employed there in 2004 and 2005, see Sarkissian et al (2009), Chapter 4.1.
2   Within her training as a shiatsu practitioner, Sophia was aware that laughter can stimulate the heart meridian, which is associated with joy (see Beresford-Cooke et al (2003), p145).

Also (according to her creativity training at Zen Renaissance College in Sydney), these two qualities are highly desirable for visualising a vibrant and healthy future. Therefore, she began introducing some laughter exercises based on those she had experienced at the Balmain Laughter Club, Sydney. For information on laughter clubs, see www.laughteryoga.org/.

Not every community may be open to such exercises, but every time Sophia has used them, she reports positive feedback.

Sophia explained her three laughs this way: In the *one-metre laugh* participants hold their left arm out to the side and bring the right arm across to meet it. Then they 'step' their right hand across their arm/chest and outstretch it to the other side, saying 'ha' with every step. When both arms are fully outstretched so that their chest is open, they just laugh: hahahahahahahah! *The silent laugh* is where people simply laugh without making any noise (this seems to reach the bottom of the lungs). *Clam laugh* is interactive: people hold their forearms across their eyes. Then they go up to another person and open their forearms (one up and one down) like a clam opening. And they laugh together with that person.

Gilt-edged Resource 3: The Gods Must Be Crazy: Script and Instructions from the *Safe Communities* Scenario, Sydney

1   SES: State Emergency Services in New South Wales: volunteers helping their communities cope with emergencies.

Gilt-edged Resource 4: Barefoot Mapping: Learning Through the Soles of Our Feet: A Participatory Design Workshop for Youth in Airds, Sydney, New South Wales

1   By Wendy Sarkissian and John Murray. An earlier version of this material appeared in the *Workshop Checklist*, Appendix A. See Sarkissian et al (2000), pp79–82.
2   We always use trained facilitators *and* recorders in participatory processes. It is essential that all recording be 'public' for all to see and that there is a strict separation between facilitation and recording processes.

3   As with all participatory processes, attention to detail is *everything!* We use large cardboard gold stars, not small adhesive ones. The ones which work best are about 10cm from point to point and available in shops which sell shop-window decorations.

Gilt-edged Resource 5: A Week with a Camera

1   See Hester (2006) and Hester (1985), pp10–12. See also Cunningham et al (1994); Cunningham and Jones (2002); and Tranter (1993).
2   We recognize environmental concerns about this method – Kodak assures that their disposable cameras, or at least parts of them, are recycled.
3   Digital photos can also be taken as long as a printer is available at the workshop.

References

Academy for Guided Imagery (2009) www.academyforguidedimagery.com/, accessed 1 May 2009

Alexander, C. (1979) *The Timeless Way of Building*, Oxford University Press, New York

Alexander, C. (2005) *The Nature of Order: An Essay on the Art of Building and the Nature of the Universe*, four volumes, Taylor and Francis, London

Ames, S. C. (1988) 'Municipal Visioning: Creating a Strategic Vision for the Future', unpublished paper, Alberta Ministry of Municipal Affairs, Edmonton, AB

Ames, S. C. (ed) (1989a) *A Guide to Community Visioning*, Steven Ames Planning, Portland, OR

Ames, S. C. (1989b) *Charting a Course for Corvallis: A Case Study of Community Visioning in Oregon*, American Planning Association (Oregon Chapter), Gresham, OR

Ames, S. C. (1993) *The Agency Visioning Handbook: Developing a Vision of the Future in Public Agencies: A Hands-on Guide for Planners and Facilitators in State and Federal National Agencies*, US Fish and Wildlife Service, Division of Federal Aid, Arlington, VA

Ames, S. C., Coppel, P. and Rains, C. (eds) (1993) *A Guide to Community Visioning: Hands-on Information for Local Communities* (revised and updated), Oregon Visions Project, Oregon Chapter, American Planning Association, Portland, OR

Armstrong, C. (2006) *Rethinking Equality: The Challenge of Equal Citizenship*, Manchester University Press, Manchester

Arnstein, S. R. (1969) 'A ladder of citizen participation', *Journal of the American Institute of Planners*, vol 35, no 4, pp216–224

Australia Department of the Environment and Heritage (1992) *National Strategy for Ecologically Sustainable Development*, prepared by the Ecologically Sustainable Development Steering Committee, endorsed by the Council of Australian Governments, December, www.deh.gov.au/esd/national/nsesd/strategy/communit.html, accessed 11 May 2009

Avasilichioaei, O. (2008) Personal communication with Dianna Hurford, 18 February – 3 March, cited in Hurford, D. (2008) 'Breaking the Line: Integrating Poetry, Polyphony, & Planning Practice', Master's thesis, School of Community and Regional Planning, University of British Columbia, Vancouver

Beauregard, R. (2001) 'The multiplicities of planning', *Journal of Planning Education and Research*, vol 20, pp437–439

Bellamy, E. (eds) (2003) *Looking Backward: 2000–1887*, edited by A. MacDonald, Broadview Press, Peterborough, ON

Beresford-Cooke C., Williams, L. and Pole, N. (2003) *Shiatsu Theory and Practice: A Comprehensive Text for the Student and Professional*, Second Edition, Elsevier Churchill Livingstone, New York

Bimber, B., Flanagin, A. J. and Stohl, C. (2005) 'Reconceptualizing collective action in the contemporary media environment', *Communication Theory*, vol 15, no 4, pp365–388

Birch, E. L. (2001) 'Practitioners and the art of planning', *Journal of Planning Education and Research*, vol 20, no 4, pp407–422

Blanchet-Cohen, N. (2006) *Growing up in Cities Canada: Civic Engagement of Young People in Vancouver*, DVD, The International Institute for Child Rights and Development (IICRD), Victoria, BC

Bolitho, A. and Hutchison, M. (1998) *Out of the Ordinary: Inventive Ways of Bringing Communities, their Stories and Audiences to Light*, Canberra Stories Group, Curtin, ACT

Booher, D. E. and Innes, J. E. (2002) 'Network power in collaborative planning', *Journal of Planning Education and Research*, vol 21, no 3, pp221–236

Booher, D. E. and Innes, J. E. (2004) 'Reframing public participation: Strategies for the 21st century', *Planning Theory & Practice*, vol 5, no 4, pp419–436

Bowers, C. A. (1995) *Educating for an Ecologically Sustainable Culture: Rethinking Moral Education, Creativity, Intelligence and Other Modern Orthodoxies*, State University of New York Press, Albany, NY

Braid, K. (2008) Personal communication with Dianna Hurford, 3 March, cited in Hurford, D. (2008) 'Breaking the Line: Integrating Poetry, Polyphony, & Planning Practice', Master's thesis, School of Community and Regional Planning, University of British Columbia, Vancouver

Brassard, M. (1989) *The Memory Jogger Plus+: Featuring the Seven Management and Planning Tools*, first edition, GOAL/QPC, Methuen, MA

Bringhurst, R. (2007) *Everywhere Being is Dancing: Twenty Pieces of Thinking*, Gaspereau Press, Kentville, NS

Brock, K. and Pettit, J. (eds) (2007) *Springs of Participation: Creating and Evolving Methods for Participatory Development*, Practical Action Publishing, Rugby, UK

Burch, M. (2000) *Stepping Lightly: Simplicity for People and the Planet*, New Society Publishers, Gabriola Island, BC

Callenbach, E. (1975) *Ecotopia: The Notebooks and Reports of William Weston*, Heyday Books, Berkeley, CA

Camino, L. and Shepherd, Z. (2002) 'From periphery to center: Pathways for youth civic engagement in the day-to-day life of communities', *Applied Developmental Science*, vol 6, no 4, pp213–220

Camino, L., Zeldin, S. and Mook, C. (2005) 'The adoption of innovation in youth organizations: Creating the conditions for youth–adult partnerships', *Journal of Community Psychology*, vol 33, no 1, pp121–135

Canadian Alliance for Community Service-Learning (CACSL) (undated) 'Home', www.communityservicelearning.ca/en/resources_links.cfm, accessed 3 January 2009

Carnegie, K. www.kashoniatoday.com/, accessed 20 June 2009

Cavers, V. with Carr, P. and Sandercock, L. (2007) *How Strangers Become Neighbours: Constructing Citizenship Through Neighbourhood Community Development*, Vancouver: Metropolis British Columbia, Centre of Excellence for Research on Immigration and Diversity, Working Paper Series No. 07–11, November

Chambers, R. (1997) *Whose Reality Counts?: Putting the First Last*, Intermediate Technology Publications, London

Chambers, R. (2002) *Participatory Workshops: A Sourcebook of 21 Sets of Ideas and Activities*, Earthscan, London

City of Portland Water Bureau (undated) 'Water Blog', www.portlandonline. com/water/index.CFM?c=39678, accessed 14 April 2009

City of Vancouver (undated) 'One day Vancouver: Small steps towards a cleaner, greener, healthier city', www.vancouver.ca/oneday/, accessed 14 April 2009

Communitybuilders.nsw (2004) 'Creating Child Friendly Cities symposium presentations', www.communitybuilders.nsw.gov.au/building_stronger/ inclusive/ccfc.html, accessed 19 June 2009

Compton, W. (2004) *Performance Bond*, Arsenal Pulp Press, Vancouver

Cone, D. and Harris, S. (1996) 'Service-learning practice: Developing a theoretical framework', *Michigan Journal of Community Service Learning*, vol 3, Fall, pp31–43

Cooper Marcus, C. (1978) 'Remembrance of landscapes past', *Landscape*, vol 22, no 3, pp34–43

Cooper Marcus, C. (1979) *Environmental Autobiography*, Working Paper 301, January, Institute for Urban and Regional Development, University of California, Berkeley, CA

Cooper Marcus, C. (1995) *House as a Mirror of Self: Exploring the Deeper Meaning of Home*, Conari Press, Berkeley, CA

Cooper Marcus, C. (2006) *House as a Mirror of Self: Exploring the Deeper Meaning of Home*, second edition, Nicolas-Hays, Inc, Lake Worth, FL

Cooperrider, D. L. and Whitney, D. (2005) *Appreciative Inquiry: A Positive Revolution in Change*, Berrett-Koehler Publishers, San Francisco

Coult, T. and Kershaw, B. (eds) (1983) *Engineers of the Imagination: The Welfare State Handbook*, Methuen, London

Creighton, J. L. (2005) *Public Participation Handbook: Making Better Decisions through Citizen Involvement*, Jossey-Bass, San Francisco

Cunningham, C. and Jones, M. A. (2002) 'How Kids Use and Think About Their Urban Environment: A review of research into children and play', Paper presented to the seminar, *Kids in Local Space*, 20 March, Melbourne Town Hall, Melbourne, Victoria

Cunningham, C. J., Jones, M. A. and Taylor, N. (1994) 'The child-friendly neighbourhood: Some questions and tentative answers from Australian research', *International Play Journal* vol 2, pp79–95

Dalton, L. C. (2001) 'Weaving the fabric of planning as education', *Journal of Planning Education and Research*, vol 20, pp423–436

Daniels, T., Keller J. and Lapping, M. (1995) *The Small Town Planning Handbook*, second edition, Planners Press, American Planning Association, Chicago

Davidson, S. (1998) 'Spinning the wheel of empowerment', *Planning*, vol 1262, 3 April, pp14–15

Dersken, J. (2006) 'Urban regeneration: Gentrification as global urban strategy', in Schier, R. (2006) *Stan Douglas: Every Building on 100 West Hastings*, Contemporary Art Gallery and Arsenal Pulp Press, Vancouver, BC

Ding, P. (2005) 'Envisioning local futures: the evolution of community visioning as a tool for managing change', *Journal of Future Studies*, vol 9, no 4 (May), pp89–100

Driskell, D. (2002) *Creating Better Cities with Children and Youth: A Manual for Participation*, Earthscan, London and Sterling, VA and UNESCO Publishing, Paris

Dunlop, R. (2002a) 'A story of her own: Female *'bildungsroman'* as arts-based educational research', *Alberta Journal of Educational Research*, vol 48, no 3, pp215–228

Dunlop, R. (2002b) 'In search of tawny grammar: Poetics, landscape, and embodied ways of knowing', *The Canadian Journal of Environmental Education*, vol 7, no 2, pp23–37

Dunstan, G. (undated) 'Peacebus.com', peacebus.com, accessed 11 May 2009

Dunstan, G., Sarkissian, W. and Nicholson, T. (Producers) (1990) *Whose Roads? Videotape of the Victorian Roads Corporation Search Conference on the Future of Melbourne's Arterial Roads*, Andrew O'Brien and Associates, Transportation Planners, Melbourne

Dunstan, G., Sarkissian, W. and Ward, R. (1994) 'Goonawarra: Core story as methodology in interpreting a community study', in W. Sarkissian and K. Walsh (eds) *Community Participation in Practice: Casebook*, Institute for Technology Policy, Murdoch University, Perth, Western Australia

Ear to the Ground Planning (undated) www.eartothegroundplanning.com, accessed 20 April 2009

Eckstein, B. J. and Throgmorton, J. A. (2003) *Story and Sustainability: Planning, Practice, and Possibility for American Cities*, MIT Press, Cambridge, MA

Ehrlich, G. (1995) *A Match to the Heart: One Woman's Story of Being Struck By Lighting*, Penguin, New York

Elkin, T. and McLaren, D. with Hillman, M. (1991) *Reviving the City: Towards Sustainable Urban Development*, Friends of the Earth with Policy Studies Institute, London

Engwicht, D. (1993) 'Just Imagine', The 1993 Meares Oration, Disability Advisory Council of Australia, Sydney

Engwicht, D. (1999) *Street Reclaiming: Creating Livable Streets and Vibrant Communities*, Pluto Press, Annandale, NSW

Fals-Borda, O. and Rahman, M. A. (eds) (1991) *Action and Knowledge: Breaking the Monopoly with Participatory Action-Research*, The Apex Press, New York

Farmer, P. (2005) *Pathologies of Power: Health, Human Rights, and the New War on the Poor*, University of California Press, Berkeley, CA

Felten, P., Gilchrist, L. Z. and Darby, A. (2006) 'Emotion and learning: Feeling our way toward a new theory of reflection in service-learning', *Michigan Journal of Community Service Learning*, vol 12, no 2, pp38–46

Finlay, L. (2002) 'Negotiating the swamp: The opportunity and challenge of reflexivity in research practice', *Qualitative Research*, vol 2, no 2, 209–230

Finney, N. and Rishbeth, C. (2006) 'Engaging with marginalised groups in public open space research: The potential of collaboration and combined methods', *Planning Theory & Practice*, vol 7, no 1, pp27–46

Floyd, J. and Hayward, P. (2008) 'Community development for ecological sustainability: Working with interiority in the cultivation of social foresight', academic paper for the stream, 'Community Development and Building Social Movements', Community Development and Ecology: Engaging Ecological Sustainability, Deakin University, Centre for Citizenship, Development and Human Rights, 26–28 March, www.deakin.edu.au/arts-ed/cchr/eco-cd-conf08/abstr-wshops.php, accessed 20 June 2009

Flyvbjerg, B. (2002) 'Bringing power to planning research: One researcher's praxis story', *Journal of Planning Education and Research,* vol 21, no 4, pp353–366

Forester, J. (1999) *The Deliberative Practitioner: Encouraging Participatory Planning Processes*, MIT Press, London and Cambridge, MA

Forester, J. (2005) 'Critical moments in negotiations: On humor and irony, recognition and hope', in U. Johansson and J. Woodilla (eds), *Irony and Organizations: Epistemological Claims and Supporting Field Stories*, Copenhagen Business School Press, Copenhagen

Foucault, M. (1980) *Power/knowledge: Selected Interviews & Other Writings 1972–1977*, C. Gordon (ed. and trans.), Pantheon Books, New York

Fox, J. (2002) *Eyes on Stalks*, Methuen, London

Fraser, N. (1997) *Justice Interruptus: Critical Reflections on the 'Postsocialist' Condition*, Routledge, New York

Freire, P. (1970) *Pedagogy of the Oppressed*, M.B. Ramos (trans.), Seabury Press, New York

Freire, P. (1985) *The Politics of Education*, D. Macedo (trans.), Bergin & Garvey, New York

Freire, P. (1992) *Education for Critical Consciousness*, The Continuum Publishing Company, New York

Freire, P. (1998) *Pedagogy of Freedom: Ethics, Democracy, and Civic Courage*, Rowman and Littlefield Publishers, Inc., Lanham, MD

Friedmann, J. (1979) *The Good Society*, MIT Press, Cambridge, MA

Friedmann, J. (1987) *Planning in the Public Domain: From Knowledge to Action*, Princeton University Press, Princeton, NJ

Fryer, M. and Newnham, J. (2005) 'Ways of responding to community issues: An overview and invitation', UBC Learning Exchange www.learningexchange.ubc.ca/__shared/assets/waysofresponding2019.pdf, accessed 23 July 2009

Gadsden, H. (2003) 'Community Engagement in Policy Development – Encouraging community capacity development and exploring innovative models in participative policy development', paper presented to the International Quality & Productivity Centre Conference, Canberra, 5–6 March

Gallant, C. (2004) *Practicing Democracy, A Legislative Theatre Project*, Gallant Solutions Inc., Vancouver, BC

Gardner, H. (1993) *Multiple Intelligences: The Theory in Practice*, Basic Books, New York

Gardner, H. (1999) *Intelligence Reframed: Multiple Intelligences for the 21st Century*, Basic Books, New York

Gardner, J., Maier, J., with Henshaw, R. A. (trans.) (1985) *Gilgamesh*, Vintage Books, New York

Gastil, J. and Levine, P. (2005) *The Deliberative Democracy Handbook: Strategies for Effective Civic Engagement in the Twenty-First Century*, Jossey Bass, San Francisco

Gawain, S. (2002) *Creative Visualization: Use the Power of your Imagination to Create What You Want in Your Life*, New World Library, Natar Novato, CA

Gayá Wicks, P., Reason, P. and Bradbury, H. (2008) 'Living inquiry: Personal, political and philosophical grounding for action research practice', in P. Reason and H. Bradbury (eds) *The Sage Handbook of Action Research: Participative Inquiry and Practice*, second edition, Sage Publications, Thousand Oaks, CA

Giddens, A. (1984) *The Constitution of Society: Outline of the Theory of Structuration*, Polity, Cambridge

Goldstein, H. A. and Carmin, J. (2006) 'Compact, diffuse, or would-be discipline? Assessing cohesion in planning scholarship, 1963–2002', *Journal of Planning Education and Research*, vol 26, pp66–79

Goleman, D. P. (1995) *Emotional Intelligence: Why it Can Matter More Than IQ for Character, Health and Lifelong Achievement*, Bantam Books, New York

Goleman, D. P. (2006) *Social Intelligence: The New Science of Human Relationships*, Bantam Books, New York

Gould, G. with the Kitchener–Waterloo United Mennonite Church Congregational Choir (1992) *Glenn Gould's Solitude Trilogy: Three Sound Documentaries*, Canadian Broadcasting Corporation, Ottawa

Greed, C. (1994) 'The place of ethnography in planning: Or is it "real research"?', *Planning Practice and Research*, vol 9, no 2, pp119–127

Greene, M. (1995) *Releasing the Imagination: Essays on Education, the Arts, and Social Change*, Jossey-Bass Publishers, San Francisco

Greenwood, D. J. and Levin, M. (2007) *Introduction to Action Research: Social Research for Social Change*, Sage Publications Inc, Thousand Oaks, CA

Griffith University (2004) '2004 1st creating child friendly cities symposium', www.griffith.edu.au/environment-planning-architecture/urban-research-program/news-events/2004, accessed 19 June 2009

Grogan, D. and Mercer, C. with Engwicht, D. (1995) *The Cultural Planning Handbook: An Essential Australian Guide*, Allen and Unwin, St Leonards, NSW

Growing Up in Cities: A UNESCO–MOST Project (undated) www.unesco.org/most/guic/guicmain.htm, accessed 15 April 2009

Hammond, P. (2009) 'Eagleby Wetlands boasts bounty of bird life', *Brisbane Courier Mail*, 30 January, www.news.com.au/couriermail/story/0,23739,24979790-3044,00.html, accessed 29 May 2009

Hancock, T. (1993) 'Creating healthier communities: Seeing the vision, defining your role', *Healthcare Forum Journal*, vol 36, no 3, pp30–36

Hart, R. A. (1997) *Children's Participation: The Theory and Practice of Involving Young Citizens in Community Development and Environmental Care*, Earthscan Publications, London

Hatherley, J. (2001) 'Pachelbel or Prozac: Music for uplifting your mood and improving your health', *Wellbeing Magazine*, no 82, February, pp72–83

Hayes Percer, L. (2002) 'Going beyond the demonstrable range in educational scholarship: Exploring the intersections of poetry and research', *The Qualitative Report*, vol 7, no 2, www.nova.edu/ssss/QR/aindex.html, accessed 23 May 2009

Headlines Theatre (1998) 'Welcome to Headlines Theatre', www.headlinestheatre.com/intro.htm, accessed 17 May 2009

Healey, P. (1996) 'Planning through debate: The communicative turn in planning theory', in S. Campbell and S. Fainstein (eds) *Readings in Planning Theory*, Blackwell Publishing, Malden, MA, Oxford, UK and Victoria, AUS

Healey, P. (1997) *Collaborative Planning: Shaping Places in Fragmented Societies*, Macmillan Press, London

Hester, R. T. (1990) *Community Design Primer*, Ridge Times Press, Mendocino, CA

Hester, R. T. (2006) *Design for Ecological Democracy*, MIT Press, Cambridge, MA

Hine, C. (2000) *Virtual Ethnography*, Sage Publications, London

Hoffman, J., Jones, K., Gallupe, C., Penn, B. and Gunn, D. (2001) *Barefoot Mapping*, The Sierra Club of British Columbia, Victoria, BC

Hogan, C. (2000) *Facilitating Empowerment: A Handbook for Facilitators, Trainers and Individuals*, Kogan Page, London

Holden, M. (2008) 'The tough minded and the tender minded: A pragmatic turn for sustainable development planning and policy', *Planning Theory & Practice*, vol 9, no 4, December, pp475–496

Hopkins, L. D. (2001) 'Planning as science: Engaging disagreement', *Journal of Planning Education and Research*, vol 20, pp399–406

Houston, J. (1982) *The Possible Human: A Course in Enhancing Your Physical, Mental and Creative Abilities*, J. P. Tarcher, Putnam, New York

Houston, J. (1987) *The Search for the Beloved: Journeys in Mythology and Sacred Psychology*, J. P. Tarcher, Putnam, New York

Houston, J. (1992) *The Hero and the Goddess: The Odyssey as Mystery and Initiation*, Aquarian/Thorsons, London

Hurford, D. (2008) 'Breaking the Line: Integrating Poetry, Polyphony, & Planning Practice', Master's thesis, School of Community and Regional Planning, University of British Columbia, Vancouver

Imagine! (2004) 'Dynamics of Group Decision-Making', vol 2, issue 2, Fall, www.imaginal.nl/vol_2_iss_2/newsletterV2I2P1.htm, accessed 26 April 2009

Infed (the informal education homepage) (2002) 'howard gardner, multiple intelligences and education', www.infed.org/thinkers/gardner.htm, accessed 13 June 2008

Innes, J. (1995) 'Planning theory's emerging paradigm: Communicative action and interactive practice', *Journal of Planning Education and Research*, pp183–189

Innes, J. and Booher, D. (2004) 'Reframing public participation: Strategies for the 21st century', *Planning Theory & Practice*, vol 5, no 4, pp419–436

International Association for Public Participation (undated) 'IAP2 Spectrum of Public Participation', www.iap2.affiniscape.com/associations/4748/files/ IAP2%20Spectrum_vertical.pdf, accessed 14 May 2009

International Society of City and Regional Planners (2007) 'Urban Trialogues – Co-productive ways to relate visioning and strategic urban projects', 43rd International Planning Congress ISOCARP, Antwerp, Belgium, 19–23 September

Kane, P. (2000) 'Play for today', *The Observer*, Sunday 22 October, www.

guardian.co.uk/theobserver/2000/oct/22/life1.lifemagazine, accessed 26 April 2009

Kane, P. (2004) *The Play Ethic: A Manifesto for a Different Way of Living*, MacMillan, London

Kane, P. www.newintegrity.org; www.newintegrity.org/documents/SpiritinBusiness-PlayEthicpresentation.ppt, accessed 1 June 2009

Kaner, S. with Lind, L., Toldi, C., Fisk, S. and Berger, D. (1996) *The Facilitator's Guide to Participatory Decision-Making*, New Society Publishers, Gabriola Island, BC

Keenan, P. (2002) *Heartstorming: The Way to a Purposeful Life*, McGraw-Hill, New York

Kershaw, B. (1992) *The Politics of Performance: Radical Theatre as Cultural Intervention*, Routledge, London and New York

Kindon, S., Pain, R. and Kesby, M. (eds) (2007) *Participatory Action Research Approaches and Methods: Connecting People, Participation and Place*, Routledge, New York, pp33–40

King, T. (2005) *The Truth About Stories, A Native Narrative*, House of Anansi Press, Toronto, ON

Korten, D. C. (2006) *The Great Turning: From Empire to Earth Community*, Berrett-Koehler, San Francisco

Korten, D. C. and Klauss, R. (eds) (1984) *People-Centered Development: Contributions Toward Theory and Planning Frameworks*, Kumarian Press, West Hartford, CT, pp299–309

Kovacs, M. G. (trans.) (1989) *The Epic of Gilgamesh*, Stanford University Press, Stanford, CA

Krall, F. (1994) *Ecotone: Wayfaring on the Margins*, State University of New York Press, Albany, NY

Lange, E. A. (2004) 'Transformative and restorative learning: A vital dialectic for sustainable societies', *Adult Education Quarterly*, vol 54, no 2, pp121–139

Lavarack, G. (2004) *Health Promotion Practice: Power & Empowerment*, Sage Publications, Thousand Oaks, CA

LeBaron, M. (2000) *Transforming Cultural Conflict in an Age of Complexity*, Berghof Research Center for Constructive Conflict Management, Berlin, Germany

LeBaron, M. (2001) *Conflict and Culture: A Literature Review and Bibliography*, Institute for Dispute Resolution, University of Victoria, Victoria, BC

LeBaron, M. (2002) *Bridging Troubled Waters: Conflict Resolution from the Heart*, Jossey Bass, San Francisco

LeBaron, M. (2003a) *Bridging Cultural Conflicts: A New Approach for a Changing World*, Jossey Bass, San Francisco

LeBaron, M. (2003b) 'Trickster, mediator's friend', in Bowling, D. and D. Hoffman, (eds) (2003) *Bringing Peace Into the Room: How the Personal Qualities of the Mediator Impact the Process of Conflict Resolution*, Jossey Bass, San Francisco, pp135–150

LeBaron, M. (2004) 'Learning new dances: Finding effective ways to address intercultural disputes' in C. Bell, and D. Kahane (eds) (2004) *Intercultural Dispute Resolution in Aboriginal Contexts: Canadian and International Perspectives*, UBC Press, Vancouver, pp11–27

LeBaron, M. (2008) 'Shapeshifters and synergy: Toward a culturally fluent approach to representative negotiation', in C. M. Hanycz, F. H. Zemans, and T. C. W. Farrow, (2008) *The Theory and Practice of Representative Negotiation*, Emond Montgomery Publications, Toronto, pp139–157

LeBaron, M. and Honeyman, C. (2006) 'Using the creative arts' in Schneider, A.K. and Honeyman, C. (eds) *The Negotiator's Fieldbook: The Desk Reference for the Experienced Negotiator*, American Bar Association, Washington, DC, pp415–424

LeBaron, M. and Pillay, V. (eds) (2006) *Conflict Across Cultures: A Unique Experience of Bridging Differences*, Intercultural Press, Boston

LeBaron, M. and Zumeta, Z. D. (2003) 'Windows on diversity: Lawyers, culture, and mediation practice', *Conflict Resolution Quarterly*, vol 20, no 4, pp463–472

Le Guin, U. K. (2001) *Always Coming Home*, University of California Press, Berkeley, CA

Leu, D. J., Kinzer, C. K., Coiro, J. L. and Cammack, D.W. (2004) 'Towards a theory of new literacies emerging from the internet and other information and communication technologies', in R. B. Ruddell and N. J. Unrau (eds) *Theoretical Models and Processes of Reading*, fifth edition, International Reading Association, Newark, DE

Loden, M. and Rosener, J. (1990) *Workforce America! Managing Employee Diversity as a Vital Resource*, Business One, Irwin, Homewood, IL

Logue, C. (1969) 'Come to the Edge', in C. Logue (ed) *New Numbers*, Cape, London, pp65–66

Louv, R. (2005) *Last Child in the Woods: Saving Our Children from Nature-Deficit Disorder*, Algonquin Books of Chapel Hill, Chapel Hill, NC

Lunch, N. and Lunch, C. (2006) *Insights into Participatory Video: A Handbook for the Field*, Insight, Oxford, UK

Macy, J. and Young Brown, M. (1998) *Coming Back to Life: Practices to Reconnect Our Lives, Our World*, New Society, Gabriola Island, BC

Malone, K. and Hasluck, L. (1998) 'Geographies of exclusion: Young people's perceptions and use of public space', *Family Matters*, vol 49, Autumn, pp20–26

Manguel, A. (2007) *The City of Words*, House of Anansi Press, Toronto

Marcus, C. Cooper (1978) 'Remembrance of landscapes past', Landscape, vol 22, no 3, pp34–43

Marcus, C. Cooper (1979) Environmental Autobiography, Working Paper 301, January, Institute for Urban and Regional Development, University of California, Berkeley, CA

Marcus, C. Cooper (1995) *House as a Mirror of Self: Exploring the Deeper Meaning of Home*, Conari Press, Berkeley, CA

Marcus, C. Cooper (2006) *House as a Mirror of Self: Exploring the Deeper Meaning of Home*, second edition, Nicolas-Hays, Inc, Lake Worth, FL

Mariechild, D. (1989) *Mother Wit: A Guide to Healing and Psychic Development*, revised second edition, Crossing Press, Freedom, CA

Mayo, M. (2000) *Cultures, Communities, Identities: Cultural Strategies for Participation and Empowerment*, Palgrave, Houndmills, Basingstoke, Hampshire, UK

McCaffery, S. (2008) *Every Way Oakly*, BookThug, Toronto

McGarva, G. (2008) Personal communication with Dianna Hurford, 15 February, cited in Hurford, D. (2008) 'Breaking the Line: Integrating Poetry, Polyphony, & Planning Practice', Master's thesis, School of Community and Regional Planning, University of British Columbia, Vancouver.

McIntyre, A. (2007) *Participatory Action Research*, Sage Publications, Thousand Oaks, CA

McKnight, J. (1977) 'Professionalized service and disabling help', in I. Illich, I. K. Zola, J. McKnight, J. Caplan and H. Shaiken (eds) *Disabling Professions*, Marion Boyars Publishers, London

McLaren, N.-J. and Edelson, N. (2004, unpublished) 'Using Talking Circles to Develop Inclusive Communities', prepared for *The United Way of Greater Vancouver 'Communities in Action Project'*, United Way, Vancouver

McLaren, N.-J. and Edelson, N. (2007) *Community Initiatives 2007*, [self-published]

McTaggart, R. (ed) (1997) *Participatory Action Research: International Contexts and Consequences*, State University of New York Press, Albany, NY

Mellon, N. (1992) *Storytelling and the Art of Imagination*, Element Books, Shaftesbury, Dorset, Rockport, MA, and Brisbane

Miller, D. and Slater, D. (2000) *The Internet: An Ethnographic Approach*, Berg Publishers, New York

Miller, W. C. (1987) *The Creative Edge: Fostering Innovation Where You Work*, Addison-Wesley, Reading, MA

Mizuno, S. (ed) (1988) *Management for Quality Improvement: The 7 New QC Tools*, Productivity Press, Inc., Cambridge, MA

Moody, J. (2000) 'Dreaming of sustainability: The role of young people', ATSE Academy Symposium, www.atse.org.au/index.php?sectionid=310, accessed 17 April 2009

Morton, K. (1995) 'The irony of service: Charity, project and social change in service-learning', *Michigan Journal of Community Service Learning*, vol 2, pp19–32

Moynihan, S. and Horton, N. (2002) 'Protest or Participate? Community Cultural Development and Globalization in Australia', in D. Adams and A. Goldbard (eds) *Community, Culture and Globalization*, Rockefeller Foundation, New York

Murray, J. and Sarkissian, W. (1998) *Learning through the Soles of Our Feet:* 'A Participatory Design Workshop for Youth in Airds, New South Wales', unpublished paper, reprinted in Sarkissian. W., Cook, A. and Walsh, K. (2000) *Workshop Checklist*, second edition, Institute for Science and Technology Policy, Murdoch University, Murdoch, Western Australia

Myers, D. and Banerjee, T. (2005) 'Towards greater heights for planning: Reconciling the differences between the profession, practice, and academic field', *Journal of the American Planning Association*, vol 71, no 2, pp121–129

New Economics Foundation (1997a) *Briefings on Different Techniques: Future*

Search, Guided Visualization, Participative Theatre, Centre for Community Visions, London

New Economics Foundation (1997b) *Creating Community Visions*, Centre for Community Visions, London

New Economics Foundation (1997c) *How to Design a Community Vision*, Centre for Community Visions, London

New Economics Foundation (1998) *Participation Works! 21 Techniques of Community Participation for the 21st Century*, New Economics Foundation, London, www.neweconomics.org

New Economics Foundation (1999) *How to Design a Community Vision, Central Briefing, Edition 1.1*, January, Centre for Participation, New Economics Foundation, London

New Integrity (Kane, P. and Adnan, I.) (undated) www.newintegrity.org/new_integrity.htm, accessed 20 May 2009

NSW Commission for Children and Young People (undated) *'Participation Kit: TAKING PARTicipation Seriously'* www.kids.nsw.gov.au/kids/resources/participationkit.cfm, accessed 18 May 2009

Ng, K. S. L. (1996) 'Community Participation and How it Influences Urban Form', unpublished Master of Urban Design dissertation, University of Sydney, Urban Design Program, Faculty of Architecture, Sydney, December

Norris, P. (2001) *Digital Divide: Civic Engagement, Information Poverty, and the Internet Worldwide*, Cambridge University Press, Cambridge, UK

Oldenburg, R. and Brissett, D. (1982) 'The third place', *Qualitative Sociology*, vol 5, no 4, pp265–284

Orr, D. W. (1994) *Earth in Mind: On Education, Environment, and the Human Prospect*, First Island Press, Washington, DC

Orr, M. (2007) *Transforming the City: Community Organizing and the Challenge of Political Change*, University Press of Kansas, Lawrence, KS

Owen, H. (1997) *Open Space Technology: A User's Guide*, second edition, Berrett-Koehler Publishers, San Francisco, CA

Patton, M. Q. (1990) *Qualitative Evaluation and Research Methods*, Sage Publications, Newbury Park, CA

Paulin, S. (ed) (2006) *Community Voices: Creating Sustainable Spaces*, University of Western Australia Press, Crawley, Western Australia

Peavey, F. (2000) *Heart Politics Revisited*, Pluto Press, Sydney

Penner, A. (2005a) 'Salmon tales: An arts-informed and literary inquiry into salmon farming in B.C.', Master's thesis, York University, Toronto, ON

Penner, A. (2005b) 'The mechanics of fracture', an excerpt from 'The promise of something grand', *Emerge*, pp84–88, Simon Fraser University Writing and Publishing Program, Vancouver, BC

Peters, T. and Waterman, R. (1982) *In Search of Excellence: Lessons from America's Best Run Companies*, Harper and Row, Publishers Inc., New York

Piercy, M. (1976) *Woman on the Edge of Time*, Knopf, New York, NY

Pinson, D. (2004) 'Urban planning: An "undisciplined" discipline', *Futures*, vol 36, pp503–513

Ponic, P. (2000) 'A herstory, a legacy: The Canadian Fitness and Amateur Sport Branch's Women's Program', *Avante*, vol 6, no 1, pp48–61

Ponic, P. (2007) 'Embracing Complexity in Community-based Health Promotion: Inclusion, Power and Women's Health', PhD Dissertation, University of British Columbia, Vancouver, BC

Ray, M. and Myers, R. (1986) *Creativity in Business*, Doubleday, New York

Reason, P. and Hawkins, P. (1988) 'Storytelling as inquiry', in P. Reason (ed) *Human Inquiry in Action: Developments in New Paradigm Research*, Sage Publications, London

Revell, J. and Norman, S. (1997) *In Your Hands: NLP in ELT*, Saffire Press, London

Rietz, H. L. and Manning, M. (1994) *The One-stop Guide to Workshops*, Irwin Professional Publishing, Burr Ridge, IL and New York

Roberts and Kay, Inc. (1999) 'Open space technology', *Best Practices*, vol 9, Roberts and Kay, Inc, published online www.robertsandkay.com/newsletters/open_space.html, accessed 23 January 2008

Roe, M. (2006) '"Making a wish": Children and the local landscape', *Local Environment*, vol 11, no 2, pp163–181

Rosenthal, A. T. (2003) 'Teaching systems thinking and practice through environmental art', *Ethics & the Environment*, vol 8, no 1, pp154–168

Rumi, 'Emptiness', in C. Barks and J. Moyne (trans.) (1997) *The Essential Rumi*, Castle Books, Edison, NJ, p27

Saltmarsh, J. (1996) 'Education for critical citizenship: John Dewey's contribution to the pedagogy of community service learning', *Michigan Journal of Community Service Learning*, vol 3, pp13–21

Sandercock, L. (1995) 'Voices from the borderlands: A meditation on a meta-phor', *Journal of Planning Education and Research*, vol 14, pp77–88

Sandercock, L. (ed) (1998a) *Making the Invisible Visible: A Multicultural Planning History*, University of California Press, Berkeley, CA

Sandercock, L. (1998b) *Towards Cosmopolis: Planning for Multicultural Cities*, John Wiley and Sons, London

Sandercock, L. (1998c) 'The difference that theory makes', in Sandercock, L. *Towards Cosmopolis: Planning for Multicultural Cities*, John Wiley and Sons, London, pp85–104

Sandercock, L. (2003a) *Cosmopolis II: Mongrel Cities of the 21st Century*, Continuum, London and New York

Sandercock, L. (2003b) 'Out of the closet: The importance of stories and storytelling in planning practice', *Planning Theory & Practice*, vol 4, no 1, pp11–28

Sandercock, L. (2005) 'A new spin on the creative city: Artist/planner collabo-rations', *Planning Theory & Practice*, vol 6, no 1, pp101–103

Sandercock, L. and Attili, G. with Cavers, V. and Carr, P. (2009) *Where Strangers Become Neighbours: Integrating Immigrants in Vancouver, Canada*, Springer, Dordrecht, The Netherlands

Sarkissian Associates Planners (2000) *Getting Out and About in Eagleby: A Report on the Community Participation Activities Conducted for SEPA-Q*, Sarkissian Associates Planners, Brisbane

Sarkissian, W. (1996) 'With a Whole Heart: Nurturing an Ethic of Caring for Nature in the Education of Australian Planners', PhD dissertation, Institute for Sustainability and Technology Policy, Murdoch University, Perth, Western Australia

Sarkissian, W. (1997) 'Listening to all the Voices: Storytelling and the Path of Expression in Community Research', keynote address, 16 September, 1997 Main Street and Small Towns Conference, Merimbula, NSW

Sarkissian, W. (2005) 'The artistry of community consultation', *Artwork*, vol 63, December, pp27–32

Sarkissian, W. and Cook, A. (2002) 'Savvy Cities: Helping kids out of the bubble wrap', keynote address to the International CPTED Association annual conference, Calgary, AB, October

Sarkissian, W. with Dunstan, G. (2003) 'Stories in a park: Reducing crime and stigma through community storytelling', *Urban Design Forum Quarterly*, vol 64, published online, www.udf.org.au, accessed 7 June 2008

Sarkissian, W. and Ludher, E. (2004) 'Are we shutting kids out?: A Review of Government Community Engagement Advisory Material', presentation to the Creating Child-friendly Cities Conference, Brisbane, October 2004, www.griffith.edu.au/__data/assets/pdf_file/0008/50885/child-symposium-sarkissian-ludher.pdf, accessed 19 June 2009

Sarkissian, W. and Perlgut, D. (1986) *The Community Participation Handbook: Resources for Public Involvement in the Planning Process*, Impacts Press, Sydney; second revised edition (1994), Institute for Sustainability and Technology Policy, Murdoch University, Perth, Western Australia

Sarkissian, W. and Perlgut, D. (eds) with Walsh, K. (1994) *The Community Participation Handbook*, second edition, Institute for Sustainability and Technology Policy, Murdoch University, Perth, Western Australia

Sarkissian, W. with Taylor, K. (1991) *Urban Land Authority, 'Welcome Home' Workshops, A Manual for Workshop Planners and Facilitators*, the Authority, Melbourne, May

Sarkissian, W. and Walsh, K. (eds) (1994a) *Community Participation in Practice: Casebook*, Institute for Science and Technology Policy, Murdoch University, Perth, Western Australia

Sarkissian, W. with Walsh, K. (1994b) 'Teamwork and collaborative planning for a new suburban development in Melbourne: The case of Roxburgh Park', in W. Sarkissian and K. Walsh (eds) *Community Participation in Practice: Casebook*, Institute for Sustainability and Technology Policy, Murdoch University, Perth, Western Australia

Sarkissian, W. and Benjamin-Mau, W. with Cook, A., Walsh, K. and Vajda, S. (2009) *SpeakOut: The Step-By-Step Guide to SpeakOuts and Community Workshops*, Earthscan, London and Sterling, VA

Sarkissian, W., Cook, A. and Walsh, K. (1997) *Community Participation in Practice: A Practical Guide*, Murdoch University, Perth, Western Australia

Sarkissian, W., Cook, A. and Walsh, K. (2000) *Community Participation in Practice: Workshop Checklist*, second edition, Institute for Sustainability and Technology Policy, Murdoch University, Perth, Western Australia

Sarkissian, W. with Cross, A. and Dunstan, G. (1994a) 'The conference of the birds: A role play within a workshop', in W. Sarkissian and K. Walsh (eds) *Community Participation in Practice: Casebook,* Institute for Sustainability and Technology Policy, Murdoch University, Perth, Western Australia

Sarkissian, W. with Dunstan, G. and Walsh, K. (1994b) '"The Gods must be crazy": A role play simulation within a search conference', in W. Sarkissian and K. Walsh (eds) *Community Participation in Practice: Casebook*, Institute for Sustainability and Technology Policy, Murdoch University, Perth, Western Australia

Sarkissian, W., Hirst, A., Stenberg, B. with Walton, S. (2003) *Community Participation in Practice: New Directions*, Murdoch University, Perth, Western Australia

Sarkissian, W., with Hofer, H., Shore, Y., Vajda, S. and Wilkinson, C. (2008) *Kitchen Table Sustainability: Practical Recipes for Community Engagement with Sustainability*, Earthscan, London and Sterling, VA

Sarkissian, W., Walsh, K. and Campbell, A. (2001) *Improving Community Participation in the City of Port Phillip: A Toolbook of Participatory Techniques CD-ROM*, City of Port Phillip, St Kilda, Melbourne,

Sarkissian, W., Walsh, K., Lindstad, A. and Roberts, S., (1995) *Children's Impact Assessment: Site Planning and Design of the Public Realm for Children*, Urban Land Authority, Melbourne, September

Sarkissian, W., Walsh, K., Shore, Y., Lindstad, A. Roberts, S. with LaRocca, S. and Fasche, M. (2002) *KidScape: Guidelines for Designing Sustainable Residential Environments for Children*. Prepared by Sarkissian Associates Planners Pty Ltd for the Urban and Regional Land Corporation, Melbourne

Scarry, E. (2006) *On Beauty and Being Just*, Duckworth, London

Scharmer, C. O. (2007) *Theory U: Leading from the Future as it Emerges: The Social Technology of Presencing*, Society for Organizational Learning, Cambridge, MA

Scharmer, C. O. (undated) 'Addressing the Blind Spot of Our Time: An Executive Summary of the New Book by Scharmer *Theory U: Leading the Future as It Emerges*' (The Social Technology of Presencing), www.ottoscharmer.com/publications/summaries.php, accessed 22 June 2009

Search Institute (2007) *Developmental Assets Tools: 40 Developmental Assets for Adolescents*, www.search-institute.org/developmental-assets-tools, accessed 5 May 2009

Seed, J., Macy, J., Fleming, P. and Naess, A. (1988) *Thinking Like a Mountain: Towards a Council of All Beings*, New Society, Philadelphia and Santa Cruz, CA

Senbel, M. (2002) 'Empathic Leadership: Effective Communicative Action for Planners', student paper and poster presentation, American Planning Association Conference, Chicago, 17 April, www.design.asu.edu/apa/proceedings02/S-SENBEL/s-senbel.htm, accessed 6 May 2009

Senge, P. M. (2005) *The Fifth Discipline: The Art and Practice of the Learning Organization*, Currency-Doubleday, New York, NY

Senge, P., Scharmer, C.O., Jaworski, J. and Flowers, B.S. (2005) *Presence: Exploring Profound Change in People, Organization, and Society*, Nicholas Brealey Publishing, London

Shipley, R. (2000) 'The origin and development of vision and visioning in planning', *International Planning Studies*, vol 5, no 2, pp225–236

Shipley, R. (2002) 'Visioning in planning: Is the practice based on theory?', *Environment and Planning A*, vol 34, no 1, pp7–22

Shipley, R. and Newkirk, R. (1998) 'Visioning: Did anybody see where it came from?', *Journal of Planning Literature*, vol 12, no 4, pp407–416

Shipley, R. and Newkirk, R. (1999) 'Vision and visioning in planning: What do these terms really mean?', *Environment and Planning B*, vol 26, pp573–589

Shore, Y. (undated) *Soul Business*, soulbusiness.com.au, accessed 1 May 2009

Sidhu, M. (1994) 'Timbarra: Five years on', in W. Sarkissian and K. Walsh (eds) *Community Participation in Practice: Casebook*, Institute for Sustainability and Technology Policy, Murdoch University, Perth, Western Australia

Silver, M. (2009) 'Heart of Business', www.heartofbusiness.com/, accessed 20 May 2009

Simpkinson, C. and Simpkinson, A. (eds) (1993) *Sacred Stories: A Celebration of the Power of Story to Transform and Heal*, HarperSanFrancisco, San Francisco, CA

Smith, S. E., Willms, D. G. and Johnson, N. A. (eds) (1997) *Nurtured by Knowledge: Learning to Do Participatory Action Research*, Ottawa International Development Research Centre, The Apex Press, New York, NY

Society for Organizational Learning (undated) 'Presence: An Exploration of Profound Change in People, Organizations, and Society', www. presence. net, accessed 4 April 2009

Starhawk (1993) *The Fifth Sacred Thing*, Bantam, New York

Stiftel, B., Rukmana, D. and Alam, B. (2004) 'Faculty quality at US planning schools: A National Research council-style study', *Journal of Planning Education and Research,* vol 24, no 1, pp6–22

Summers, I. (undated) 'Heartstorming Newsletter', www.presence.net, accessed 22 April 22 2009

Think Salmon (2009) Pacific Salmon Foundation and Fraser Basin Council, www.thinksalmon.com, accessed 30 March 2009

Tranter, P. J. (1993) *Children's Mobility in Canberra: Confinement or Independence?,* Department of Geography & Oceanography, ADFA (Australian Defence Force Academy), Canberra

United Nations Economic Commission for Europe (UNECE) (2006) 'Blogs: Are there Applications for Statistical Agencies?', United Nations Statistical Commission and Economic Commission for Europe Conference of European Statisticians, presented at the UNECE Work Session on Statistical Dissemination and Communication, Washington, DC, 12–14 September

University of British Columbia (undated) 'Learning Exchange', www.learningexchange.ubc.ca/Welcome.html, accessed 21 March 2009

Urbanthinkers (undated) 'Urban Thinkers: Child and Youth Engagement in Sustainable Transportation', www.urbanthinkers.ca/, accessed 15 February, 2009

VicUrban (Melbourne, Victoria) (undated) www.vicurban.com/cs/Satellite?c=VPage&cid=1155711917237&pagename=VicUrban%2FLayout&site=VicUrban, accessed 29 May 2009

von Oech, R. (1973) *A Whack on the Side of the Head: How You Can Be More Creative,* Business Plus, New York, NY

Walker, P. (1994) 'Community visioning: Outline project proposal', New Economics Foundation, London, 24 March

Walsh, K. with Cook, A. (1994) 'The beginning of something: The Timbarra "Welcome Home" workshops', in W. Sarkissian and K. Walsh (eds) *Community Participation in Practice: Casebook,* Institute for Sustainability and Technology Policy, Murdoch University, Perth, Western Australia

Walsh, K. with Sarkissian, W., Dunstan, G. and Cook, A. (1990) 'A report on the Timbarra "Welcome Home" Workshop, Sunday 24 June 1990', prepared for the Urban Land Authority by Sarkissian Associates Planners, Pty Ltd, Melbourne

Warland, B. (2005) 'Nose to nose', in B. Warland (ed) *Only This Blue*, Mercury Press, Toronto, ON

Wates, N. (2000) *The Community Planning Handbook: How People Can Shape their Cities, Towns and Villages in Any Part of the World*, Earthscan, London

Wates, N. (2008) *The Community Planning Event Manual: How to Use Collaborative Planning and Urban Design Events to Improve Your Environment*, Earthscan, London

Welfare State International (undated) www.welfare-state.org, accessed 2 May 2009

White, R. (1998) *Public Spaces for Young People: A Guide to Creative Projects and Positive Strategies*, Australian Youth Foundation in partnership with the National Campaign Against Violence and Crime, Canberra

Whitecross, P. (2004) Personal communication with Graeme Dunstan and Wendy Sarkissian, 16 July

Wilson, P. A. (2004) 'The Inner Practice of Civic Engagement', *Fieldnotes: A newsletter of the Shambhala Institute*, February, issue 3, pp1–6

Winnipeg Committee for Safety (1991) *No Paper Rights: A Safer Winnipeg for Women and Children*, City of Winnipeg, Winnipeg, MB

Wittel, A. (2000) 'Ethnography on the move: From field to net to Internet', *Forum: Qualitative Social Research*, vol 1, no 1, www.qualitative-research.net/index.php/fqs/article/view/1131, accessed 24 April, 2009

Young, I. M. (1997) *Intersecting Voices: Dilemmas of Gender, Political Philosophy, and Policy*, Princeton University Press, Princeton, NJ

Young, I. M. (2000) *Inclusion and Democracy*, Oxford University Press, Oxford

Ziegler, W. (1995) *Ways of Enspiriting: Transformative Practices for the Twenty-first Century*, FIA International LLC, Denver, CO

Ziegler, W. (1996a) *Enspirited Envisioning™: A Guide Book to the Enspiriting Approach for the Future*, FIA International LLC, Denver, CO

Ziegler, W. (1996b) *Enspirited Envisioning™ for Groups, Organizations, and Communities: A guidebook to the enspiriting approach to the future*, FIA International LLC, Denver, CO

Zittel, T. and Fuchs, D. (2007) *Participatory Democracy and Political Participation: Can Participatory Engineering Bring Citizens Back In?*, Routledge, New York, NY

Appreciations

All three authors would like to acknowledge:

Our publishers, Earthscan, and specifically Rob West, Alison Kuznets, Claire Lamont and Camille Bramall. Our editor, Barouir Ara Nalbandian. And Nick Wates, Leonie Sandercock, Yollana Shore and all of our friends and colleagues who generously agreed to be interviewed for this book or who made contributions in manifold ways.

This book is about important things – about what's not often spoken about in planning. One special person deserves our appreciation at the start.

Leonie Sandercock's radical spirit is everywhere in this book – not simply in the interview with her. We thank Leonie for all her beautiful risk-taking: norm-breaking writing, experimental film and persistent art infusion into the theoretical planning imagination. Leonie, you have given the planning field and this book a beautiful new interactive room to walk into.

Wendy Sarkissian

In 1967, I completed a Master's thesis on Robert Browning's long poem, *The Ring and the Book*. I remember that it's 21,000 lines long and I wrote about truth. I expected I'd become a high school English teacher, as that was what I'd been trained for. So who would have imagined, over 40 years later, my co-authoring a book about creativity and community engagement?

With a poet for a co-author!

Many tributaries flow into the stream of my creativity – and this book. I have many appreciations to express. My father, Gordon Sarkissian, a pianist and dreamer, gave me a love of music that endures and daily brings me joy. Norman Etherington, my first partner and intellectual mentor, sustains a fierce passion for history, the arts and letters that filled our lives with music and poetry. He taught me how to think, how to write and how to listen. I learned every breath in difficult Mozart concerti as he played his bassoon every evening in his study. Don Perlgut's love of film opened me to that artistic mode with weekly trips to Sydney's funky Roseville Cinema.

The blessings that the courageous and poetic Clare Cooper Marcus continues to bring to my life are chronicled in many places in this book. We've been friends since 1973. We wrote a book together, *Housing as if People Mattered*, in 1986 and it's still in print! I can attribute most of my journeying in creative and spiritual realms to her spirited encouragement. Although I was never, formally, Clare's student, I *am* that student. And I bow deeply in gratitude to my mentor.

When I was living in Adelaide in 1975, a friend introduced me to Leonie Sandercock, then in Canberra. Initially 'pen friends', we built the most nourishing and beautiful friendship imaginable. During the lonely months of my bush sojourn for my PhD, I was encouraged by long, handwritten letters from Leonie, always giving permission. That's it: *giving permission*. Leonie's remarkable work about communities and cultural diversity – the multiplicities of differences we find everywhere – gives us permission to write a book about poetry and dreaming in planning. In fact, Leonie and I have been cooking up ideas for a book on 'Poetry and Planning' for decades. But we never actually wrote it. It took poet Dianna Hurford finally to prepare a thesis on that topic!

Meeting John Forester several years ago in Brisbane was an experience I will never forget. Hours after our formal interview was finished, we were still talking about community engagement. He was still listening to my stories. When he wrote that 'listening is the social policy of everyday life', he was referring to himself. I'm honoured by his Foreword to our book and blessed by his support and enthusiasm for this work.

My dear friend, Colette Meunier, fellow Canadian and former planning student of mine, graces this book with her astute observations of planning and community engagement in the United States and Canada. I thank her for that contribution and for three decades of generous friendship.

Graeme Dunstan has been driving me crazy for 20 years. And I know it's mutual. If ever I were to wander into a bourgeois life, take a straight job or decide to live in suburbia, I could count on Graeme to remind me what's important. He puts flesh on the bones of his activism in endlessly astonishing ways. I thank him for introducing me to chicken wire, glue guns, bamboo poles, banners, stencils, lanterns and 'cardboard art'. His watchful eye has been on me throughout the preparation of this book as he sat sewing banners on my sewing machine. He just wants us to make a difference with it!

My two co-authors, formerly my students in the School of Community and Regional Planning at the University of British Columbia, have been the greatest delight to work with. Both have made light work of heavy and otherwise boring tasks. Chris's care and passion for social justice have kept our feet to the fire. Dianna's poetic touch, calm persistence and artful shepherding of the manuscript made it much better than I could have ever dreamed.

In a poem in early 2008, I wrote about their 'bright faces'. Here's a fragment:

Bright faces
Green hearts
Poetic old souls in young bodies

Bring tears to weary eyes
Warmth to eager heart.

As I seek to become more than an author – a writer – I find great support just when I need it. In this regard, I am deeply grateful to Vivienne Simon in Boston and Anne Gorman in Sydney.

In other Earthscan books, I've offered my heartfelt thanks to my Beloved, Karl Langheinrich, the best cook in Australia. Not every man would persevere with a woman who wanted to write three books in one year without protesting that perhaps some paid work would be nice... Educated in the school of hard knocks and formally in philosophy, sociology, politics and social work, Karl's read every word we've written and made astute comments for which I am most grateful.

I'm blessed with a circle of friends who have supported me in many ways during the writing of this book. I give thanks especially to Marnee and Ollie, Peter and Jan, Anne, Anne, Viv, Ann, Leonie, Michelle, Wendy T., Nadia, Katherine, Yollana and Will, Cathy, Wiwik and Noel, Colette and Mark, Andi, Kelvin, Kevin and Kate, Shelagh and Casimir, Jean and Hugh, Joan, Jane, Lis, Vanda, Angela and Jack, Clare, Nancy and my sister, Margaret Sarkissian.

Finally, my contribution to this book acknowledges the love and sustenance of the living Earth. The kookaburras laughing loudly from the tree behind where I sit writing remind me that we live in difficult times. There's a lot of fear around. When we're working with communities, remembering what's sustains us, what's really important and finding ways to express our creativity will help us demonstrate – and receive – love and care.

Dianna Hurford

My creativity has been fed, cultured and weathered by many delightful beings.

Thank you

: to my co-authors. Wendy, for being such a brave, passionate and compassionate creation. I am ecstatic to celebrate the importance of your work and to continue our creative friendship. Christine. What a pleasure! We clicked through so much together with spontaneous ease. Let there be opportunity for more.

: to Leonie Sandercock, for shaking me from language sleep with beautiful writing and new imagination. A special thank you also to Leonie for inviting poets and poetry into the planning discourse and agreeing to supervise my Masters thesis. You have prepared me for flight. Thank you also to John Friedmann for writing *The Good Society* (1979).

: to Aileen Penner for our many parallels and intersections, to *The Writer's Studio* (TWS) and to Cathie Borrie, Deb McVittie, Rob Madden, Jenni Uitto, Kim Lundsbye and Danielle Arsenault of *em dash* writers collective for friendship, commitment to writing and ongoing critique of my work.

: to poets Wayde Compton, Oana Avasilichioaei, Graham McGarva and Kate Braid for your evocative insights into the relationships between planning and poetry. I have been inspired by your thoughts and textual music. Thank you also to Betsy Warland, Jeff Derksen, Robert Bringhurst and Glenn Gould.

: to friends and mentors, Norma-Jean McLaren and Nathan Edelson, for all collective thoughts in how to stay in creative cross-cultural planning conversation without giving up.

: to family, mom for her beautiful belief and dad for knowing how the earth will grow it. Also to my Wolferstan family, for pioneering this life on water and especially for the gift of Linquenda to alter course, live gently and write. Thank you to the Gillespies for creative life living, lifelong friendship and utopian dinner conversations.

: to the Vancouver Art Gallery (VAG), Centre Pompidou and the trio of herons circling the writing of this work while in port along the Loire.

To Jonathan, the artist of my everyday. Geo-typographer. Engaged public space advocate. Sea poet. (My heart belongs to you.)

Christine Wenman

Wendy and Dianna auspiciously appeared in my life at a time of transition – a pause for reflection after a few years' flurry of action. I'm deeply grateful to Wendy for affording me the opportunity of collaborating on this project. The brainstorming, reading, writing and discussing have been among many welcome sources of new, connected and expanded ideas during the past two years.

I want to express my thanks to some of the people who have made these times beautiful:

To Wendy for her loving warmth and the model she has set by bravely exploring the edges of her practice throughout her career.

To Dianna whose quiet and gentle leadership, expansive thinking and poetic advice are inspirational.

To Susan, my mentor and friend who has most poignantly taught me the importance of caring for the individuals within collective communities.

To my family, whose loving support shelters me from far to near.

To Patrick, whose unconditional companionship softens all the bumps.

To my home community and adopted '282' family – Aaron, Chris and Nana – for sensing just the right moments and gestures to uplift.

Thank you.

Graeme Dunstan

At the beginning of this work, we decided to dedicate this book to a community cultural developer with many years of creative community engagement experience. As authors sending our hopes and ideas for creative and positive change out into world, we would like to end with Graeme's morning prayer, as he acknowledges all of our pasts and our futures on this beautiful Earth.

Graeme's Morning Prayer

Ancestors, hear my cry!

All you whose dust is in my blood and in my bones.
All the mothers and fathers who brought me here.
All those whose dust is in this place, in the Earth, in the rocks, in the trees, in the birds, in the air, in the water I drink, in the food I eat...

Bless me, guide me and protect me that I might serve to the benefit of all beings, near and far, seen and unseen, born and yet to be born.

May I make art that builds community
and builds community resistance,
sustainable resistance.

Bless me with good health, energy and creativity.

Bless my deeds with auspiciousness.

Bless my words with the power to persuade.

Bless me with many uplifting friends and companions on this path.

For the Earth!

Sources for Photographs

All photographs are by Wendy Sarkissian with the exception of the following

Photograph of Graeme Dunstan (page v): Thorsten Jones

Photograph of John Forester (page xi): Kevin Stearns

Chapter 3: Wendy coordinating the Embodied Affinity Diagram exercise (page 32): Graeme Dunstan

Chapter 6: Images on page 77: Angela Hirst

Chapter 8: Carnegie Community Centre (p111): Christine Wenman

Chapter 12: Images on pages 168 and 169: Arthur Orsini

Photograph of Wendy Sarkissian (page 297): Angel Kosch

Photograph of Dianna Hurford (page 298): Sally Andrew

Photograph of Christine Wenman (page 299): Susan Wenman

About the Authors

Wendy Sarkissian

Wendy Sarkissian is committed to finding spirited ways to nurture and support an engaged citizenry in the pursuit of sustainable futures. She holds a Master of Arts in English Literature, a Master of town planning and a PhD in environmental ethics. She has taught in schools of planning, landscape architecture and architecture internationally and lectures in ethics for the Planning Insitute of Australia.

As a consultant, Wendy has pioneered innovative planning and development approaches in a variety of contexts, earning 40 professional awards. She is co-author of the award-winning *Housing as if People Mattered: Illustrated Site Design Guidelines for Medium-density Family Housing* (1986) and the award-winning suite of five books: *Community Participation in Practice* (1994–2003).

Wendy is author of two previous books in the Earthscan Tools for Community Planning series: *Kitchen Table Sustainability: Practical Recipes for Community Engagement with Sustainability* (2008) and *SpeakOut: The Step-by-Step Guide to SpeakOuts and Community Workshops* (2009).

Wendy's doctorate explored ways of nurturing an ethic of caring for Nature in the education of town planners. This approach – focusing on the caring instinct – is a hallmark of her writing and speaking. Wendy's career as consultant and academic provides firsthand knowledge of many contexts.

She is a Fellow of the Planning Institute of Australia, Adjunct Associate Professor, Curtin University Sustainability Policy Institute (CUSP), Western Australia and Adjunct Professor in the School of Sustainable Development, Bond University, Queensland.

Dianna Hurford

Dianna Hurford MAP is a poet | planner.

Over the past ten years, Dianna has worked in the field of affordable housing and homelessness in Vancouver, BC, Canada, as both a consultant and as a research coordinator for a non-profit agency.

She holds a Master of Arts in planning from the School of Community and Regional Planning, University of British Columbia and a Bachelor of Arts (with a double major in English literature and political science) from the University of Victoria. Dianna is also a graduate of the creative writing program, *The Writer's Studio* (TWS) from Simon Fraser University and a member of *em dash Vancouver* writers collective.

Writing her Master's thesis, 'Breaking the Line: Integrating Poetry, Polyphony and Planning Practice' (2008), was a metamorphic process for Dianna. The work beckoned her from language paralysis, aligning the fragments of her professional and creative self. Her research ignited her further commitment to reflective and critical word play and poetic research for inclusive community engagement.

Her poetry has been published in *emerge* and she has participated in numerous literary readings, including the *Vancouver International Writers & Readers Festival* (2005).

Christine Wenman

Christine Wenman, BSc, MSc, is a community and natural resource planner.

While completing a BSc in environmental science at the University of Ottawa, she became increasingly aware of the gap between our substantive knowledge base and what is effectively implemented in policy. Her professional focus has since shifted to include governance, education and citizen engagement.

Facilitating a water and sanitation program with a non-profit organization in Mexico called *Atzin* further sensitized her to the strength and fragility of the human spirit, the intricate connections of environment, emotion and health and the exclusive societal forces subtly at play both locally and globally. The experience would lead her to a Masters from the School of Community and Regional Planning at the University of British Columbia.

Christine has also worked in multicultural planning and engagement, environmental education, non-profit housing and as a caregiver and server in British Columbia, Ontario, Quebec, and overseas.

Index